Governance for Health Care Providers

The Call to Leadership

More Praise for *Governance for Health Care Providers: The Call to Leadership*

"Boards of Trustees will be critical actors in transforming our health care system. This book is an important resource in giving providers the knowledge they need to be successful board members."

Maulik S. Joshi, DrPH, Senior Vice President for Research, American Hospital Association; President, Health Research & Educational Trust

"The arrival of this book on health care governance couldn't be more timely. The Institute of Healthcare Improvement has declared *Getting the Board on Board* as a key element in its 5 Million Lives campaign, recognizing the importance of board leadership and effectiveness in furthering national goals of patient safety and quality health care. The authors/editors have assembled an impressive list of experts who cover well specific elements of effective health care governance. This book will be at the top of the list of 'required reading' for current and new health care board members, and indeed all physician and senior administrative leaders."

Martin D. Merry, MD, CM, Adjunct Clinical Associate Professor of Health Management and Policy, University of New Hampshire

"Staffing shortages, increased reporting requirements, and calls to improve patient safety are just a few of the challenges that boards face that require clinical leadership. Health care providers are by definition already leaders—but have a responsibility to become the best leaders they can be by serving in governance roles. Whether you are on a board now, have just been asked to serve, or want to prepare yourself for serving in the future don't wait to read this book. *Governance for Health Care Providers: The Call to Leadership* will help to prepare you in a very effective way."

Susan B. Hassmiller, PhD, RN, FAAN, Senior Advisor, Robert Wood Johnson Foundation for Nursing

Governance for Health Care Providers

The Call to Leadership

Edited by

David B. Nash ◆ William J. Oetgen ◆ Valerie P. Pracilio

Foreword by Michael D. Connelly, MA, JD, FACHE

CRC Press
Taylor & Francis Group
Boca Raton   London   New York

CRC Press is an imprint of the
Taylor & Francis Group, an **informa** business

A PRODUCTIVITY PRESS BOOK

Productivity Press
Taylor & Francis Group
270 Madison Avenue
New York, NY 10016

© 2009 by Taylor & Francis Group, LLC
Productivity Press is an imprint of Taylor & Francis Group, an Informa business

No claim to original U.S. Government works
Printed in the United States of America on acid-free paper
10 9 8 7 6 5 4 3 2 1

International Standard Book Number-13: 978-1-4200-7853-4 (Hardcover)

Library of Congress Cataloging-in-Publication Data

Governance for health care providers : the call to leadership / editors, David B. Nash,
    William J. Oetgen, Valerie P. Pracilio.
        p. cm.
    Includes bibliographical references and index.
    ISBN 978-1-4200-7853-4 (alk. paper)
    1. Health services administrators. 2. Leadership. 3. Health facilities administration.
I. Nash, David B. II. Oetgen, William J. III. Pracilio, Valerie P.

RA971.G628 2008
362.1068--dc22   2008046486

Visit the Taylor & Francis Web site at
http://www.taylorandfrancis.com

and the Productivity Press Web site at
http://www.productivitypress.com

To my children, Leah, Rachel, and Jake.

—DBN

To my wife, Pam, and to Susan and Casey, Matt
and Sarah, and Gracie and Lucy.

—WJO

To my parents, Robert and Antoinette, for their
endless support and encouragement.

—VPP

To all providers answering the call to leadership.

Contents

Foreword

Reports of conflicted governance have become routine media events since the Enron Corporation debacle. Issues such as restated financials, excessive executive compensation, unprepared trustees, transparency, and conflicts of interest are today the fodder of trustee responsibilities. One might argue that this new level of expectation is a metamorphosis of board accountability similar to President Theodore Roosevelt's use of federal law to change the market rules for corporate titans a century ago. The Sarbanes-Oxley legislation of 2002 created a similar seismic shift.

What prompted the need for such radical change? My reflection, after serving on more than 25 boards, is that two main drivers have created this need for reform. The first is that boards have not kept pace with rapid changes in corporate America. Boards have not evolved into continuous learning organizations— dedicating the time, energy, and intentionality of assuming responsibility for the corporation's results. This level of commitment is expected of a trustee in today's world. Trusteeship, historically, has been viewed more as a social "contribution" rather than a social "responsibility," especially in the tax-exempt sector. This mindset results from governance being viewed as a contribution of time to a worthy cause rather than as an obligation to assume responsibility for the performance of a corporation. Given the voluntary, part-time nature of governance, this traditional way of thinking is understandable. Unfortunately, that mindset is no longer adequate for trustees—just ask the trustees at the Red Cross, Smithsonian, and J. Paul Getty Museum.

The second significant factor in influencing the concern over board performance is the dominant influence of the chief executive officer (CEO). The work of trusteeship has grown significantly, and the corporate CEO has filled that void by assuming responsibility for more of the board's work. This evolution has created an imbalance of power between the CEO and the corporate board. The old adage of "power corrupts and absolute power corrupts absolutely" seems to be an appropriate reference in this context. Much of Sarbanes-Oxley is about restoring that balance of power to the board of trustees.

Trustees today need a well-defined road map to understand their new level of responsibilities and a crisp curriculum to prepare them for their increased obligations of accountability.

This book, *Governance for Health Care Providers: The Call to Leadership*, put together under the able leadership of Dr. David Nash, Dr. William Oetgen, and Ms. Valerie Pracilio, provides trustees with a comprehensive, thoughtful, and disciplined review of critical knowledge needed for health care governance. It organizes for trustees essential materials needed to fulfill their expanded responsibilities. Though this book will undoubtedly be useful for all health care board members, it has a special focus on preparing providers for health care governance responsibilities. The set of knowledge and skills for these responsibilities has not generally been present in the academic curricula of health care professionals.

A recent informal survey of board members of health care organizations shows that up to one-third of board members may be physicians, nurses, pharmacists, or social workers by profession. This text creates a customized curriculum particularly for health care board trustees who are also health care professionals. The breadth and depth of that curriculum ranges from legal duties to current trends in quality, strategy, finance, conflicts of interest, corporate structure, and governance best practices. Of particular note is the faculty that has prepared the curriculum—they represent the leading experts in the field.

Governance today requires a new level of preparation and education—in short a commitment to continuous learning. This text represents a superb opportunity to prepare for those new accountabilities. This commitment to preparation is also an essential step to balancing the equilibrium of power between the board and the CEO. *Governance for Health Care Providers: The Call to Leadership* will guide trustees down the road to more fully accept the responsibility for the mission of the corporations they lead.

Michael D. Connelly, MA, JD, FACHE
President and Chief Executive Officer
Catholic Healthcare Partners

Preface

We are thrilled to bring you *Governance for Health Care Providers: The Call to Leadership.* The contributors have been very carefully selected and have worked tirelessly to bring you this book, which is intended to prepare you for board membership. The expectations of a board member are not always clear, and education is lacking. Health care providers are often overlooked but remain important contributors to boards of directors. This book was written to prepare provider board members to become key contributors and to give them a comprehensive learning tool.

Governance is receiving more attention now than ever before. As the health care industry takes a step back and focuses on the key decision makers, the role of a board member will become increasingly important. The board is faced with difficult decisions and is ultimately responsible for the health of the organization. This book comes at a time when health care is being scrutinized and accountability is on the rise, a daily reminder to organizations of the importance of governance.

Throughout this book we use the term *provider* to include physicians, nurses, pharmacists, administrators, and all other health care professionals, who are the primary audience for this work. We hope this book will serve as an educational tool at the graduate level in schools of medicine, nursing, health care administration, public health, business administration, law, and other fields. The book has been organized to provide an overview of the key components of board oversight and to provide recommendations to prepare for the future of health care governance.

We thank our colleagues that have supported us in this endeavor, especially the leadership of Thomas Jefferson University and Georgetown University. One of us (DBN) would especially like to thank several key leaders at Jefferson. Our university president, Robert L. Barchi, MD, PhD, and our hospital CEO, Thomas J. Lewis, have both been strong supporters of our work. Two former deans, Drs. Joseph S. Gonnella and Thomas J. Nasca, had the vision to help us build a medical school department of health policy. Finally, thanks to the corporate board and management leadership of Catholic Healthcare Partners, in Cincinnati, Ohio, the best teachers about the true meaning of governance mission and vision.

Another of us (WJO) thanks the board and executive leadership of MedStar Health, Inc., who have worked so diligently to make MedStar the trusted leader in caring for people and in advancing health in the Baltimore–Washington region. Special thanks are extended to E. F. Shaw Wilgis, MD, current chair of the MedStar Health Board, to James R. Hyde, his immediate predecessor as chair, and to Kenneth A. Samet, president and CEO of MedStar Health—all of whose vision and leadership have made MedStar board membership a wonderful, rewarding, and educational experience. Fellow board members are also deserving of profound gratitude for their generosity and friendship: Ed Brody, Dr. Chandra Banerjee, Drew Berry, Win Churchill, Esq., Ed Civera, Dr. Don Cooney, Dr. Paul Corso, Dr. Jack DeGioia, Dr. Don Dietrick, Steve Harlan, Dr. Barbara Heller, Terry Hyman, Dr. John Kirkpatrick, Catherine Meloy, Tuck Nason, Bill Roberts, Pauline Schneider, Esq., Dr. Stuart Seides, Pat Smyth, Sara Watkins, and Togo West. Thanks are also graciously extended to the MedStar senior executive leadership: Mike Curran, Dr. Bill Thomas, Michael Rogers, Alton Knight, Mike Ryan, Esq., Elizabeth Simpson, Esq., Chris Swearingen, Steve Cohen, Catherine Szenczy, Eric Wagner, Jan Bahner, Joel Bryan, Brad Holmes, Steve Neitz, David Noe, Larry Smith, Esq., Carl Schindelar, Dr. Joy Drass, Dr. Rich Goldberg, Larry Beck, Joe Oddis, Ed Eckenhoff, Harry Rider, Pete Monge, Jim Caldas, Dr. Janis Orlowski, and Dr. Neil Weissman. Special appreciation is given to Jamie Padmore, Kelly Kimberling, and Patti Noe for all they do and have done.

Finally, VPP thanks Neil Goldfarb and David B. Nash for their ongoing mentorship and for the opportunity to participate in this project. We also acknowledge our readers for taking the first step toward understanding the importance of the role of board member by reading this book. We hope you will find it a valuable resource as you take your seat at the boardroom table.

As editors, we take full responsibility for any error of commission or omission in the final version of this text. We hope that our readers will recognize the enormity of the role of a board member and utilize *Governance for Health Care Providers* when answering *The Call to Leadership*.

David B. Nash, William J. Oetgen, and Valerie P. Pracilio

Contributors

F. Kenneth Ackerman, Jr., FACHE, FACMPE
Chairman
Integrated Healthcare Strategies
Minneapolis, Minnesota
ken.ackerman@ihstrategies.com

Barry S. Bader
President
Bader & Associates
Potomac, Maryland
bbader@GreatBoards.org

Janet A. Benton, JD, MHA
Administrative Fellow
Allina Hospitals & Clinics
Minneapolis, Minnesota
janet.benton@allina.com

Caryl E. Carpenter, MPH, PhD
Professor
Health and Medical
  Services Administration
Widener University
Chester, Pennsylvania
cecarpenter@widener.edu

John R. Combes, MD
President and Chief Operating
  Officer
Center for Healthcare Governance
Chicago, Illinois
jcombes@aha.org

Michael D. Connelly, MA, JD, FACHE
President and CEO
Catholic Healthcare Partners
Cincinnati, Ohio
mdconnelly@health-partners.org

Jennifer DuBose, MS
Research Associate II
College of Architecture
Georgia Institute of Technology
Atlanta, Georgia
Jennifer.Dubose@coa.gatech.edu

John K. Dugan, CPA
Partner
PriceWaterhouseCoopers
Philadelphia, Pennsylvania
john.k.dugan@us.pwc.com

Gary L. Filerman, PhD
Chair
Department of Health Systems
  Administration
Georgetown University Medical
  Center
Washington, D.C.
glf3@georgetown.edu

Kanak S. Gautam, PhD, MBA
Associate Professor
Department of Health Management
  and Policy
Saint Louis University
St. Louis, Missouri
gautamk@slu.edu

Barbara R. Heller, EdD, RN, FAAN
Senior Vice President
Strategic Initiatives and Product
  Development
Health Sciences
Laureate Education, Inc.
Baltimore, Maryland
barbara.heller@laureate-inc.com

Molly K. King, MHA
Director of Volunteer and
  Educational Program Development
MedStar Health, Inc.
Columbia, Maryland
Molly.K.King@medstar.net

Alton F. Knight, MBA, MS
Senior Vice President
Audit and Compliance
MedStar Health, Inc.
Columbia, Maryland
Alton.F.Knight@medstar.net

David B. Nash, MD, MBA
The Dr. Raymond C. and Doris N.
  Grandon Professor of Health Policy
Chairman
Department of Health Policy
Jefferson Medical College
Philadelphia, Pennsylvania
david.nash@jefferson.edu

Stephen J. Neitz, MA, CPA
Vice President
Office of the CEO
MedStar Health, Inc.
Columbia, Maryland
Stephen.Neitz@medstar.net

Gene J. O'Dell
Vice President
Strategic and Business Planning
American Hospital Association
Chicago, Illinois
godell@aha.org

Catherine C. Oetgen, JD
Associate Counsel
Perlman & Perlman, LLP
New York, New York
catherine.oetgen@gmail.com

William J. Oetgen, MD, MBA
Clinical Professor of Medicine
  (Cardiology)
Georgetown University
Washington, DC
oetgenw@georgetown.edu

P. Michael Peterson, EdD
Professor
College of Health Sciences
University of Delaware
Newark, Delaware
pmpeter@udel.edu

Valerie P. Pracilio
Project Manager for Quality
  Improvement
Department of Health Policy
Jefferson Medical College
Philadelphia, Pennsylvania
valerie.pracilio@jefferson.edu

Lawrence D. Prybil, PhD
Professor
College of Public Health
The University of Iowa
Iowa City, Iowa
lawrence-prybil@uiowa.edu

Jona Raasch
President
The Governance Institute
San Diego, California
jraasch@governanceinstitute.com

James Rice, PhD, FACHE
Vice Chairman
The Governance Institute
Practice Leader
Governance and Leadership
Integrated Healthcare Strategies
Minneapolis, Minnesota
Jim.Rice@IHStrategies.com

Frederick Ruccius
Vice President
Strategic Development Initiatives
Development and Alumni Relations
Thomas Jefferson University
Philadelphia, Pennsylvania
frederick.ruccius@jefferson.edu

Blair L. Sadler, JD
Senior Fellow
Institute for Healthcare Improvement
Past President and CEO
Rady Children's Hospital
San Diego, California
bsadler@chsd.org

Elizabeth A. Simpson, JD
Senior Vice President and General
  Counsel
MedStar Health, Inc.
Columbia, Maryland
Elizabeth.A.Simpson@medstar.net

William L. Thomas, MD, FACP
Executive Vice President Medical
  Affairs
MedStar Health, Inc.
Columbia, Maryland
William.L.Thomas@medstar.net

Craig Zimring, PhD
Professor
College of Architecture
Georgia Institute of Technology
Atlanta, Georgia
CRAIG.ZIMRING@coa.gatech.edu

Chapter 1

Welcome to the Board

Valerie P. Pracilio, David B. Nash,
and William J. Oetgen

Contents

Executive Summary

Physicians, nurses, pharmacists, and other health care providers are increasingly accepting positions at the board's table. While these professionals are well versed in the clinical aspects of medicine, the business side of health care is often unfamiliar to them. Education to prepare providers to become active members of the board is essential. Basic governance principles as well as the board's role in decision making are crucial to the success of the organization. As a health care provider and board member, you are called to learn about your role on the board as a decision maker and steward. *You have been called to leadership.*

Learning Objectives

1. To gain a better understanding of the role of a health care provider serving on a governance board.
2. To identify key governance issues.
3. To identify cultural differences between the clinical and business aspects of health care.
4. To understand how this book can be an educational tool for trustees.

Key Words

- Board of directors
- Center for Healthcare Governance
- Disruptive governance
- Governance Institute
- Trustee education

Introduction

Congratulations, you have been appointed to the board of directors of a health care organization. You have been selected in the hopes that you will be a committed leader for the organization. The fundamental question is: Are you ready? While your clinical or administrative training is complete, you may not be familiar with the intricacies of the health care business. This book is your answer. Health care providers enter into a position on a board of directors with minimal or no training in governance. In this role, providers are being asked to make decisions that determine the future of the health care organization. There is a cultural gap that exists between clinical practice and the business of health care. Providers as board members must find a balance between these clinical and business cultures in order to govern effectively. This book was written as a primer for providers about to enter or currently fulfilling a term on a board of directors. While providers' clinical knowledge is an asset to the board, it needs to be paired with an understanding of health care governance in order to comprise an exceptional board.

Leadership is a team sport. However, problems arise when board members assume that being a physician, nurse, or pharmacist is qualification enough to lead a complex organization.[1] Education of incoming trustees is important preparation for the role, but it is not a common practice. There is simply not enough room in professional curricula for elective courses in health care governance. As a result, health care providers who enter into a role on a board during their careers frequently assume the position unaware of the expectations. So how can you be prepared for your role on the board? Some organizations such as the Governance Institute in San Diego, California, and the Center for Healthcare Governance in Chicago, Illinois, have developed tools to prepare trustees, but health care professionals are often overlooked. The expectation is that providers are aware of the issues and concerns facing the board. Clinical training prepares you for practice, but what prepares you for the boardroom? This book will provide you with information necessary to understand your role on a health care board of directors. Chapter 1 is organized to provide background information on health care governance and the board's role in facing key issues at the board table. This chapter is the gateway to tools and resources that will help you make well-informed decisions as a board member. It describes your call to leadership in this role.

Health Care Boards of Directors

Health care governance has entered an era of heightened scrutiny. Expectations are on the rise because of external forces shaping the work of the board.[2] As pay-for-performance creates a stronghold in the marketplace, provider participation on boards will also contribute to the organization's economic growth. Boards are entering an era of disruptive governance, where refocusing on new ways to govern and changing existing governing practices are the goals.[3] Becoming an exceptional board requires a good relationship among board members, strategic partnerships with management, and nurturing a team-based approach. How the board chooses to spend its limited time together and where to focus its efforts define the difference between a good board and an exceptional board.[3] Building strategic partnerships with hospital and health system leadership can be accomplished by engaging providers as members of the board. The participation of health care providers on a health care organization's board of directors will arguably be the most crucial element defining the success of health care boards in the twenty-first century.

In the United States, there are 5747 registered hospitals.[4] The board of directors of each of these hospitals has the fiduciary responsibility for its respective institution. More than half of these organizations are nonprofit; less than 16% are for-profit, and the remainder are governmental organizations.[4] The common link among these organizations is the inevitable presence of providers on the board of directors.[4] While composition of a health care board of directors is often diverse, the presence of physicians, nurses, pharmacists, and other trained medical professionals is the common link between hospital and health system boards. Generally, each board member enters the role with a different background, some related to health care and others unrelated.

A typical health care board is comprised of stakeholders who have a common interest in the organization. These stakeholders often include payers, clinicians, and other employees of the health care organization, accreditors and regulators, in addition to members of communities and the public.[5] It is difficult to concisely define governance given its complexity, but most agree that it is the process of making important decisions about the services the organization provides, to whom, and the cost of providing those services.[5] There is a distinction between single organization and system governance. The defining characteristic of the system board is that it is comprised of multiple boards of its subsidiaries with a hierarchical structure.[6] There are three main components of any governance model that determine the success of the health care organization: board composition, structure, and function.[5] These components tend to vary according to status as a for-profit or nonprofit institution. In order to make decisions of this magnitude, you should understand how the three components of the governance model determine a board's effectiveness.

Board Composition

Every organization, upon its inception, develops a mission that guides the work of that entity. It is the work of the board of directors to carry out the organization's mission through the decisions that are made. But before the organization can define its direction, the "right people need to be on the bus."[7] Jim Collins is not simply describing the importance of the team overshadowing the vision of the organization; rather, he is pointing out that the organization that realizes the "who" questions must be answered before the "what" questions is on the way to becoming a great organization.[7] The average board is composed of 13 members[5] of various disciplines, and it has been cited that fewer than 20 members is most effective.[3] Health care providers are increasingly playing an important role on health care boards as discussions about patient safety and quality of care are enhanced by a clinical perspective. Up to this point, we have not made any distinction among hospital, long-term care, acute care, and home health agencies. The common link among these organizations is the presence of physicians, nurses, pharmacists, and other medical professionals on the organization's board.

Board Structure

The financial status and ownership of a health care organization determine its board structure. Board members are chosen by the shareholders in the for-profit health care sector. Nonprofit health care organizations, on the other hand, self-elect board members to represent all stakeholders.[8] The intention of the board is to represent a balance of interests between shareholders and stakeholders.[8] Governance has traditionally been a hierarchical structure, usually represented by a triangle, with the board at the top and the chief executive officer (CEO), administration, and medical staff below. Because of increasing board accountability, which will be described throughout this book, the structure is becoming more horizontal than ever before. The board now relies on the medical expertise of health care providers and the analytic and financial savvy of the administration to present a dashboard of the organization's performance.

Board Function

The role of the twenty-first century health care board will be evident as you read each chapter of this book. Boards are in a period of transformational change. Accountability for quality is becoming the norm and is a result of the evolving role of the board. The Robert Wood Johnson Foundation studied 12 health care systems over a period of 3.5 years to demonstrate that an organization-wide commitment to quality leads to improved patient care. The study identified five critical elements that formed the framework for organizational transformation. Impetus to transform, leadership commitment to quality, improvement initiatives that engage staff in problem solving, alignment with the organization's goals, and integration to bridge intraorganizational boundaries were among the elements. The purpose of this longitudinal study was to move toward achievement of the Institute of Medicine's (IOM) goals presented in *Crossing the Quality Chasm* in 2001.[9] These elements involve the participation of health care providers and administration on multiple levels. This model, combined with transparency and communication with trustees, could function to transform health care at the organizational, system, and national levels.

The foundation of the board is built upon the composition of its members, the structure of the board, and the functions that are defined. Participation of health care professionals on the board is an essential component of board composition. Board accountability is increasing, and the need to review the care being provided to patients is the key to achieving high-quality care. The role and expectations of a health care provider on a board should be understood before taking your seat at the boardroom table. You will be provided the tools and resources needed to understand this role in the following chapters.

The Board's Role in Health Care Governance

Now that you have accepted a role on a health care board of directors, you need to know where to turn for advice. This book will serve as a primer for all you need to know about your new responsibilities. There are also governance organizations such as The Governance Institute (http://www.governanceinstitute.com) and the Center for Healthcare Governance (http://www.americangovernance.com), which remain the authorities on the topic. The Governance Institute is the leading source of governance information and education for health care organizations in the United States.[2] The Institute functions to provide education from the perspective of governance experts in the form of conferences, materials, training, and publications. The Center for Healthcare Governance is a partner of the American Hospital Association and functions to provide resources to both new and seasoned board members. The Center is comprised of a community of board members and executives with experience in health care governance.[10] Many of the authors of *Governance for Health Care Providers: The Call to Leadership* are affiliated with these organizations and have prepared chapters on their area of expertise for this book.

There are six core responsibilities of boards: financial oversight, quality oversight, setting strategic direction, board self-assessment and development, management oversight, and advocacy.[2] Every 2 years, the Governance Institute reports on its survey of chief executive officers of nonprofit acute care hospitals and health systems across the United States.[2] The report describes CEO perceptions of their institution's governance practices as they relate to the core responsibilities. This is an exercise to increase transparency of the work done by health care boards of directors and is a means to increase accountability. Respondents cover health systems, independent hospitals, hospitals that are part of a system, and government-sponsored hospitals. Of the 718 organizations that responded, there was an average of 2.5 physicians serving on a board. The respondents claimed spending up to $20,000 per year on board member education; however, the extent of the education was not reported.

There has been an increase in the number of boards reporting committees focusing on quality, audit and compliance, finance, and community benefit, among others. While results vary based on type of organization and relationship to a health system, the importance of these key committees and their contributions should not go unnoticed. Overall, boards rated performance lower in 2007 than in 2005, but the Governance Institute speculates that increased expectations were the cause, rather than decreased performance. Boards are being scrutinized now more than ever, which supports the need for proper trustee education to ensure competency to make decisions that affect health care organizations, systems, and members of the community.[2]

The core responsibilities are a framework for trustee training, and the biennial survey is a tool to understand the needs of hospitals and health care systems. The report demonstrated that boards rated above the 50th percentile for all core responsibilities with the exception of advocacy. Over 75% of respondents rated the quality and management oversight of their board as excellent or very good. Quality oversight was defined as reviewing quality measures quarterly and patient satisfaction annually. Management oversight included the maintenance of a succession plan for the organization. While the results of this survey are specific to nonprofit health care entities, they represent the majority of health care organizations in the United States; therefore, they can be generalized. All decisions at the board level should be made with these core responsibilities in mind, in addition to the duties of care, loyalty, and obedience, which will be expanded upon in subsequent chapters. Donald Berwick, president and CEO of the Institute for Healthcare Improvement, described the board's obligation to be stewards of health care: "Until leaders own that problem, I don't think spread is going to happen. The buck stops in the board room."[11]

Governance Issues

As expectations rise, so does the need for performance benchmarks. Health care is moving to a system of definitions and measurement. Transparency is becoming the norm, and reimbursement is increasingly being based on performance. Pay-for-performance programs are a prime example. While governance organizations make recommendations about structure, health care governance in the United States remains disjointed. Without a formal educational program for new board members, they enter the role with different perceptions and knowledge of the board's role in a health care organization. Lack of education presents a fundamental problem because the playing ground is not level from the start. The result? Key decisions are being delegated to management without informed board oversight.

Core Dimensions of Governance

Because of the lack of quantifiable measures in governance, Moody's[12] describes seven core dimensions that are displayed in those boards considered effective. These dimensions pertain to nonprofit health care organizations and include:

1. Development of organization's mission
2. Selection and evaluation of senior management
3. Board composition and performance
4. Understanding and interpretation of financial reporting
5. Use of performance metrics based on external benchmarks to regularly review institution's performance
6. Maintaining and building the organization's financial resources
7. Avoidance of conflicts of interest[13]

A challenge that many organizations face is translation of the mission into strategy. Often the mission contains guiding principles for the organization, but translation into strategies that accomplish a high level of performance is difficult. The mission of the organization establishes performance objectives for its board members. However, the lack of formal education and defined competencies for board members makes it difficult to establish such objectives. At the board level, decisions must be made on behalf of the organization as a whole.

Transparency among committees and board members is critical to the success of the organization in the decision-making process. The board, as the organization's advocate, has an obligation to make sound decisions for the benefit of the community. The difference between good and great leaders is apparent in "a culture wherein people have a tremendous opportunity to be heard and, ultimately, for the truth to be heard."[7] While transparency allows for information sharing, knowledge of what to do with the information once obtained is critical to a board's success. A clear definition of board member roles and responsibilities is essential to accurately assess the board's effectiveness.

Assessment

The shift of board structure from vertical to horizontal focuses on the need for collaboration. The diversity of board membership creates a challenge that must be met head-on, and a trusting relationship must be built to foster collaboration among members.[14] A collaborative relationship must support physicians as partners. "The board must embrace and communicate continuously its belief that the hospital and physicians are in a symbiotic relationship—one cannot achieve the desired level of success without the other."[14] Providers and administration must work together with other members of the board to make sound decisions to ensure all parties' needs are met. Chapter 3 provides additional information about the duties and responsibilities of board members with an eye on the provider's role.

Collaborative relationships among board members also play an important role in the quality of care being delivered by health care organizations throughout the country. Evan Benjamin, MD, FACP, vice president for Healthcare Quality at Baystate Health in western Massachusetts, has a clear understanding of the importance of a board that embraces quality improvement. Benjamin developed a quality improvement infrastructure where physician leaders serve on performance improvement teams that ultimately report to the board. Benjamin's advice as a health care leader in an organization that has physicians serving as one-third of its board's members is: "Engage with the lay board members. The lay board members are often scared to address quality and safety because they feel it is complicated. It is important to recognize that we are asking the board to be active in quality and safety. Work closely with lay board members. There is not a mystery to quality and safety. Engaging the lay board members is key." Diversity among a health care board of directors can be a challenge, but leadership that embraces physicians as partners and actively engages lay board members will succeed.

Cultural Competence

Notable differences in the mindsets of board members is the difference between members engaged in medical professions and those in business occupations. Health care practitioners' training and education differ philosophically from the training and education in the business community. Society deems most health care occupations to be professions. The distinction that Starr suggests is that a profession "is an occupation that regulates itself through systematic, required training and collegial discipline; that has a base in technical, specialized knowledge; and that has a service rather than profit orientation, enshrined in its code of ethics."[15]

Differences in cultural alignment may be present among board members of health care organizations (Table 1.1). These differences may affect how individuals approach solutions to problems. Those board members with clinical mindsets will have spent their careers focused on individual patients, will have worked

Table 1.1 Clinical versus Business Mindset of Board Members

Mindset	Focus	Goal	Working Unit	Measure of Success	Accountability
Clinical	Patient	Health	Individual professional	Cure or amelioration	Individual
Business	Organization	Maximize wealth	Teams	Return on assets	Group and individual

most frequently as individuals, whose goal has been cure or amelioration of disease, and will have been personally accountable for their actions. Board members with business mindsets will have focused their careers on organizations, will have worked frequently in teams whose ultimate goal was maximization of shareholder wealth, and will have had group as well as personal accountability.

These cultural differences are vital to the health care board's ability to function appropriately. The benefit of this professional cultural diversity is the reason that health care boards seek members who are health care providers. To function most effectively in the unfamiliar milieu of the boardroom, however, health care practitioners must educate themselves on the skills and knowledge of their business colleagues.

Need for Board Education

On April 30, 2007, the State of New Jersey made a landmark decision to require all hospital and health system board members to complete training certified by the Department of Health and Senior Services (DHSS):

> Hospital trustee training must be completed no later than six months after the date the person is appointed as a member of the board … the subject matter of the training will include (but not necessarily be limited to) types of financial, organizational, legal, regulatory, and ethical issues that a hospital trustee may be required to consider in the course of discharging his/her governance responsibilities.[16]

The legislation was signed by Acting Governor Richard Codey and made New Jersey the first state to require trustee training. The actual components of the training had not been decided at the date of publication, but the New Jersey Hospital Association, the Hospital Alliance of New Jersey, and the New Jersey Council of Teaching Hospitals are working collaboratively to develop the training. Assemblyman Gary Schaer, a health care trustee himself, identified the need for the training and proposed the idea. The law states that the training will be a full day of education for new hospital trustees, the goal of which is to level the playing field for anyone taking a role on a health care board of directors. At present, the incentives and penalties remain unclear.[17] While legislators in New Jersey recognize the importance of trustee education, this is not the case in other states. Absent national policy or a similar law in other states, trustee education is determined by individual institutional policies.

Key Issues Facing Boards Today

Health care boards today face myriad challenges, which present themselves in five significant areas: financial, organizational, legal, regulatory, and ethical.

The cost of health care continues to rise because of increasing specialization, technological progress, and an aging and less healthy population. Rates of payment for health services are either flat, falling, or rising at a rate lower than the rate of rising costs. The narrowing margins are forcing health care boards to demand cost trimming and improvements in productivity and efficiency. Philanthropy is much more predominant in the financial planning of health care organizations than it has previously been.

Boards also must deal with serious organizational questions, which range from strategic planning decisions to nursing staff shortages to replacement of aging plants and equipment.

Legal issues are prominent in the health care environment. Medical malpractice, compliance with coding, billing, and antifraud legislation, and prosecutorial assaults on the nonprofit status of health care organizations are more frequently demanding the time and attention of health care boards.

The quality and patient safety initiatives of health care organizations are under increasingly microscopic scrutiny by regulatory agencies and the media. Local, state, and federal regulatory agencies are imposing demands on health care organizations. These requirements are generally operational in nature, but the potential threat demands that these issues be fully understood by board members. Finally, as part of a broader societal concern for ethical behavior in business organizations, health care boards are dealing with issues of justice, integrity, and conflict-of-interest with more formal and documented procedures.

Educating Health Care Providers

The educational pathways of physicians traditionally have included courses in preclinical sciences, such as anatomy and physiology, and clinical sciences, such as internal medicine and surgery, and some courses with public health or sociological bases. In this regard, programs leading to degrees in nursing have followed a path generally similar to programs leading to medical degrees. The academic curricula of health professions have not, in general, included courses with a business orientation, which would be helpful to health care professionals serving on the boards of health care organizations. The exceptions to this general rule are the curricula that lead to a Doctor of Pharmacy (PharmD) degree.[18]

One of the expressed goals of the PharmD degree program is to manage the business of the pharmacy. To that end, business management is one of the six major areas of instruction for PharmD curricula. The area of study is generally considered pharmacy administration, and it consists of courses in microeconomics, financial accounting, management, information technology, marketing, retail merchandising, and law, as it relates to pharmacy as a profession.[18] Though these courses present the fundamentals of business, which are helpful in the setting of the boardroom, they do not touch on the techniques and principles of governance, which are the relevant skill set for board members.

Historically, curricula leading to the degree of Doctor of Medicine have not included business- or governance-related courses. There are data, however, that suggest that in recent years this trend has reversed. In its 2004–2005 survey of curricula of 125 accredited medical schools in the United States and Canada, the Association of American Medical Colleges (AAMC) documented high frequencies of course offerings that may qualify for business or governance relevant education.[19] Ninety-three of 125 (74%) responding medical schools require courses in health care financing, for example, and 43 (34%) provide health care financing as an elective course. Ninety-four (75%) schools offer a required course in health care quality improvement, and 33 (26%) offer elective courses in this subject. One hundred seven (86%) schools offer required health care systems courses, and 57 (46%) offer electives. Other relevant required courses and their frequency among responding medical schools are: medical informatics (84%), medical jurisprudence (83%), medical licensure and regulation (48%), medical socioeconomics (80%), practice management (54%), health policy development (59%), and health care workforce (54%).

Medical schools are also responding to the increasing demand for economic, management, governance skills, and knowledge by offering dual-degree programs combining the MD curriculum with a master's degree in business administration.[19] These MD-MBA programs usually require 5 years of study (as opposed to 6 years, if the degrees were pursued separately). Currently, 49 schools (34% of AAMC membership) offer these dual-degree programs.

Beyond courses offered in the curricula of medical schools and joint medical-management degree programs, there is evidence that a cultural change is evolving in the way medicine is taught, and ultimately in the way it will be practiced. In November 2007, Darrell G. Kirch, MD, president of the AAMC, urged academic medical centers to undertake radical change: "While higher education and health care have held fast to their traditional, individualistic culture," Dr. Kirch noted that "the world has fundamentally changed to a greater emphasis on collaborative, coordinated, and integrative efforts in research, patient care, and medical education."[20]

Schools of nursing have broadened their curricula to include topics that will be helpful to members of that profession who are called upon to serve on health care boards. The American Association of Colleges of Nursing (AACN) has published documents that delineate the essential characteristics of curricula for bachelor, master's, and doctorate degrees in nursing.[21]

In the 1998 document for baccalaureate education for nursing practice, the AACN delineated five components for professional nursing education[21]: a liberal education, professional values, core competencies, core knowledge, and role development. Among the core competencies were knowledge of "health care systems and policy," including "an understanding of the organization and environment in which nursing and health care is provided." The baccalaureate graduate in nursing is expected to have the knowledge and skills to:

- Understand the organization and financing of health care delivery systems
- Identify economic, legal, and political influences on health care
- Participate in efforts to influence health care on behalf of others
- Understand cost factors in health care
- Understand the effects of legal and regulatory pressures on health care[21]

The AACN is in the process of revising "The Essentials of Baccalaureate Education for Professional Nursing Practice,"[21] and the new requirements will include emphasis on leadership theory and skills, communication, patient safety, and team work. All of this knowledge and these skills, as well as those identified earlier in the AACN 1998 document, will enhance nurses' professional clinical practice and will be the educational basis for effective board membership in the nurses' careers.

Graduate medical education altered radically in 1999 when the Accreditation Council for Graduate Medical Education (ACGME) proposed changes in the competencies for training future physicians.[22] Implemented in 2007, the requirements contain two new competencies, practice-based learning and improvement and systems-based practice, which call for skills not previously part of residency programs. Knowledge and technical skill in quality improvement processes, information technology, health care delivery systems cost-effectiveness, and team theory that are now required of all residents will improve their medical care in the present and will prepare them for board membership and efficacy in the future.[23] While these new requirements will help prepare future providers, the challenge of educating providers currently in practice still remains.

Book Organization

Each chapter in the book has been structured to maximize clarity and facilitate learning. Following the chapter title there is a brief executive summary, which provides an overview of the chapter's contents. A list of learning objectives details what you can expect to learn once you have read the chapter. A list of key words helps the reader focus on important terminology contained in the chapter. A brief introduction precedes the central content of the chapter. A succinct conclusion follows, and in each chapter, the authors include a case study that emphasizes the most important issues addressed in the chapter and may serve as a source for further thought and more formal analysis of these issues. Next, the authors list several study and discussion questions, which may be helpful to assess the accomplishment of the learning objectives at the conclusion of the chapter. This section will also prove to be useful when the book is utilized in the academic environment. The authors also provide "Suggested Readings and Web Sites" for additional resources related to the chapter's content. Finally, the references relevant to the chapter material are provided as an additional source of information.

This book is a tool for health care providers about to take a role on a health care board of directors. The authors that have been chosen as contributors to *Governance for Health Care Providers: The Call to Leadership* are key thought leaders on health care governance. They have vast experience in the governance arena and have contributed significantly to the field. Each of the 15 chapters has been organized with careful detail to current hot topics in health care governance. Each chapter provides a primer on an area of health care governance and defines the provider's role. The topics covered in this book will provide you with the tools necessary to make well-informed decisions and answer *the call to leadership*.

Conclusion

As a health care provider, your role on a board of directors will expand your view of the health care landscape and provide a vision for the organization's future. Armed with the knowledge this book provides, you will be prepared for the role and have a clearer understanding of the evolving responsibilities of a health care board of directors. While the composition, structure, and function are the foundation on which a board of directors is built, each of these vary by the type of organization.

A discussion of the core responsibilities and dimensions of governance provide a basic understanding of what can be expected. However, it is apparent that board education in advance of board membership is imperative. This book recognizes the need for provider education, and therefore addresses this group of trustees that are often left out of governance discussions. The subsequent chapters contain principles and concepts of governance that will help you define your role and prepare for the responsibilities that lie ahead. Use this book as a tool and as a guide throughout your journey on a health care board of directors.

Case Study

Gloria Sheehan locked her car door and began to walk across the parking lot to the entrance of Saint Mary's Hospital. She was going to have to hurry or she would be a little late for her first meeting as a member of the hospital board of trustees. She did not have quite enough time to study the 300-page meeting information packet that she had received the week before.

Before Gloria had reached the door, she was stopped by Rita Purcell, Saint Mary's chief nursing officer, a position that Gloria had held for 5 years until her retirement 2 years ago.

"Gloria," said Rita, "I was delighted to hear that you had been elected to the board. We had been hoping that they would select a nurse. You will bring so much patient care experience to the board. They really need that. And listen, you've got to make them ease up on the budget limitations for hiring agency nurses. I can't staff the floors without agency nurses. Our turnover rate for employed nurses has soared since the new president came in."

Gloria thanked Rita for her good wishes and made a mental note about the agency nurse budget problem. It was the first she had heard of an agency nurse funding problem. Two years ago, they had not used agency nurses at Saint Mary's.

In the lobby of the hospital, Gloria ran into Dr. Tom Clemens, chief of surgery at Saint Mary's and, for the past 40 years, practice partner of Dr. James Sheehan, Gloria's husband. "Gloria, you've got to get the board off their rear ends and make a decision on the SurgiCenter Joint Venture that Jimmy and I are proposing. The strategic planning wonks have been studying it for 6 months, and while they've been dithering, Memorial Medical has broken ground on their center two blocks away."

"I'll look into it, Tom," she said as she slipped onto the elevator just as the doors closed.

Fifteen seconds and two floors later, the doors opened, and Gloria walked out, nearly colliding with a young man who introduced himself: "Mrs. Sheehan, I am Nick Reynolds, the new hospital CFO. Welcome to the board. I hope you had a chance to look at the financials. I won't be able to go into detail because they've cut my time to 10 minutes, but I wanted to let you know that I have reviewed the numbers, and the days in AR is 64, not 57, and the cash on hand is 80 days, and, oh, yeah, our ratios have slipped a little, and we are close to technical default on the covenants for the last bond offering."

Gloria felt as though she was staggering as she opened the door and walked into the boardroom. The meeting was already in progress.

"Gloria, welcome," said Bob Davidson, the board chair. "We were just reviewing the committee assignments for this year. I'd like you to chair the audit committee."

Study and Discussion Questions

1. What human resources issues can Gloria expect to deal with in the near future as a board member?
2. Does Gloria have any potential conflict-of-interest problems that would reduce her effectiveness as a board member?
3. Will the hosptial's strategic plan be an important document to Gloria in the near future?
4. How will Gloria best understand the financial issues that have been suggested to her?
5. Should Gloria agree to serve as audit committee chair?

Suggested Readings and Web Sites

Readings

Collins, J. 2001. *Good to great*. New York: HarperBusiness.

Fuchs, V. R. 1974. *Who shall live? Health, economics, and social choice*. New York: Basic Books.

Gawande, A. 2002. *Complications: A surgeon's notes on an imperfect science*. New York: Metropolitan Books.

Gawande, A. 2007. *Better: A surgeon's notes on performance*. New York: Metropolitan Books.

Pointer, D. D. and Orlikoff, J. E. 2002. *Getting to great: Principles of health care organization governance*. San Francisco: Jossey-Bass.

Porter, M. E. and Teisberg, E. O. 2006. *Redefining health care: Creating value-based competition on results*. Boston: Harvard Business School Press.

Starr, P. 1982. *The social transformation of American medicine*. New York: Basic Books.

Web Sites

American Hospital Association: http://www.aha.org
Center for Healthcare Governance: http://www.americangovernance.com
The Governance Institute: http://www.governanceinstitute.com
Health Affairs: http://www.healthaffairs.org
Institute for Healthcare Improvement: http://www.ihi.org
Joint Commission: http://www.jointcommission.org
MedStar Health, Inc.: http://www.medstarhealth.org/
Thomas Jefferson University Department of Health Policy: http://www.jefferson.edu/dhp/

References

1. Menninger, B. 2005. Do MDs or MBAs make better leaders? *HealthLeaders*.
2. The Governance Institute. 2007. *Boardsx4* Governance structures and practices*. San Diego, CA.
3. Orlikoff, J. E. and M. K. Totten. 2001. *The trustee handbook for health care governance*. 2nd ed. Chicago: Health Forum.
4. American Hospital Association. 2007. *Fast facts on U.S. hospitals*. Washington, DC.
5. Kovner, A. R. 2002. Governance and management. In *Health care delivery in the United States*, ed. A. R. Kovner and S. Jonas, chap. 13, 339–61. 7th ed. New York: Springer Publishing Company.
6. Center for Healthcare Governance. 2007. *Building an exceptional board: Effective practices for health care governance—Report of the Blue Ribbon Panel on Health Care Governance*, 68. Chicago.
7. Collins, J. 2001. *Good to great*. New York: Harper Business.
8. Pointer, D. D. and J. E. Orlikoff. 1999. *Board work governing health care organizations*. San Francisco: Jossey-Bass Publishers.
9. Lukas, C. V., S. K. Holmes, A. B. Cohen, J. Restuccia, I. E. Cramer, M. Shwartz, and M. P. Charns. 2007. Transformational change in health care systems: An organizational model. *Health Care Management Review* 32:309–20.
10. Center for Healthcare Governance. http://www.americangovernance.com/americangovernance_app/index.jsp (accessed January 11, 2007).
11. Schyve, P. M. 2006. An interview with Donald Berwick. *Joint Commission Journal on Quality and Patient Safety* 32:661–66.
12. Goldstein, L. 2008. *Clinical quality initiatives have positive long-term impact on not-for-profit hospital bond ratings*. Moody's U.S. Public Finance. New York: Moody's Investors Service.
13. Viacava, D. F. 2005. *Governance of not-for-profit healthcare organizations*. New York: Moody's Investors Service.
14. Kazemek, E. A. 2006. Physician collaboration. *Healthcare Executive*, July/August, p. 54.
15. Starr, P. 1982. *The social transformation of American medicine*. New York: Basic Books.

16. New Jersey State Legislature—Bills 2006–2007. New Jersey Office of Legislative Services. http://www.njleg.state.nj.us/bills/BillView.asp (accessed October 13, 2007).

17. Becker, C. May 28, 2007. Getting schooled in governance: New Jersey enacts law that will require trustees to receive certified training through class, special leadership curriculum. *Modern Healthcare* 37(22):6–7, 16, 1.

18. American Association of Colleges of Pharmacy. The PharmD curriculum. http://www.pharmcas.org/advisors/pharmdcurriculum.htm (accessed December 9, 2007).

19. Association of American Medical Colleges. AAMC curriculum management & information tool. http://services.aamc.org/currdir/section2/04_05hottopics.pdf (accessed December 9, 2007).

20. Kirch, D. G. AAMC president calls on medical education leaders to focus on culture change. http://www.aamc.org/newsroom/pressrel/2007/071104a.htm (accessed December 9, 2007).

21. Association of American Colleges of Nursing. http://www.aacn.nche.edu/Education/pdf/BEdraft.pdf (accessed December 9, 2007).

22. Accreditation Council for Graduate Medical Education. http://www.acgme.org/outcome/comp/GeneralCompetenciesStandards21307.pdf (accessed December 9, 2007).

23. Moskowitz, E. and D. B. Nash. 2000. Accreditation Council for Graduate Medical Education competencies: Practice-based learning and systems-based practice. *American Journal of Medical Quality* 22:351–82.

Chapter 2

Governance: Back to Basics

Jona Raasch and James Rice

Contents

Executive Summary

The governance structure of an organization is linked to its success. The first challenge that any board faces is defining how it will govern its organization. For provider trustees, understanding the organization's governance structure is essential to understanding the organization's priorities. There is a fine line between governance and management that is not always clear. A successful board collaborates with and regularly evaluates upper-level management to ensure alignment of goals. Creating a board culture of excellence starts with getting the right people to the table, educating them about the role of a trustee, and providing them the tools to fulfill the role.

Learning Objectives

1. To understand the challenge of defining governance and board structure.
2. To understand the distinction between boards and management and the importance of regular evaluation to maintain alignment of board actions with the organization's mission.
3. To understand the importance of selecting trustees committed to creating a board culture that supports ongoing education and development.

Key Words

- Board education
- Continuing education
- Culture of excellence
- Efficacy
- Governance
- Performance evaluation
- Recruitment and selection

Introduction

High-performing hospitals and health systems are governed by a board of trustees that directs the plans, policies, and funds to best achieve the organization's mission and vision. As a provider, you are attuned to the work of trustees, and you understand the focus of the board's efforts; however, your role as a trustee may not be as clear. High-performing boards orient more to the future than to the past, more on the strategic than on the tactical, and more to guide and support management than to do the work of management.

This chapter explores practical strategies being employed by high-performing boards across the United States, but also anchors this scan of effective practices within a broader global recognition that governance matters for health care and health gain. The micro level of the health provider institution is not the sole focus. The meso and macro levels of societies must also be understood to make sound governance decisions. Health care providers can leverage their talents by exploring ways to understand, engage in, and master all levels of hospital and health system enterprise governance.

The Challenge of Defining Governance

There is now a global consensus that a major, urgent effort must be made to strengthen health system performance if the public in both developed and developing nations is to achieve good value for their money and enhanced health care and health gain. Better governance is an essential prerequisite to this enhanced performance. World Bank leaders observe that health system strengthening is neither an end in itself nor a single-sector effort. "Adequate financing, a sound regulatory framework for private-public collaboration, good governance, robust insurance schemes, provider payment and incentive mechanisms, timely and accurate information, well-trained personnel, and a basic facility infrastructure must all be in place to ensure equitable access to effective health, nutrition and population interventions and a continuum of care to save and improve people's lives."[1]

This new-found focus on governance in health sectors needs to include evaluation of institutional governance, the micro level of governance, which is the focus of this book. It also should include a focus on the meso level, the study of interrelationships among institutions within a nation's health sector. How society balances its investments of human and financial resources for better health and health care, health protection, health funding and insurance, health provision by health professionals, and new forms of diagnostic and surgery centers and hospitals are meso-level considerations. The macro level encompasses the interplay among nations in such challenging arenas as global bioterrorism, pandemics, response to natural disasters like regional war and tsunamis, and cross-border threats from economic competition and movement of scarce health workers. The meso governance challenges are usually addressed by the country's ministry of health and legislative bodies. The macro level of governance is managed by varied cross-national governance bodies as the World Health Organization, World Bank, Organization for Economic Cooperation and Development, and World Trade Association.

In the U.S. health sector, of almost 4000 hospitals, 85% are tax-exempt. This status is determined either by virtue of their ownership by a local city or county government (about 10% of all hospitals, which usually have elected or appointed boards from seven to nine members), or because they have been accepted by the federal and state governments to be operating as a charity. Those organizations deemed to deliver charity care are engaged in health care delivery and education on behalf of the public's health. Most have boards of 11 to 15 members who are invited to serve as community volunteers. There are approximately 100,000 community leaders who volunteer to serve on these boards; the majority (over 87%) does not receive compensation for service on behalf of their communities.

The governing boards of these tax-exempt organizations are generally an organized group of elected or appointed people with the authority to control and direct the organization. Most case law and governmental regulations have defined that these boards are legally responsible for the operations (quality, fiscal vitality, and policies) of the enterprise. The board is responsible for establishing the strategic direction for the organization in concert with its mission or reason for being, establishing policies that guide the enterprise to achieve its mission and plans, maintaining quality patient care, providing for sound institutional management, and ensuring the protection and enhancement of the financial well-being of the organization. The governing board delegates day-to-day management to the chief executive officer (CEO) and patient care to the medical staff, but the board is ultimately held accountable by the public and the government on behalf of the public's interests. Performance and ethical behavior of the organization in pursuit of its charitable purposes for the public's health and health care are the board's responsibility.

In the United States, the average board size for all types of hospitals and systems is 13 members—health system boards tend to have more voting board members (18) and government-sponsored hospitals have fewer (seven to eight). For nearly half of the organizations (48%), the CEO is a voting board member (on 14% of boards the CEO is a nonvoting board member), and on 38% the CEO is a non–board member but regularly attends meetings. In approximately 43% of the organizations, the head of the medical staff (chief of staff or president of the medical staff) is a voting board member. However, 11% with this designation are nonvoting board members, 36% are non–board members but regularly attend meetings, and 10% do not attend meetings. In most organizations the CEO and the chief of staff are present at board meetings, even when these positions are not designated as *ex officio* board positions. Other management positions commonly represented as nonvoting members that regularly attend meetings are the chief operating officer (COO), vice president of medical affairs (VPMA), chief financial officer (CFO), and chief nursing officer (CNO). The average number of medical staff physicians who are voting board members is two. Most frequently these are physicians who are on the medical staff but who are not employed by the organization.[2]

Most organizations do have provider representation on the board—either *ex officio* (chief of staff, for example) or board appointed—the average is two providers who are virtually always physicians. In addition to the CEO, other representatives from the executive team usually attend board meetings (but are not board members). The most frequently noted executive management in attendance are the chief financial officer, chief medical officer or vice president of medical affairs, chief nursing officer, and chief operating officer. Only in rare instances do these positions have a formal seat at the boardroom table.[2]

Managing Gray Lines between Boards and Management

The line between governance and management can sometimes blur. In fact, we believe there is no real line between the two. The distinction can more accurately be characterized as interplay between distinguishable units—like the movement of the ocean and its waves breaking on a beach—subject to constant movement as environmental circumstances change.[3]

The health care board must represent and balance the interests of its diverse constituents. This is best accomplished by focusing board efforts on policy governance—the area where the board is best positioned to add value to the organization. Sometimes, however, boards drift into the responsibilities of management, to the detriment of the organization. Boards must give their management enough freedom to do its job creatively while observing and ensuring appropriate direction and oversight from the governing body. This is difficult to accomplish, but it is central to the job of governing.

Management must accomplish tasks necessary to meet the organizational goals established by the board. It also serves as the in-house expert on the day-to-day activities of the organization and the interpreter of local, regional, and national trends in the health care industry. The success of a health care organization depends greatly on the working relationship between the board and executive management. Neither can be effective without the other. Together, they make the organization dynamic, robust, and strong.

There has been an increasing tendency for the lines of responsibility drawn between management and governance to blur slightly as boards and managers redefine their roles. Boards stray into operations and away from policy for three main reasons: they pursue what is most familiar to them; they feel the need to step in when they replace their CEO; and they lose faith in the CEO (Tables 2.1 and 2.2).

There are several summary points on the distinction between management and governance that merit emphasis:

Table 2.1 Top 10 Causes of Board Member Frustration with Management

1. Surprises at board meetings (i.e., a large deal or capital project has all of a sudden sprung onto the table).
2. Giving long speeches at board meetings, leaving little time for quality discussion on important, future-oriented issues.
3. Overwhelming the board with management detail; not enough easy-to-read and easy-to-understand information in graphic or picture form.
4. Treating board members as figureheads, when they should be treated as valuable and respected assets from which to invite counsel on strategic directions or community relations.
5. Waiting to seek board counsel until the problem has reached crisis stage.
6. Often being at odds with the physicians.
7. Spending too much time on analysis before taking action.
8. Lack of clear criteria for CEO performance evaluation.
9. Weak orientation and not enough ongoing education about the complexities of finance and quality in the health sector.
10. Lack of clear expectations of what one needs to do to be a great board member, and assessments of the board member's performance against the criteria.

- The distinction between governance and management varies from organization to organization and, from time to time, within each organization.
- When the board steps outside its governance domain, it can make matters worse, and this usually results in a rift between the board and executive management.
- The very nature of governance roles helps boards to take strategic approaches to issues rather than focus on operational matters.
- By fulfilling their policy-making role, boards most clearly follow their governance directive.
- Most health care boards need to spend more time formulating policy, specifically nonoperating policy.

Ideally, the board and the CEO have a symbiotic relationship, each being accountable to the other while pursuing the same goals. Optimal organizational performance is a joint endeavor.[4] Great hospital performance is a function of great governance. Great governance is related to great board–CEO relations.

Table 2.2   Top 10 Causes of CEOs' Frustration with Boards

1. Poor meeting attendance or lack of preparation for the discussions on the agenda.
2. Waffling on support of difficult and controversial decisions in meetings after they said they were ready to move forward.
3. Treating the health system "just like any other business" and focusing on achieving the best financial results without regard for vision and mission.
4. Having direct or indirect conflicts of interest (especially physicians), even after the board's adoption of a compliance plan, and expecting the CEO (rather than the board or committee chairman) to discipline trustees who violate compliance plans and policies.
5. Board members (especially board officers) who seek, encourage, or allow the COO, CFO, and other senior administrators to communicate directly with them without the CEO's knowledge.
6. Encouraging or allowing medical staff members to use social or family relationships to "inform the board" or lobby for specific decisions or actions.
7. Failure of the board to elect new members who (1) bring needed experience to the board, (2) have talents that complement, rather than duplicate, those of existing members, and (3) are able to be objective when difficult decisions need to be made.
8. Unwillingness to devote time needed to (1) learn about health care as a different business than those in which they are experienced, and (2) keep up with changes in health care, health care financing, and health care governance.
9. Pressuring the hospital to work with local vendors that do not give the best service or price.
10. Board chair who does not (1) establish priorities for work of the board and each board committee each year (in consultation with the CEO), (2) approve the agenda for each meeting, and (3) require each committee chairman to complete specific priority work during the year and report to the board chair and the board on the committee's work.

One of the most important roles of the board is the hiring, support, and development of a talented CEO. There should be a formal succession plan developed for the CEO, and the CEO should periodically report on the parallel plans for his or her direct reports. There should be a formal annual CEO performance planning meeting with the board chairperson and executive committee before the start of the fiscal year.

Good CEO performance assessments provide an opportunity for mutual definition of CEO and board expectations for the year's performance targets and related strategies. The CEO should have a mid-year progress review and an end-of-year performance review that is related to incentive compensation. High-performing boards periodically survey CEO employment arrangements at comparable organizations to ensure the reasonableness and competitiveness of the CEO's compensation package. The Internal Revenue Service is now more assertive in its calls for reporting of executive compensation arrangements on Form 990. This may generate media reviews that should be carefully anticipated by the CEO and board leadership.

Although there are no panaceas, one essential prerequisite reported by boards and CEOs from across the United States is to build and nurture CEO–board chair relations. While a strong relationship between the board chair and CEO does not guarantee a strong relationship between the CEO and the board, it is almost impossible to achieve this relationship without starting with that of the board chair and CEO. The overall relationship needs to be built on T^3: trust, transparency, and truthfulness. An essential ingredient for the embrace of these three facets is communication, which should address the C^3, F^3, and I^3 features of the relationship:

- Community, cash, and conflicts (common foci of board–CEO communications)
- Formal, friendly, and frequent (the style of board–CEO communication)
- Ideas, issues, and initiatives (the outputs of board–CEO communication)

Importance of the CEO Performance Evaluation

The Joint Commission (formerly the Joint Commission on Accreditation of Healthcare Organizations [JCAHO]) mandates routine assessment of chief executive performance, and observers clearly view this activity as a primary indicator of good governance.

This is not a responsibility many board members enjoy, but it is fundamental to good governance. It aligns the organizational mission, values, goals, and objectives with the organization and CEO's performance. The chief executive may have anxieties about being evaluated, but the need to know typically outweighs any fears, and in fact, executives usually want and need structured performance evaluations.

Both the board and the CEO need a clear vision of where the organization should be. The vision helps delineate an overall plan to guide the CEO's activities. As the CEO executes the plan, the board needs assurance that the CEO's leadership and direction remain compatible with the organization's vision and goals. Performance evaluation gives both the board and the CEO an opportunity to measure progress. At this level, CEO and organizational performance are largely inseparable.

The Value of a Good Performance Evaluation

The board deals with many issues and responsibilities, but its primary function is to establish and maintain a framework for the effective, legal, and ethical operation of the organization. It does this through a combination of directives and specifications: the mission statement, board bylaws, board policies, strategic plan, short-term and long-term goals and objectives, and the selection and routine evaluation of the chief executive. The CEO is responsible for implementing board policies, adhering to the mission and values of the organization, managing the organization in accordance with the mission and policies, and working toward organizational goal achievement by being the board's leadership partner.

Great boards should expect an effective CEO evaluation to accomplish at least the following:

1. Clarify the board's expectations of the CEO.
2. Provide clear goals to help the CEO identify and prioritize work to be accomplished.
3. Educate the board about the nature of the CEO's responsibilities, roles, and duties.
4. Focus the CEO on things that really matter to the board and to the direction of the organization.

An *effective* evaluation also benefits the CEO:

1. It helps the CEO develop and upgrade competencies and experiences.
2. It gives the CEO an opportunity to engage in self-assessment of personal performance.
3. It provides the CEO with honest feedback, direction, and reaffirmation regarding performance.
4. It eliminates surprise—the "well-known board-to-CEO evaluation pattern known as 'good job, good job, good job—gone!'"[5]

A good performance evaluation ultimately nurtures the growth and development of both the chief executive and the organization.[3,4]

The Efficacy of Board Committees

Establishment of board committees balances the need for board members to become better informed in selected aspects of board work, ensures focused and disciplined attention to board challenges and an equitable division of labor among board members. These committees and related meeting structures significantly improve the efficiency and effectiveness of board work, and enhance the use of the time and talents of the executive team.

The median number of committees reported by the Governance Institute's 2007 Biennial Survey of Hospitals and Healthcare Systems is 4.86. Only 6% of respondents do not have board committees. There has been a statistically significant increase over the last 2 years in the percentage of organizations reporting the following committees: governance and nominating, quality, strategic planning, and executive compensation.[2] High-performing boards trust their committees, but avoid having too many. Contemporary boards are merging committees to better use the time and talents of their board members and executives. For those that have board committees, meeting frequency varies. Over half of the respondents said their finance committees meet monthly, but the other committees tend to meet less frequently.

Board committees do not act in place of the board, but serve at their request to ensure that policy decision making is based on as much good information and analysis as possible, without unnecessarily consuming the board's time.

A desirable core set of committees are:

Strategy and finance: This combination better integrates the functions of strategic and financial planning.

Quality and professional affairs: This combination embraces a focus on patient quality and the role of credentialed health professionals to accomplish higher levels of quality and patient safety.

Governance and mission effectiveness: This combination ensures that the board is focused on such related tasks as board competency definition, board member recruitment, orientation, education, and processes to ensure mission achievement. The board should measure their performance utilizing a board self-assessment.

Executive: This committee meets infrequently when urgency precludes the full board's convening. It can also lead the CEO's performance planning, appraisal and compensation philosophy work.

Committee membership: Each board committee or task force should be chaired by a member of the board. Non–board members can be invited to serve on any board committee with or without vote, and the work of committees must move to the full board for final action or ratification. Committees are expected to consist of approximately three to seven members. Health care professionals are increasingly invited to serve on these board committees.

Committee charters and work plans: Each committee should follow a charter (purpose and authority, desired member competencies, duties and responsibilities, evaluation) and should establish a calendar of routinely scheduled meetings. It should follow an annual committee action plan that is adopted before the commencement of the fiscal year of the organization. When possible, committees should undergo an annual formal effectiveness evaluation.

Creating a Board Culture of Excellence

The culture of the board is defined to mean the "pattern of beliefs, traditions, and practices that prevail when a board of directors convenes to carry out its fiduciary duties."[6] It includes "the norms and values that boards hold and the way board members work together."[7]

The characteristics of a good board culture are similar to those of any good relationship, personal or professional. Actually, they closely resemble the characteristics of a partnership. Evidence of good board culture includes the following[8]:

- Board work and conversations that demonstrate commitment to the organization's mission
- Trusting relationships
- Open, candid, and transparent discussions
- Mutual respect
- Active participation
- Strong board leadership
- Collegial and professional relationships
- Humor

The responsibility to create an effective board culture ultimately rests with each member of the board, but it is most often established and nurtured by the board chairperson and CEO. The board should regularly discuss the aspects of a good board culture and identify actions for its enhancement.[8]

Board enthusiasm increases in a positive culture when the board wisely uses the time of its board and committee members, as well as that of its executive team. To balance a need for rigorous oversight of the affairs of the health system and the cost-effective use of the time and talents of the governance participants, an effective practice is to rely on an annual calendar with these key characteristics:

■ The board meets every other month and receives written reports from management and committees in the intervening months.
■ High-performance committees meet variably according to their work plans, usually four to nine times per year.
■ Board members are expected to attend at least 70% of all meetings in a year, in person or via teleconferencing.
■ The board engages health professionals in a concept of clinical governance.

As hospitals and health systems expand the range of clinical services into more fully integrated care systems with multiple service delivery venues and levels of care, their boards recognize the importance of engaging health professionals in the institution's governance processes. Whether invited to serve on the board or one of its committees, or invited into one of the governance decision-making processes (for example, strategic planning, community health improvement, quality assurance, capital allocations, investing in the recruitment of scarce health manpower), the health care professional will need to prepare for the effective and efficient investment of time and talents.

Great boards continuously scan the horizon for new concepts and tools for enhanced governance. Increasingly these strategies will explore the new concepts of shared governance,[9] clinical governance, and various forms of internal operational governance bodies that balance leadership of physicians, nurses, allied health professionals, and members of the overall fiduciary board. The U.K. National Health Service's development of clinical governance holds promise for high-performing hospitals and health systems in the United States.

When health professionals are invited to participate in the board's activities, they must be clear on the role they are assuming. If they are participating as a board member, they must accept and place the role of a board member as the top priority, and they must ensure that they are thinking, operating, and participating with the organization's mission and strategic plan in mind at all times. Conflict-of-interest must be understood, and policies must be in place that enable board members to proactively and consciously participate effectively.

Support System for the Board

The high-performing board continuously drives toward open access to information that enhances board member knowledge and the confidence to ethically apply the knowledge for ever smarter governance effectiveness. New digital forms for knowledge management are needed in modern health system governance.

The board needs to develop enhanced monitoring processes and systems for performance of the care system and facilities. There should be a consensus reached prior to each fiscal year using a balanced scorecard of key quarterly or, in some cases, monthly performance measures that the board will monitor during the year, in these common performance dimensions:

- Quality and patient safety
- Service expansion and enhancement
- Financial vitality
- Human capital development
- Growth
- Community relations

Wherever possible, these measures should be available in easy-to-read, electronic (online) charts and graphs that facilitate board member understanding of trends and patterns of performance against industry benchmarks, including the organization's prior year performance, and a range of performance measures that the board and management have agreed to at the start of the fiscal year.

The board should continue to enhance its reliance on modern digital means of reporting and performance monitoring by using an intranet Web site that provides continuous access to a password-protected site with information such as:

- Photographs and biographies of all board members, senior managers, and physician leaders
- Board orientation manual, including board roles and responsibility policy statements
- Board policy and procedure manual
- Board educational white papers or related reading materials
- Periodic communiqués from the CEO and board chairperson
- Hospital events board members might be expected to attend
- Committee charters and work plans
- Committee meeting calendars
- Minutes of committee meetings
- Links to governance best practice information sites
- Links to tools and surveys used in the annual board self-assessment and CEO performance review

Board Education and Development

High-performing boards continuously enhance their orientation program and educational development plans and budget. These programs should focus on three levels: the board as a group, each committee, and each individual board member. Board members should also have a simple, personal, and customized development strategy that identifies topics they would like to develop in the coming year. Board members should be encouraged to participate in at least one educational activity each year, whether at board meetings, state hospital associations, or out of state at conferences with similar hospitals and experienced board leaders. More senior board members can serve as mentors to help orient new board members. Each board member should participate in a formal orientation program and tour of the organization's facilities within 60 days of joining the board.

The governing board has the ability to shape the best possible future for the health care organization. What a hospital or health system becomes will depend largely on the values its trustees hold and the leadership they provide.

A governing board should be made up of people with a variety of skills and expertise, community connections, occupations, ages, and backgrounds. Board members need to have time, commitment, interest, and the ability to work together. Boards should actively seek knowledge of recommended or best practices. They should identify those best practices that will benefit their own board work, and modify them so they fit the culture and values of the board to become part of the way the board operates on an ongoing basis. High-performing boards do much more than the minimal actions to maintain legal compliance.

Trustee Selection and Recruitment

Prior to identifying prospective board members, a profile and evaluation of the existing board should be completed. This will identify skills and abilities of current board members. The hospital's strategic plan should be examined to identify the skills and abilities needed to enable the board to meet the hospital's future needs. Selection criteria should be developed for new board members. Board member candidates should be continually recruited (the board, administration, medical staff, and community members may identify candidates). Prospective board members must understand their role, responsibilities, and the time commitment.

For some organizations, especially in rural settings or smaller communities where outstanding leaders are already participating on numerous boards, it is becoming more difficult to identify and recruit board members. Some organizations are holding informational meetings and receptions inviting individuals or organizations to learn more about the hospital, the important role the hospital plays in the community, and what it takes to be a board member.

These are common criteria for selecting board members:

- Dedication to mission, vision, and organizational success
- Sufficient time and energy
- Financial and business sense
- Integrity
- Specific skills or expertise needed by the hospital or health system's strategic plan
- Ability to evaluate managerial skills and performance
- Principles of medicine, insurance, law, and real estate
- Corporate and civic leadership
- Involvement in the community
- Flexibility
- Creativity
- Ability to function as part of a team

Board tenure and method of election and appointment for public hospital board members are usually specified by state statutes, hospital district enabling legislation, or city or county charters. Other tax-exempt hospitals and health systems typically seek term limits of 3 years. However, not all hospital boards have term limits; overall, 58% of U.S. nonprofit hospitals (including government-sponsored hospitals) have term limits in place.[2]

Board Orientation and Continuing Education

Board education is an ongoing process beginning with new trustee orientation and continuing education opportunities for the entire board. The objective of board education is to increase trustees' knowledge and understanding of the hospital's programs and services, future opportunities and direction, financial issues, the many changes occurring in health care and how they affect the hospital and the board's roles and responsibilities. Having and using a board manual, participating on committees, reading articles, and attending board retreats and trustee conferences are forms of trustee education.

The Governance Institute, a leading resource for hospital and health system boards, executives, and physician leaders, reports a significant increase—especially in the last 2 years—of health care provider attendance at its leadership conferences. These providers attend health policy and governance-related sessions, side by side with trustees. According to one Governance Institute executive, this increase is being driven by increased scrutiny from lawmakers and regulators, and a growing emphasis on accountability for organizational integrity, quality of care, and patient safety. It is imperative that organizations not only provide excellent board member orientation and continuing education, but also nurture opportunities for board members and health providers to jointly participate in these endeavors.

The Board Manual

A governing board manual provides direction as the board carries out its responsibilities.

The manual should be unique to the organization and should contain:

- A history of the organization
- The organization's:
  - Vision statement
  - Mission statement
  - Goals
  - Articles of incorporation
  - Governing statute (public hospitals)
  - Code of ethics
  - Bylaws
- Service area description
- Organizational chart
- Governing board:
  - Board job description
  - Board chair job description
  - Board member job description
  - Board self-assessment process
  - List of members
  - Officers
  - Committees
  - Liability indemnification policy
  - Conflict-of-interest policy statement
- Annual report
- Annual budget summary
- Long-range strategic plan
- Affiliations and agreements
- Physical layout of the facilities
- Chief executive officer:
  - CEO job description
  - Contract with CEO
  - CEO evaluation process

- Medical staff:
  - Medical staff bylaws
  - Committee structure
  - Types of appointments and privileges
- Quality assurance and patient safety plan
- Corporate compliance plan
- Board calendar of meetings and events
- Board policies

A Checklist for Governing Board Excellence

A review of high-performing boards indicates that an effective board will:

√ Focus on where the hospital is going and how the board will know when it gets there
√ Develop a positive and dynamic relationship with their chief executive officer
√ Set policy, direction, and strategy but not manage the hospital
√ Encourage each trustee to share and contribute his or her talents and skills to the board and the hospital
√ Create an environment of respect and cooperation where trustees can be truthful, ask questions, and speak their concerns
√ Invest in two-way communication with the medical staff
√ Listen to and hear one another
√ Perform an annual board self-evaluation

Conclusion

Governance of a health care organization can be considered the result of a coordinated effort between the board of directors and the executive staff. The board of directors is responsible for the establishment of plans, policies, and funding for the organization, and the executive staff is responsible for direction of all activities that implement the organization's mission. Health care providers, as members of the governing board, can bring a unique and invaluable perspective to the board's functions.

To do this most effectively, health care providers and their fellow board members must have a sophisticated understanding of the similarities and differences between governance (primarily board functions) and management (primarily executive staff functions). Health care providers must also understand in detail the relationships among the board, the board chair, and the CEO of the organization.

Health care provider board members must be actively and appropriately involved in the board committee structure, and they must strive to work toward a board culture of excellence—both individually and collectively as a contributing member of the governing board. These responsibilities will take active effort on the part of most health care provider board members, because traditional health care educational pathways do not include training to build these skills.

Serving as a member of a board is a commitment that requires participation in continuing education efforts and in development and recruitment of talented trustees who will ensure the continuity of board excellence into the future. The present function and future success of all health care organizations are fully dependent on their governing boards, and health care provider board members are called to exemplify excellence.

Case Study

A 180-bed community hospital on the East Coast invited a retired nurse to its board of 15 members. On the board for only 1 month, the nurse missed her board orientation and has not yet had an opportunity to meet with her assigned board mentor. Eager to gain a sense of the pulse of the employee and nurses' morale since she retired from the hospital last year, she stopped by yesterday unannounced to visit a few medical surgical units in the hospital. She was warmly welcomed as a new board member and received an earful about the needs for better medical equipment and requests for enhanced patient quality training for physicians and nurses.

On her way home, she happened to meet an acquaintance from church who works as the editor at the local newspaper. In an unguarded moment she comments: "The hospital is making great strides in its medical services, but really needs to expand its programming for clinical care quality." Now intrigued, the editor calls the board chairman and asks: "I understand that the hospital is not yet doing enough to protect patient safety and quality, and I am curious what the board plans on doing to improve the situation?" The board chairman, ever eager to nurture a positive rapport with the media, agrees to meet tomorrow over lunch to continue the discussion.

Study and Discussion Questions

1. If you were a leader of the management, the medical staff, or the nursing staff, what challenges do you see in this situation, and how should the board chairman best approach the lunch meeting?
2. Who should the chairman talk with and perhaps include in the lunch meeting? Should the lunch meeting be postponed, and if so, why and how?
3. What should the CEO think about the situation, and how should he or she respond if the chairman calls for guidance the evening before the lunch?
4. How should the new board member be approached so as to avoid the real difficulties that are likely to arise in such a situation, and also help her become a better board member?
5. How do high-performing hospital boards and leaders avoid the challenges outlined in this brief case?

Web Sites

Forum for Shared Governance: www.sharedgovernance.org
The Governance Institute: www.governanceinstitute.com
NHS Clinical Governance Support Team: www.cgsupport.nhs.uk/

References

1. Preker, A. S. and A. Harding. 2003. *Innovations in health service delivery: The corporatization of public hospitals.* Washington, DC: World Bank.
2. The Governance Institute. 2007. *Boardsx4* governance structures and practices.* San Diego, CA.
3. The Governance Institute. 2002. *Elements of Governance™: The distinction between management and governance.* San Diego.
4. Pointer, D. and C. Ewell. 1994. *Really governing: How health system and hospital boards can make more of a difference.* Albany, NY: Delmar.
5. Ewell, C. M. 1997. CEOs, remember who hired you. *Modern Healthcare* 27:86.
6. Prybil, L. D. 2006. Characteristics of effective boards. *Trustee* 59:20–23.

7. Center for Healthcare Governance. 2007. *Building an exceptional board: Effective practices for health care governance—Report of the Blue Ribbon Panel on Health Care Governance*, 68. Chicago.

8. Killian, R. P. 2007. Health system governance: Board culture. *BoardRoom Press*, December.

9. Forum for shared governance. http://www.sharedgovernance.org/ (accessed February 25, 2008).

10. Klein, R. 2004. Britain's national health service revisited. *New England Journal of Medicine* 350:937–42.

Chapter 3

Defining a Great Board: Duties and Responsibilities

Barry S. Bader

Contents

Executive Summary

The challenges facing hospitals and health systems to sustain their vital mission in the face of economic, demographic, and regulatory pressures underscore the importance of effective governance to organizational success. In this environment, all trustees must understand their fiduciary duties, roles, and responsibilities in the context of the heightened public accountability and transparency expected of corporate and nonprofit organizations' boards. Health care providers serving as trustees should be aware of the special value they bring to board work, but they also need to be sensitive to potential conflicts of interest and confidentiality concerns that may arise. The effective trustee functions as a team member and supports a healthy board culture of accountability, integrity, candor, and continuous learning.

Learning Objectives

1. To understand the history and meaning of governance and its relationship to management.
2. To understand the fiduciary duties, roles, and responsibilities of governing boards and individual trustees.
3. To learn how external forces are raising the bar for fiduciary conduct and overall board performance.
4. To understand the importance of board culture for achieving effective governance.
5. To learn how to practice tri-modal governance, incorporating fiduciary, strategic, and generative modes of governance.

Key Words

- Board culture
- Conflict-of-interest
- Duty of care
- Duty of loyalty
- Duty of obedience
- Fiduciary
- Generative governance

- Governance
- Independent trustee
- Inside trustee
- Institutional integrity
- Shared governance
- Subsidiary board
- System (parent) board

Introduction

Governance matters. When boards excel, they ensure that their organizations have exceptional executive leadership and clear direction, and they provide a powerful connection to stakeholders and customers. When boards falter, the mission suffers, public trust weakens, and organizations can fail.

High-profile governance failures on Wall Street and at highly regarded non-profit organizations have put the need for effective governance in the spotlight as never before, with attention from Congress, courts, the Internal Revenue Service and other federal agencies, state taxing agencies, the news media, and the public.

Both investor-owned and nonprofit organization boards face an environment of heightened corporate accountability and transparency. Boards of nonprofit organizations generally—and boards of charitable hospitals specifically—once enjoyed a public presumption of doing good works for unselfish motives. Today, they face a growing list of mandates to demonstrate their institutional integrity, that is, showing transparently that they deserve their tax-exempt status and the public's trust by virtue of their measurable community benefit services, steward-ship of financial resources, corporate integrity and compliance with laws and regulations, clinical quality and patient safety, and ethical conduct.

Effective governance begins with a thorough understanding of the meaning of governance, its difference from and relationship to management, and the three fiduciary duties of boards and directors. These duties have remained unchanged in recent years, but the expectations of what boards must do to fulfill their duties have escalated in the form of increased transparency, new regulations, and new research into effective governance practices.

This chapter will address the fundamentals of governance, and then it will go further, because today's challenging environment demands that boards view fulfillment of their fiduciary duties as the floor, not the ceiling of governance effectiveness. We will explore how—in a culture of trust, accountability, candor, and continuous learning—boards must demonstrate visionary, strategic leadership and engage in what several governance experts have termed generative governance.

Fiduciary Duties and Responsibilities of Trustees

What Is Governance?

Reduced to its simplest terms, a board is "an organized group of people with the authority collectively to control and foster an institution that is usually administered by a qualified executive and staff."[1] Today, new corporations create governing boards at birth, but historically, both for-profit and nonprofit boards came about in a different way that forms the foundation of their fiduciary duties and roles today.

Before the industrial revolution, most private companies were owned and run by individuals or families. It was not until companies needed to raise capital by issuing stock to outside investors that a board of directors became necessary to represent the interests of shareholders and to ensure that management acted in their best interests.

Many nonprofit organizations began as groups of devoted citizens or members of religious communities who created an organization to carry out good works in education, health, and other social services. These founding volunteers did the work and also created boards to oversee and perpetuate their work as they passed on.

The Brotherhood of Mercy was established in Florence, Italy, around 1240, and for seven centuries has been governed by a board and an unpaid administrative head.[1] The oldest hospital in the United States is Pennsylvania Hospital, founded by Benjamin Franklin, Dr. Thomas Bond, and other Philadelphia leaders in 1751. Franklin served as the first secretary and later as second president of what was the board of managers, and cofounder Dr. Bond was the first physician to serve on a hospital board.[2]

The nonprofit corporation's board possesses ultimate authority over the organization's management, finances, and programs. Until approximately the last 60 years or so, many hospital boards continued the Franklin tradition. They recruited wealthy and influential local citizens to serve as boards of volunteer managers, overseers, and fund-raisers.

The nonprofit hospital board's role began to change in the United States after World War II. Hospitals became more complex enterprises requiring professional management, and fundraising became less critical to survival as

Medicare, Medicaid, and employer-financed health insurance provided financial stability from operations. The concept of a board of managers faded into obscurity, replaced by boards of trustees and directors who saw their role as ensuring that professional management operated the organization responsibly in the best interests of its stakeholders, that is, those who derive benefits from the organization's good works. As a guidebook published by the American Bar Association for nonprofits put it, "A Director directs, but does not perform, the corporation's activities."[3]

Special Considerations for Health Care Providers on Hospital Boards

For health care providers who serve on a hospital or health system governing board, the position of director or trustee is different from their role in caring for patients or running a health care practice or company in various respects:

- *One part of the whole*: A trustee exerts authority only as a part of the board, not as an individual with control over subordinates. Trustees who "freelance," expecting they can issue orders to the chief executive officer (CEO) or senior executives as if they were direct reports, do not understand the limits of their authority. A physician who practices in the hospital does not gain the authority to control management by virtue of a board seat. Even the chairperson of the board must be cautious to differentiate when speaking as an individual or on behalf of the board. A chair represents the board only when acting in accordance with board-approved goals, policies, or specific delegated authority, such as the power to negotiate the CEO's compensation and to bring a proposal back to the compensation committee for approval. This is not meant to minimize the chairperson's powers, importance, and influence—for when a chair speaks, only a foolish CEO fails to listen—only to underscore the fact that each officer and trustee acts as one part of the whole.
- *Representing the stakeholders*: As a trustee, a provider must act and vote like any other board member in the best interests of all the stakeholders, not in the narrow interests of a single constituency. Because the board is accountable to the stakeholders, a trustee must understand the organization's mission and its work, as well as the needs of all its stakeholders. It needs to have measures of how well the organization is fulfilling its mission. Health care providers can bring perspectives and expertise from their work and constituencies to assist the board in conducting business, but as trustees, they have one master: the stakeholders.

■ *Stakeholders have diverse needs*: The stakeholders of a large, urban teaching hospital, for example, may include a mixture of patients from the inner city who are poor and reliant on the hospital for primary care; better-insured suburban residents who can choose among competing providers based on service, price, and quality; and medical residents and faculty focused on the missions of education and research, as well as patient care. The communities the hospital serves may be home to a broad mix of ethnic groups and patients with special health needs. While a practicing physician, for example, takes an oath to care for each patient as an individual, the physician as trustee must seek to understand and represent the collective interests of all the stakeholders; this is not an easy task.

■ *Balancing mission and financial viability*: Like any corporation, a nonprofit hospital must earn a positive financial margin from fees, grants, and philanthropy to cover its expenses and replace its physical stock, or it will not survive. The term *nonprofit* does not mean that the organization is expected to lose money—it means that the organization must reinvest positive financial returns into its mission, including capital investments, to keep facilities and technology up to date. Yet, the nonprofit hospital's mission may require engagement in some financially draining activities, such as educating medical students, running community clinics, and offering financial assistance and discounts to the poor. Nonprofit hospital trustees must weigh both mission and financial considerations when they make major strategic and financial decisions, such as how much they can afford to subsidize services for the poor and whether to keep or divest an unprofitable clinical service line, nursing home, or home care agency. A trustee who is also a surgeon on the medical staff may personally want an abundance of nurses, the latest technology, and operating room facilities, but the surgeon-trustee must consider these needs in the context of the overall budget and resources for all clinical programs to meet stakeholders' needs.

■ *Ambassadors to the stakeholders*: It is good practice for reasons of consistency and expertise that a CEO is the primary spokesperson for the organization, but because nonprofit trustees often come from stakeholder groups, they can be effective ambassadors. The physician or nurse trustee does not represent the medical or nursing staff, but can communicate that constituency's perspectives to the board and can, in turn, convey objective, credible information about the hospital board's decisions and rationale to professional colleagues.

Fiduciary Duties of Trustees

A fiduciary is a person entrusted with assets owned by another party (the beneficiary), and is responsible for seeing that those assets are managed in the beneficiary's best interests. Directors and trustees of nonprofit or charitable organizations have a fiduciary duty to the mission, constituencies, and communities for whose benefit the organization is established.

The laws relating to the duties of trustees of charitable organizations have grown out of a century of litigation, mostly involving business corporations, but the principles apply equally to nonprofits.[3] Generally, a trustee is expected to exercise his or her fiduciary responsibilities and authority: (1) in good faith; (2) with the care an ordinarily prudent person in a like position would exercise under similar circumstances; and (3) in a manner that he or she reasonably believes to be in the best interests of the organization. To demonstrate due diligence, directors should prepare for, attend, and actively participate in meetings of the board and committees and in other official board activities. Meeting minutes should sufficiently document both attendance and discussion.

Any voting board member has fiduciary responsibilities, whether he or she is an inside director (for example, employee or medical staff member) or an outside director (member of the community served). Often, a governing board's fiduciary duties are grouped under three categories:

- *Duty of obedience*: Requires fidelity to the charitable purpose of the organization. This duty compels trustees to make decisions and act in a manner consistent with the purpose or mission of the organization. Thus, when a nonprofit's trustees approve budgets, strategic plans, and major transactions, one reference point must be how the proposed action supports the mission. However, the duty of obedience does not compel a board to maintain a financially failing activity. To the contrary, the mission prevents the board from allowing financial problems in one part of the enterprise to jeopardize the whole. A nonprofit organization that wishes to sell all or part of its enterprise generally must seek the approval of the state attorney general, who will look for evidence that the board has considered the transaction in the light of the mission and has ensured that any proceeds of the transaction are retained or applied to support the mission. In addition, as William G. Bowen notes, the duty of obedience does not "imply that nonprofits, while concentrating their activities in pursuit of a defined mission, are precluded from expanding, entering new territories, and so on.... How far to go in these directions is a key question for board members of many non-profits, since they must respect both the boundaries of a relatively fixed definition of the mission of the institution and the applicable provisions of the law."[4]
- *Duty of loyalty*: Requires trustees to act in good faith based on the best interests of the organization and the community or constituencies it serves, not their personal or professional interests or the narrow interests of a single person or constituency group. According to an American Bar

Association (ABA) guidebook, "The basic legal principle to be observed here is a negative one: The trustee shall not use a corporate position for individual personal advantage."[3]

- *Conflicts-of-interest*: The duty of loyalty is the basis of the board's policies on conflict-of-interest and confidentiality. As the ABA guidebook notes, "Conflicts-of-interest involving a trustee are not inherently illegal nor are they to be regarded as a reflection on the integrity of the board or of the trustee. It is the manner in which the trustee and the board deal with a disclosed conflict that determines the propriety of the transaction."[3]

  A conflict-of-interest exists when a trustee (or immediate family member or business associate) has a material personal interest in a proposed contract or transaction to which the organization may be a party. It is not uncommon that board members are employees, partners, or owners of law firms, financial institutions, medical practices, medical supply companies, car dealerships, and so on, that do business with hospitals or other health care facilities on whose boards they sit.

  Health care providers serving on health care boards should recognize that they may have conflicts to disclose. A physician who is a hospital employee, has contracted to provide hospital services, or has privileges to care for patients as a medical staff member has a conflict. So does the nurse who is the dean of a college that contracts with hospitals to help train student nurses and allied health professionals. A trustee has a duty to disclose actual and potential conflicts of interest annually in a written statement and immediately when a new conflict situation arises.

  A committee of independent trustees who themselves have no material conflicts should decide how the conflict should be addressed. At a minimum, the trustee should take no part in the decision and should leave any meetings where the matter is discussed or voted on. The minutes should thoroughly document the disclosure of the conflict and board's resolution of the matter. The duty of loyalty is also the basis of board policies on corporate opportunity, which states that a trustee may not use a position or information gained as a board member for personal advantage. Thus, a trustee who learns about a new business opportunity from his board work may not use that information to open a competing business.

  The duty of loyalty also compels a trustee to maintain the confidentiality of board discussions, particularly on sensitive priority or personnel matters, before the board has finalized its decision and approved public communication.

■ *Duty of care*: Requires a trustee to act in a reasonable, diligent, and informed manner in carrying out the work of the board by preparing for and attending meetings, participating in discussions, asking questions, making sound and independent business judgments, and seeking independent opinions when necessary. The board is entitled to rely on information and recommendations from both outside experts and management when a careful review is performed and an independent judgment is made before taking action. The duty of care is the basis for board policies requiring a minimum level of attendance and for limiting voting by proxy. It is the reason many attorneys are recommending that minutes of board and committee meetings sufficiently describe the information reviewed by the board and summarize any discussion or questions that occur prior to a board vote.[5]

It is common and good practice for a board to delegate some functions, such as approving expenditures below predetermined thresholds and approving investment transactions consistent with a board-approved investment policy, to committees or management, but the board should specify the limits of delegated authority in a board-approved policy and also approve a monitoring and control procedures, such as regular committee reporting, circulating minutes and summary reports, and independent audits.

Learning from Governance Failures

Brief Anatomies of Failed Governance

When a private corporation or nonprofit organization faces a financial failure, ethical scandal, or embarrassing strategic miscalculation, the first question that investors, community leaders, public officials, news media, and a thousand Monday morning quarterbacks ask is: Where was the board? It is a reasonable question, since the board is supposed to oversee management.

A look at some highly publicized cases of corporate failures and accounting fraud reveals some important lessons for the practice of good governance. No one disputes that a board should build a partnership with its CEO and use its abilities to help the CEO run a successful enterprise. A board needs to trust and empower its CEO, and remain engaged at the level of strategy and policy, not operations. Yet, when boards turn trust into blind trust, and delegation becomes abrogation of the responsibility to oversee management, the risk for organizational failure heightens. Consider these examples:

- *The Smithsonian*: The importance of due diligence. In 2007, the Smithsonian Institution's Board of Regents adopted sweeping governance reforms. The changes came in response to an inspector general's report, subsequent congressional inquiries, and two board-commissioned independent reviews (all covered by the news media) that criticized the board's oversight—or rather, the lack of it—of executive compensation, executives' travel and expenses, and excessive participation by senior executives on for-profit corporate boards, for which they were richly compensated. The Smithsonian, a nonprofit organization chartered by Congress, boasted a talented board that showed excessive deference to its CEO and simply failed to exercise the oversight required by the duty of due care. As attorney Michael Peregrine writes, the deficiencies in board oversight included "the failure of the board to routinely receive or demand information necessary to support informed decision-making; the absence of critical relationships necessary to bring to the board important issues and concerns; and the inability of internal monitoring systems to raise the necessary 'warning flags' to the board when circumstances warranted."[6] Board meetings were brief and perfunctory. The board tolerated a marked lack of transparency: the CEO blocked the board from access to the chief financial officer and general counsel, who might have alerted the board to problems. As a result, the Smithsonian suffered "a loss of trust in both senior management and in the Board of Regents' ability to exercise effective oversight of the institution."[6–8]

■ *Enron*: The importance of culture. On the national stage, Enron failed when serious accounting and ethical breaches destroyed investors' confidence in its financial reports and sent its stock price plummeting. The Enron board, like the Smithsonian's, was unwilling to raise hard questions of management, even when confronted with warning signs, such as a letter from an internal whistleblower warning of accounting shenanigans, the need to give the chief financial officer a conflict-of-interest waiver to do business with the company, and a guarded prognosis from its external auditors. The problem was a culture of excessive collegiality and deference to management. "What distinguishes exemplary boards," he writes, "is that they are robust, effective social systems." They do not hesitate to ask questions and "they know how to ferret out the truth, challenge one another, and even have a good fight now and then."[9]

■ *Allegheny Health Education and Research Foundation*: The importance of culture and streamlined structure. When this multibillion-dollar health system went bankrupt in 1998, press reports and a classic study by Lawton Burns found the CEO and board chair had fostered a culture of "fear and reprisal."[10] They stifled board questioning of what would prove to be imprudent decisions to take on debt, expand the system, overpay to acquire physician practices, and assume Medicaid risk contracts. Compounding the problem was a Byzantine structure of multiple boards and committees that were manipulated by management so everyone assumed some other entity had thoroughly vetted decisions, but no one really knew where board oversight authority resided.

In board failure after board failure, a primary contributor was a culture of excessive deference to management, coupled with failure to follow good governance policies and practices, to adopt effective structures such as working committees, and to require transparency of accurate and timely information—both good and bad—to the board. When a nonprofit board values collegiality over candor and defers to management rather than holding it accountable, it fails to protect the mission and the stakeholders.

New Expectations for Institutional Integrity

Current Issues Involving Fiduciary Duties

In the wake of multiple corporate governance failures, Congress enacted the Sarbanes-Oxley Act to curb accounting abuses and restore investors' confidence. The act required corporations to adopt and enforce policies to promote accountability and transparency in their accounting and governance practices. Boards were expected to exercise independent oversight and judgment over management's performance and recommendations.

Although Sarbanes-Oxley generally does not apply to nonprofit organizations, many of its provisions are becoming a *de facto* standard for the tax-exempt sector. For example, emulating the requirements of Sarbanes-Oxley, according to the Governance Institute's 2007 survey of board practices, some 29% of hospital and health system boards have established audit committees (separate from finance committees), and another 24% have audit and corporate compliance committees.[10] Some 62% are holding executive sessions without the CEO in attendance to discuss CEO performance.[11] External auditors and governance experts alike recommend that these committees, like their private industry counterparts, be composed of independent trustees, select the external auditor, and meet with the external auditor at least annually without management present. All these practices are drawn from the Sarbanes-Oxley Act.

Boards of tax-exempt hospitals and health systems generally function under Section 501(c)(3) of the Internal Revenue Code, as well as under rules adopted by state governments and local revenue agencies to grant an exemption from local property, sales, and other taxes. Thus, boards of tax-exempt organizations have a fiduciary responsibility to see that their organization's resources support their charitable purpose and are not used for the private benefit of an individual or business.

Undeniably, nonprofit hospitals provide enormous benefits for their communities, even as they face serious economic and competitive pressures on their financial viability. Despite an exemplary record industry-wide, nonprofit hospitals have become the target of congressional and Internal Revenue Service (IRS) criticisms that they overcharge the poor and are indistinguishable from their for-profit competitors.[11] The IRS conducted compliance checks that found wide variability in hospital community benefits and oversight of executive compensation.[12] Many state governments also require hospitals to report spending on community benefits, and some jurisdictions are challenging local hospitals' tax exemptions.

A nonprofit hospital's community benefit responsibilities are defined by Congress and the IRS, but the federal community benefit standard for hospitals is rather broad and has been subject to interpretation. Community benefit includes not only charity care but also activities such as community health education, disease screening programs, clinics in medically underserved areas, medical research, and health professions education. However, hospitals have defined and measured community benefit activities in different ways. Some have included bad debts as charity care; others have not. Some have included losses incurred treating Medicare patients because of below-cost reimbursement rates; others have not. A report in 2007 by Moody's, an independent bond rating agency, concluded, "Currently, there is no agreed-upon uniform methodology of calculating charity care and community benefit by industry participants, which presents a challenge in reporting comparable data."[13]

The Catholic Health Association (CHA) and VHA, Inc., attempted to fill this void by proposing a clear definition and measurement guidelines. CHA and VHA said, "Community benefits respond to an identified community need and meet at least one of the following criteria:

■ Generate a low or negative margin
■ Respond to needs of special populations, such as minorities, frail elderly, poor persons with disabilities, the chronically mentally ill, and persons with AIDS
■ Supply services or programs that would likely be discontinued if the decision were made on a purely financial basis.[14]

In late 2007, the IRS offered some clarification as to its heightened expectations of tax-exempt organizations by releasing new disclosure requirements for nonprofits.[15] The new Form 990 that charitable organizations must file annually includes new schedules for hospitals and for tax-exempt bond activities. Hospitals must report the specific amounts expended for charity care, community benefit, and other community-building activities; information on the organization's bad debt expenses, Medicare revenues, and collection practices; and the names of management companies, facilities, and joint ventures. Hospitals must also provide information on their charity care policy, including the formula, based on Federal Poverty Guidelines, for determining whether patients are eligible for receiving free and discounted care, respectively.

The new Form 990 delves deeper than ever into areas of governance, management, and disclosure, inquiring about such items as:

- The number of voting trustees and how many are independent (discussed later).
- Whether trustees and key employees have any family or business relationships.
- Whether the full board received the Form 990 before it was filed, and the process the organization uses to review the 990.
- Whether the organization has a conflict-of-interest policy, whether annual disclosures are filed, and how the organization regularly and consistently monitors and enforces compliance with the policy.
- Whether the organization has a written whistleblower policy and document retention policy.
- Whether the process for determining executive compensation includes a review and approval by independent persons, comparability data, and contemporaneous substantiation of the deliberation and decision.
- Whether the organization participated in a joint venture or similar arrangement and, if so, whether the organization has adopted a written policy or procedure requiring an evaluation of compliance with applicable laws.

A common thread links the increased scrutiny of nonprofit organizations that is coming from multiple sources. In 2006, the Governance Institute published a white paper explaining that nonprofits, and hospitals in particular, have entered a new era of "institutional integrity."[16] Gone are the days when nonprofits were trusted to do good works for unselfish motives. Today, the report said, nonprofit hospitals and health systems must demonstrate their institutional integrity by documenting transparently their organization's community benefit, financial stewardship and corporate compliance, and oversight of quality and patient safety, as well as the ethical conduct of trustees and officers.

Implications of Institutional Integrity

Institutional integrity raises a number of implications for trustees generally, and more specifically for health care providers serving on health care boards.

1. *Conflicts-of-interest*: Boards must be able to document their independent oversight of the organization. A health care provider who serves as a voting trustee of a hospital or health system board has a conflict-of-interest if he or she is an employee, has a contract to provide services, or simply has privileges to admit and treat patients. If the trustee is an interested person in an economic relationship with the organization, he or she must disclose the conflict and refrain from participating in or appearing to influence discussions or decisions related to the relationship. Some conflicts are so material that an individual should not serve as board member. Examples are spouses or other immediate family of senior management and investors or key employees of direct competitors.

2. *Independent trustees*: All trustees are expected to exercise independent judgment, but some board functions should be carried out only by independent trustees whose impartiality cannot be questioned because they are not dependent on the hospital's business. For example, the board's committees for oversight of audit and executive compensation should include only independent trustees (or at least a majority of independent trustees).

   A board should specify how it defines an independent trustee in a written policy. There are two general approaches. The more stringent definition says an independent trustee has absolutely no economic relationship with the organization. A more pragmatic approach is a *de minimus* definition saying that trustees may be defined as independent if they engage in transactions with the organization that are so small that a reasonable person would not question the trustee's ability to be independent. *De minimus* criteria might include business transactions that fall below a specific dollar threshold (typically $50,000 to $100,000, depending on the organization's size) or that represent a small amount of the trustee's income or company's revenues. Clearly, a physician who is a full-time employee of the organization or is a member of a group with an exclusive contract for hospital-based services such as radiology or emergency medicine is not independent. Some policies categorize any physician on the medical staff as nonindependent, meaning they should not serve on the audit or executive compensation committees. The rationale is self-evident. For example, even a nonemployed, noncontract physician may have personal interest in the hospital's decisions about physician recruitment and employment, availability of operating rooms, purchase of medical technology, and contracts with managed care plans. A physician with such potential self-interests should not be in a position to either reward or punish the CEO as a member of the executive compensation committee.

3. *Corporate opportunity*: The duty of loyalty requires that a trustee not disclose or use any information gained as a trustee for personal or private

advantage. This prohibition should be defined in a written policy on corporate opportunity. Thus, a trustee who learns about a potential business opportunity at the board table should not disclose that information to others or pursue the opportunity privately. A violation should subject the trustee to dismissal from the board and possible legal action.

4. *Self-assessment of fiduciary duties*: A number of organizations have recommended good governance practices to help a board oversee community benefit, external and internal audits, corporate compliance, executive compensation, the organization's clinical quality and patient safety, and the board's ethical conduct. Among them are guidelines published by the Governance Institute, the Center for Healthcare Governance of the American Hospital Association, Independent Sector, and the IRS.[18] The Governance Institute has published a self-assessment of 72 practices designed to promote institutional integrity.

Roles and Responsibilities of Health Care Boards

An effective board governs; it does not seek to manage the organization. All new trustees should receive a written description of their roles and responsibilities.

Position Description for a Health Care Board Trustee

- *Provide for excellent management*: Select, support, advise, and evaluate the chief executive officer.
- *Executive compensation and development*: Approve an executive compensation and development philosophy and program for the CEO and other senior executives. Approve annual and incentive compensation for the CEO.
- *Policy making*: Approve and periodically review major policies affecting the organization and the operation of the board.
- *Approve strategic direction and monitor performance*: Approve the organization's mission, core values, vision, and long-range strategic plan. Review and approve the annual strategic plan update, major transactions, and significant new programs and services for consistency with the strategic direction. Monitor organizational performance against strategic goals.

- *Ensure financial viability and integrity*: Approve long-range financial goals and a long-range financial plan. Approve the annual operating budget and capital budget for consistency with the mission and long-range financial goals. Monitor performance versus budgetary goals. Approve investment policies and monitor performance. Oversee the external and internal audit processes.
- *Ensure clinical quality, patient safety, and customer service excellence*: Approve annual plans and goals for clinical quality, patient safety, and customer service excellence, and monitor performance compared to internal goals and external benchmarks.
- *Ensure quality of medical staff*: Approve medical staff bylaws and oversee the process for appointment and reappointment of members of the medical staff and delineation of clinical privileges. Review and approve appointments, reappointments, and clinical privileges for individual practitioners, based on fully documented medical staff recommendations.
- *Community benefit and mission effectiveness*: Oversee the performance of the organization's programs to benefit the community for their consistency with the mission and external requirements.
- *Monitor subsidiary performance*: Monitor the performance of subsidiary organizations and ensure they are aligned with the health system's mission, vision, and values, and are meeting their performance goals.
- *Build relationships*: Build relationships and support the organization's policies with key stakeholders, political leaders, and donors.
- *Ensure compliance*: Approve and oversee a corporate compliance program, including a corporate compliance plan.
- *Ensure board effectiveness*: Elect members of the parent board and subsidiary boards. Establish an effective structure for the conduct of board business. Ensure the effectiveness of board governance through regular self-assessment and continuous improvement.

EXPECTATIONS OF INDIVIDUAL TRUSTEES

- *Accountability*: A board member is ultimately accountable to act in the best interests of the organization and its mission. The board member carries out his or her responsibilities in recognition of a fiduciary responsibility and does not act based on self-interests or the interests of any constituency or individual.

■ *Exercise of authority*: A board member carries out the powers of his or her office only when acting as a voting member during a duly constituted meeting of the board or one of its appointed bodies. A board member respects the responsibilities delegated by the board to the CEO, management, and the medical staff, avoiding interference with their duties but insisting upon accountability and reporting mechanisms for assessing performance.

■ *Chain of command*: If a member of the community or medical staff brings a specific issue, concern, or complaint to a member of the board, the board member should handle it through appropriate channels. In general, complaints and concerns about hospital operations or medical staff issues should be directed to the CEO. Unresolved, significant complaints and concerns should be brought to the board, or to the appropriate board committee, only after pursuing other avenues for resolution.

■ *Attendance*: A board member regularly attends board meetings, assigned committee meetings, and board retreats. All board members are expected to serve on one or more committees.

■ *Participation*: A board member comes to meetings prepared, asks informed questions, and makes a positive contribution to discussions. A board member treats others with trust and respect.

■ *Confidentiality*: A board member does not disclose proprietary, sensitive, or personnel-related information.

■ *Public support*: The board member explains and supports the decisions and policies of the board in discussions with outsiders, even if the board member voiced other views during a board discussion. This expectation is not intended to limit a board member's fiduciary obligation to speak out if he or she believes the board has failed to fulfill its legal or ethical responsibilities.

■ *Conflict-of-interest*: The board member avoids conflicts of interest and fully complies with the board's conflict-of-interest policy and other policies on individual conduct.

- *Education*: The board member takes advantage of opportunities to be educated and informed about the board, the organization, and the health care field.
- *Self-evaluation*: The board member participates in the self-evaluation of the board and individual members.

There are four primary roles that a governing board fulfills. Each role functions to achieve the organization's mission. The roles include:

1. *Approve the organization's goals and priorities*: The board approves the organization's mission, vision, and values and establishes quantitative goals when it approves budgets, strategic business plans, and strategic quality plans. It also chooses among competing priorities as it allocates resources.

2. *Make major policies and decisions to support the organization's goals*: A board's most important decision is to select—and then to support, evaluate, and provide compensation for—the CEO. Boards also approve major policies and make major decisions. Boards should not rubber-stamp proposed budgets, plans, and transactions. Boards should actively participate in goal setting and decision making.

3. *Oversee performance and exercise accountability for results*: A board and its committees should receive regular reports comparing the organization to board-approved goals. Underperformance should be accompanied by an analysis and corrective action plans from management. Dashboards and balanced scorecards, financial statements, external audits, accreditation reports, community benefit reports, and customer perception studies are examples of information the board should review regularly and take appropriate action. Boards should understand the information they review, ask questions, demand transparency, and seek independent sources of information when necessary.

4. *Build relationships with the organization's key stakeholders*: The board of a nonprofit organization typically is selective because members come from key stakeholder groups. Thus, trustees are in a position to assist the organization to build relationships with the donor community, political and public policy leaders, and the local community. Trustees act as ambassadors, helping the board understand the needs and perspectives of its stakeholders and build their understanding and support for the organization's initiatives.

A governing board carries out its four primary roles to discharge its responsibilities in seven key areas, which are described in the position description and subsequent chapters in this book:

- Mission and strategy
- CEO selection, evaluation, and compensation
- Financial viability
- Quality, patient safety, customer service, and physician credentialing
- Mission effectiveness and community benefit
- Corporate compliance and organizational ethics
- Board evaluation and continuous development

Distinguishing Board from Management Responsibilities

It is tempting for all trustees to believe they are doing their jobs by getting into operational details, and the temptation is greater for health care providers who understand aspects of the enterprise and have strong ideas about how things should be done. It is a temptation to avoid. Boards who meddle in operations undermine the CEO's credibility and authority and create a culture that tolerates interference in operations from any trustee, including those who do not bring special expertise.

There is not always a clear line distinguishing governance from management. In crisis situations, especially financial turnarounds, a board may need to get more involved in details. Otherwise, a board functions best when focusing on higher-level, future-oriented matters of strategy and policy. But where is the dividing line between strategy and operations? One rule of thumb is that strategy refers to organizational decisions that impact at least 10% of an organization's revenues. A decision on whether to expand major clinical service lines such as cardiology, oncology, and orthopedics would be a strategic matter. Planning how to implement the expansion is management's responsibility, although major capital expenditures would require board approval.

A policy is a prospective statement of the principles, guidelines, or practices to be applied in certain situations. Organizations have hundreds of operational policies governing various aspects of personnel, finance and billing, and patient care. These are not board matters, unless board approval is required by law or regulation. Policies requiring board approval should have a major impact on the organization or on the conduct of the board. Common hospital board policies address such matters as conflict-of-interest, charity care and community benefit, executive compensation, CEO evaluation, physician recruitment and competition, and public transparency. A board's policies should be compiled into a manual that is available for reference at any board or committee meeting and distributed to every trustee.

To avoid wandering from governance into management, boards should consider these ideas:

- When overseeing programs, focus on whether management has established an effective program mechanism rather than trying to review or micromanage details. Thus, the board should ensure management has created effective mechanisms for financial management, strategic planning, quality measurement and improvement, physician credentialing, community benefit, and other important functions.
- When reviewing performance, focus on outcomes, not processes. If performance meets or exceeds expectations, there is no need for the board to get into operational details.
- When a challenging question comes before the board, consider whether the board has or should adopt a policy to provide guidance for this and similar decisions in the future.
- When organizing meetings, place routine items into a consent agenda to discourage routine reports and free up time for more important matters of policy and strategy, as well as board education. Supporting materials for consent agenda items are mailed in advance, and trustees are expected to review them; the consent agenda is then voted on without further discussion at the meeting. A board policy should describe the types of routine business suitable for the consent agenda. The policy also should provide a procedure for the board, on approval of a motion, to remove an item for a separate discussion and vote.

System and Subsidiary Board Responsibilities

Many health care boards function as part of health systems in which governance responsibilities are distributed between a board at the parent or corporate level and boards of subsidiaries, operating entities, or affiliates.

In order to ensure that subsidiaries are aligned with the purposes and goals of the organization as a whole, it is common that parent boards hold reserved powers over major financial, strategic, and transactional decisions by their subsidiaries, as well as over board election (see "Most Common Reserved Powers" box).

A white paper published by the Governance Institute found that health systems are moving decision-making authority for financial and strategic matters to the parent corporate level to drive higher system-wide standards for performance and accountability.[11] Although some systems have eliminated hospital boards in favor of a single parent board with fiduciary authority for the entire system,

---

MOST COMMON RESERVED POWERS

- Approve changes to the mission or corporate purpose.
- Approve budgets, debt, and major financial transactions.
- Select the external auditor and oversee the audit process.
- Approve strategic plans.
- Approve the selection and, if necessary, removal of the CEO.
- Establish and oversee the system-wide executive compensation program.

---

most have adopted some sort of shared governance model that splits authority and responsibility between parent and local boards.

However, when the system board calls the shots on the big financial, strategic, and management decisions, local trustees sometimes question if they have a meaningful role or are just window dressing, kept around for their name and philanthropic contributions. The right model for allocating authority varies, depending on a system's characteristics. However, if subsidiary boards are retained, their responsibilities need to be clearly communicated and meaningful, enabling local trustees to make a contribution that adds value above and beyond what the parent board can do. Otherwise, the subsidiary board will be unable to recruit and retain high-caliber individuals.

Local hospital boards typically fall into one of four categories, outlined in Table 3.1, depending on their relative shares of advisory and fiduciary responsibility.[18]

Tri-Modal Governance: Understanding and Mastering Fiduciary, Strategic, and Generative Models of Governance

The effective trustee knows and accepts his or her duties, roles, and responsibilities, but individual excellence is not enough. The effective trustee functions as part of a team and supports a healthy board culture of accountability, integrity, candor, and continuous learning. Effective boards help individual trustees achieve their full potential by adopting an intentional and systematic approach to the components or building blocks of governance. These include board succession planning and recruitment, orientation and continuing education, and streamlined structures, including working committees with charters and annual

Table 3.1   Types of Subsidiary Boards[20]

Type I: Purely Advisory Board	The board has no fiduciary responsibilities or formal authority, but is asked for its counsel on programs and community relationships, and assists with fund-raising, community outreach, and advocacy.
Type II: Quality-Focused Board	The board has delegated fiduciary responsibility for the quality and safety of patient care and medical staff credentialing, is kept informed about organizational performance, and is consulted as management develops strategic plans, budgets, and other major proposals.
Type III: Shared Authority Board	The board has fiduciary responsibility for quality, patient safety, and medical staff relations and monitors other areas of hospital performance. The system board gives considerable deference to its review and recommendations of strategic plans, budgets, and other major decisions.
Type IV: Operating Board	This board is delegated significant responsibilities for oversight and decision making, subject only to the system's reserved powers, such as approval of large capital expenditures and major transactions.

goals. Effective board meetings utilize consent agendas to dispense with routine business efficiently and enable the board to focus the majority of its time on major, future-oriented matters of policy and strategy. The effective board regularly seeks improvement through regular board self-assessment, which was discussed in Chapter 2.

As important as the building blocks are, some boards are frustrated by the sense that something is missing in their quest for governance excellence. In their book *Governance as Leadership: Reframing the Work of Non-Profit Boards*, Chait, Holland, and Taylor introduce some much needed fresh thinking into the never-ending search for board effectiveness.[19] The authors argue that traditional board improvement approaches that focus on redesigning board structures, policies, and practices fall short. "What if one of the central problems plaguing the board is not, in fact, uncertainty about its important roles and responsibilities, but rather a lack of compelling purpose in the first place?" the authors ask. "We maintain that many board members are ineffectual not because they are confused about their role but because they are dissatisfied with their role."

"Limited purpose produces limited performance," Chait said in an interview about the book.[20] "Our assertion has been that as the work of the board becomes truly more consequential, meaningful, and influential, the performance of the board will rise. Most boards of larger, more mature organizations go to great lengths to attract talented, bright, successful trustees. Then, the board underperforms because the opportunities are not commensurate with their capacity, and they become bored."

The authors recommend reframing board work around three modes of governing:

1. The fiduciary mode, in which the board exercises its legally required responsibilities of oversight and stewardship.
2. The strategic mode, in which the board acts on management recommendations regarding major decisions about resources, programs, and services.
3. The generative mode, in which the board engages in deeper inquiry, exploring root causes, underlying values, optional courses, and new ideas.

Generative governance engages and challenges trustees intellectually, says Chait. "It's what leaders do best. Yet, most boards spend their time mainly on fiduciary work, and they devote little time to the generative mode."

An example of how the three modes function in governance practice would be a college board asking, "Should we build a new fitness center for students and equip it with climbing walls and hot tubs?" The fiduciary question is: "Do we have the money and the space?" The strategic question is: "Should we do this to keep up with the competition?" The generative questions are: "What produced this amenities arms race? Will it ever stop? Do we want to pass or play? If we play, what are our principles? If the fiduciary mode is all we do," Chait concludes, "we will have created procedural accountability, not performance accountability. We will put a huge emphasis on compliance rather than on performance. Under the worst of circumstances, you can imagine an organization that is both lawful and financially viable—and of no social purpose. You have got to get the fiduciary mode right.... But if boards spend all their time on financial literacy, integrity, compliance, and legal liabilities, we will have missed the boat on what governance should be."

Conclusion

The position of hospital or health system trustee carries enormous responsibility and takes a significant and increasing amount of time, but it is also enormously rewarding. By exercising vision, leadership, and ambassadorial skills, an effective board can foster a financially viable, higher-quality, and more compassionate health care system in its part of the world.

Health care providers, drawn from the front lines to the boardroom, can enrich and inform the seemingly sterile policy making, decisions, and oversight work of the board by bringing the reality of patient care to the boardroom. As you think about the fiduciary duties, roles, and responsibilities of the board, also think about what you, as a health care provider, can bring to your health care board. What knowledge, skills, and perspectives do you offer, and how will you communicate them as a trustee—not as a clinician or manager? Your role is special, and so too are the contributions you can make.

Case Study

The board of Memorial Hospital had already been meeting for 3 hours, as it did every month. Several members were looking at their watches, and 3 of the 21 members had already left. The next item on the agenda was the president's report. CEO Cal Cool began, "Dr. Johnson, the head of the Downtown Medical Group, approached me this week and revealed he had been talking for months with our competitor about buying their practices."

Most of the board members suddenly paid attention—this was news to them, and important too, because through referrals and admissions, the 30-member group accounted for a quarter of the hospital's revenues. The only members who did not look surprised were on the finance committee; the CEO had briefed them in a special meeting earlier today. "Dr. Johnson said talks had broken down, and wanted to know if Memorial would be interested. I would like the board's approval to get an independent evaluation of their practice and make them an offer—we can't afford to delay."

"I agree," said Mike Manley, the board chair, in his booming voice. "We've got to strike while the iron is hot. We can convene the executive committee to review the deal when you're ready."

"I move approval," said Charley Bosworth, a long-time board member and Mike's business partner.

"Wait a minute," said Sally Diamond, the chair of the strategic planning committee and one of two women on the board. "I understand the group's importance, but we've never acquired a group of this size, and if we do this, what will be the impact on other medical staff? We've had no time to consider this in the context of the strategic plan."

"I agree," said Dr. Tom Farley, an internist in a small practice near one of Downtown's clinics. "Why wasn't this information shared earlier?"

"Because we just heard about it," snapped Cal.

More board members jumped in, asking questions and offering opinions about why the hospital needed to employ so many doctors, the costs, the risks, and so forth. All this frustrated the CEO, who saw this as a golden opportunity.

After an hour, the chair called the question and the board voted 9 to 4 to approve making an offer to acquire the Downtown Group, subject to final approval of the deal by the executive committee.

Questions for Consideration

- How well did the Memorial board fulfill its fiduciary duties, roles, and responsibilities?
- How well were strategic considerations evaluated in this board's actions?
- In this challenging development, what opportunities were presented for the board to practice in the generative mode of governance?

Study and Discussion Questions

1. Do all your board's members understand their fiduciary duties, roles, and responsibilities? Is there a mechanism in place to measure a board member's level of understanding? Does the board have a current position description that is discussed with prospective board members and explored more fully in new trustee orientation?

2. How does your board know when it is getting enough information or if information is too filtered? How would the board get independent, less biased information pertinent to its responsibilities?

3. How would you describe your board's culture? Does the board's culture encourage or discourage trust, management transparency, diligent oversight, candid discussion, strategic thinking, timely and clear decision making, and full use of each board member's talents?

4. Does your board make efficient and effective use of its time? Does it devote sufficient time to discussion of strategic issues? Does it practice tri-modal governance?

Suggested Readings and Web Sites

Readings

American Bar Association 2002. *Guidebook for directors of nonprofit corporations.* Chicago: Committee on Nonprofit Corporations.

Chait, R. P., W. P. Ryan, and B. E. Taylor. 2005. *Governance as leadership—Reframing the work of nonprofit boards.* Hoboken, NJ: John Wiley & Sons.

The Governance Institute. 2007. *Boardsx4* governance structures and practices.* San Diego, CA.

Independent Sector. 2005. *Strengthening transparency, governance, and accountability of charitable organizations: A final report to Congress and the nonprofit sector.* Washington, DC.

Nadler, D. A., J. Sonnenfeld, C. Montgomery, and R. Kaufman. 2004. Building the best boards (HBR article collection). *Harvard Business Review*, May 1.

Web Sites

Board Source: http://www.boardsource.org/

Center for Healthcare Governance: http://www.americangovernance.com/american-governance_app/index.jsp

The Governance Institute: http://www.governanceinstitute.com/

Great Boards: http://www.greatboards.org/

Independent Sector: http://www.independentsector.org/index.htm

References

1. Houle, C. O. 1989. *Governing boards.* San Francisco: Jossey-Bass.
2. History of Pennsylvania hospital. University of Pennsylvania Health System. http://www.uphs.upenn.edu/paharc/features/bfranklin.html (accessed February 11, 2008).
3. Overton, G. W. and J. Carmedelle Frey, eds. 2002. *Guidebook for directors of nonprofit corporations.* Chicago: American Bar Association, Section on Business Law, Committee on Nonprofit Corporations.
4. Bowen, W. G. 1994. *Inside the boardroom.* New York: John Wiley & Sons.
5. Graham, K. 2005. How detailed should meeting minutes be? *Great Boards*, Summer, p. 8.
6. Peregrine, M. 2007. Smithsonian controversy spawns "second generation" best practices. *The Exempt Organization Tax Review*, September, p. 277.
7. Grimaldi, J. V. 2007. Smithsonian documents detail chief's expenses. *Washington Post*, March 19, sec. A.
8. Grimaldi, J. V. and J. Trescott. 2007. Smithsonian's Small quits in wake of inquiry. *Washington Post*, March 27, sec. A.
9. Sonnenfeld, J. A. 2002. What makes great boards great. *Harvard Business Review* 80:106–13.

10. Burns, L. R., J. Cacciamani, J. Clement, and W. Aquino. 2000. The fall of the house of AHERF: The Allegheny bankruptcy. *Health Affairs (Project Hope)* 19:7–41.
11. The Governance Institute. 2007. *Boardsx4* governance structures and practices.* San Diego, CA.
12. Grassley, C. F. 2006. *Memorandum to reporters and editors.* Press release issued in Washington, DC, by Senator Grassley.
13. Internal Revenue Service. 2007. *Executive compensation initiative—Errors on and omissions from annual returns by exempt organizations.* Washington, DC.
14. Goldstein, L. 2007. *Mission vs. margin: Better reporting of community benefits may temper scrutiny of not-for-profit hospitals' tax-exempt status.* Moody's Special Comment. New York: Moody's Investors Service.
15. Catholic Health Association. 2006. *A guide for planning and reporting community benefit.* St. Louis, MO.
16. Internal Revenue Service. IRS Form 990. Washington, DC.
17. Bader, B. S., E. A. Kazemek, and R. W. Witalis. 2006. *Emerging standards for institutional integrity: A tipping point for charitable organizations.* San Diego, CA: The Governance Institute.
18. The Governance Institute. 2005. *Pursuing systemness: The evolution of large health systems.* San Diego, CA.
19. Chait, R. P., W. P. Ryan, and B. E. Taylor. 2005. *Governance as leadership—Reframing the work of nonprofit boards.* Hoboken, NJ: John Wiley & Sons.
20. The Governance as leadership: An Interview with Richard P. Chait. *Great Boards,* Summer 2005.

Chapter 4

Bringing Quality to the Table

Kanak S. Gautam

Contents

Executive Summary

In the last decade, a climate for improving health care quality has been created nationally. Boards that traditionally focused on finance and strategy are diverting their attention to quality. While trustees with clinical knowledge, often in the minority, are comfortable dealing with quality, lay trustees with no clinical knowledge or experience, often in the majority on boards, remain uncomfortable with their new role and need guidance. This chapter explains why quality has risen to prominence in health care and provides environmental, legal, practical, and ethical reasons for boards to focus attention on quality. Difficulties boards face in adopting a leadership role in quality are discussed, and measures are recommended for helping boards as they focus on trustee education, appointing providers as trustees, defining the board's role, forming a board quality committee, and establishing quality benchmarks. A remarkable change is unfolding as health care organizations define quality goals and trustees' responsibilities for quality. Understanding the immediate concerns and proactively defining ways to address them will help boards prepare for the transition.

Learning Objectives

1. To understand why health care boards must focus on quality in the current environment.
2. To understand why health care boards find it difficult to adopt a leadership role in quality and define measures.
3. To understand the operational problems that health care boards face in adopting a leadership role in quality, and how to resolve those problems.

Key Words

- Core mission
- Dual-pyramid structure
- Legal responsibility for quality
- Medical staff organization
- Medical staff reform
- Physician autonomy
- Quality
- Quality committee
- Quality management structure
- Trustee ignorance

Introduction

A national agenda focusing on health care quality is unfolding as quality improvement initiatives proliferate in the industry. Despite exhortations by the field in recent years, health care boards have been slow to focus attention on the oversight of quality. This chapter describes the board's responsibility to oversee quality, barriers faced in discharging this responsibility, and how barriers can be overcome. There are three questions that will be addressed throughout this chapter: (1) Why must health care boards play a leadership role in advancing quality today? (2) Why are many boards unable to adopt a leadership role in quality, and how can they do so? (3) What operational problems do boards face after adopting a leadership role, and how can these problems be resolved?

Definition of Quality

The Institute of Medicine (IOM) defines quality as "the degree to which health services for individuals and populations increase the likelihood of desired health outcomes and are consistent with current professional knowledge."[1] Further, the IOM laid out essential characteristics (safety, timeliness, effectiveness, efficiency, equity, and patient centered [STEEEP]) of a high-quality health care system and recommendations for how care should be delivered.[1] The IOM's definition is consistent with modern thoughts on quality. First, quality of care depends on achieving desired clinical outcomes, not just conforming to care processes such as administering required tests and drugs. Second, desired health outcomes are not based on individual physician opinion, but on professional standards of care. Traditionally, physician autonomy has been prized; patients have received treatment unique to their doctor's practice methods, and wide variation in treatment practices has existed for the same medical condition. Today, the emphasis is on conformity with professional rather than individual standards of practice and narrowing practice variation around care standards. Finally, how high-quality care should be delivered is defined and emphasized—care delivery must meet central patient needs (equity, safety, timeliness, effectiveness), and it must address economic priorities (efficiency).

Imperatives for Boards to Focus on Quality

Traditionally, health care boards have had greater familiarity with finance than with quality and patient safety. Most board trustees belong to nonclinical professions such as business, law, government, and similar industries, and therefore lack clinical knowledge or health care experience. Transformation of the definition of quality has led many boards to realize that oversight is a daunting challenge. It is natural for hospital trustees to question why they need to divert greater attention to quality than before. Understanding the reasons for focusing on quality can enable trustees to enhance their commitment and prepare for the challenges ahead.

The Environmental Imperative

The evolving health care environment is one important reason for boards to focus on quality. In 1999, the IOM report *To Err Is Human* cited evidence that suggested up to 98,000 preventable deaths occur in hospitals each year, and it moved patient safety and quality to the forefront.[1] The report spawned multiple quality improvement initiatives nationally. The Institute for Healthcare

Improvement's (IHI) 100,000 Lives Campaign, involving 1800 hospitals, the Leapfrog Group's rewarding of breakthrough practices in safety and quality, and the Hospital Quality Alliance's (HQA) introduction of Hospital Compare, a Web site tool for public reporting of comparative quality indicators, are a few of the initiatives. Several positive results followed. Many U.S. hospitals participated in large-scale quality initiatives, observed positive results firsthand, and learned tactics for implementing such projects. Private and public quality reporting programs made available comparative data on hospitals, allowing consumers to seek information, such as mortality and complication rates, to select hospitals and physicians. In 2003, the Centers for Medicare and Medicaid Services (CMS) introduced a 3-year pay-for-performance pilot program to pay 300 hospitals for meeting quality goals. Bonuses for reaching benchmarks totaled $7 million per year, signifying that quality and finance would be interrelated in the future. Pay-for-performance is reshaping the health care industry and creating a nationwide climate for improving quality and patient safety. Trustees cannot afford to ignore this movement since it is likely to remain undiminished.

The Legal Imperative

Board attention to quality is imperative since quality oversight is the board's legal responsibility. Traditionally, nonprofit boards have served as fiduciaries, safeguarding hospital resources and ensuring they are used to meet community needs. Board responsibility for quality is of recent origin. For many years, responsibility for hospital quality had rested solely with the medical staff. Court rulings in *Pepke v. Grace Hospital* (1902)[2] and *Schloendorff v. Society of New York Hospital* (1912)[3] denied hospitals and their boards any responsibility for physician credentialing or medical care quality. In the 1950s and 1960s hospitals expanded in size and scope, and courts began to ask how hospitals were taking care of patients. State statutes were revised to remove doubts about the ultimate responsible for quality—many states held hospitals ultimately responsible. Finally, in *Darling v. Charleston Community Memorial Hospital* (1964),[4] a case alleging negligent care by an improperly credentialed physician, the Illinois Supreme Court ruled that hospitals must do more than furnish facilities for treatment. Patients rightfully expect hospitals to attempt to provide therapeutic benefits and to protect them from harm. This responsibility cannot be abdicated to nurses and the medical staff. The hospital board of trustees has the ultimate responsibility for the quality of patient care and for oversight of the medical staff as evidenced by the court ruling in *Johnson v. Misericordia Hospital* (1980),[5] indicating that the medical staff was responsible to the governing board for medical care quality.

Today, a hospital board's oversight of quality includes approval of quality programs and goals, monitoring performance relative to those goals, and approving physician appointments, reappointments, and clinical privileges based on a well-documented, effective credentialing process. Board responsibility for quality is unique to hospitals as reflected in the hospital's dual-pyramid structure, with separate medical staff and management hierarchies reporting to the board. Medical staffs are not hospital employees but operate as independent contractors using hospital facilities and staff to provide care. As independent contractors, medical staffs are organized as an autonomous medical staff organization with bylaws and rules of self-governance, allowing them to establish professional quality standards and quality assurance activities. However, the actions of the medical staff organization are subject to approval by the board. While the board may ask questions and demand action on quality, key decisions are generally made in medical staff committees, with the board providing cursory review and approval of most decisions. While the board has *de jure* responsibility for quality, the medical staff has *de facto* authority. The challenge for boards is to acquire *de facto* authority.

The Practical Imperative

In addition to the environmental and legal imperatives, attention to quality is a practical imperative because the board is organizationally best situated to lead the organization's quality agenda. In 2001, an IOM report titled *Crossing the Quality Chasm* called for transformational leadership in health care organizations to improve quality through radical restructuring and reengineering.[6] Yet, the unanswered question was: Who would provide such leadership? Marren, a leading author on quality, argued that the hospital board must lead the way: "It is unreasonable, illogical and irresponsible for trustees to believe that physicians will lead the quality initiative in their organization. There are simply too many disincentives and too many demands on physicians for them to engage and lead solutions to the quality challenges facing every health care organization. The answer is that quality will be led by Trustees or not at all."[7] Marren's argument about the physician's role in quality is valid, but he leaves the role of providers as trustees unaddressed. Participation of provider trustees in quality discussions raises concern for providers with dual interests. Providers employed by and serving on the board of the same organization present a potential conflict-of-interest. This book discusses the role of provider trustees and the strength they add to a board of directors; however, those in conflicted positions should abstain from quality discussions. For providers serving on the board of a health care organization for which dual interests are not a concern, participation in quality discussions is acceptable and beneficial.

Research studies have demonstrated clear advantages of boards overseeing quality—the higher the board involvement in quality-related activities, the higher the participation of clinicians in quality activities.[8] Boards also play a mediatory role between medical staff and administration in promoting a quality culture. Without this role, hospital administration and medical staff would be at odds about quality.[9] Boards are also "a nexus for planning, implementing and institutionalizing quality."[8] Given disagreements on issues of quality between management and medical staff, especially reluctance of the medical staff to accept changes impacting physician autonomy, the board is the logical choice to lead the organization's quality agenda.

The Moral Imperative

Board leadership of quality is a moral imperative. Quality must be the board's priority because it is the right thing to do. Shortell describes the need for health systems to return to their core mission: "The system needs leaders who understand that the enterprise begins and ends with the patient.... The system needs leaders who understand that 'integration' is not about acquisitions, mergers, ownership of health plans or physician practices, or similar economic transactions, but rather is about coordinating care for patients across providers, activities, and settings over time."[10] A hospital's core mission is delivering the best possible patient care. Its moral purpose is not to meet financial goals or make profits, important as these are; it is to provide high-quality care to the community for which ends profits are a means.

Reasons for Board Failure to Lead on Quality

Despite the landmark ruling in *Darling v. Charleston Community Memorial Hospital*, many hospital boards remain unprepared and uncommitted to quality. Why have boards had greater success in overseeing finance than quality? Several reasons exist and need to be addressed if boards are to assume a leadership role in quality.

Trustee Ignorance and Insecurity

As mentioned earlier, many hospital trustees remain unaware of the board's role in overseeing quality. They often have business backgrounds and do not understand the complexities of health care, the medical staff organization, and related quality issues. Hospital trustees are often unaware of the full extent of their responsibility for quality, because it is insufficiently described in trustee orientations and continuing education sessions. Trustees generally learn of their responsibilities the hard way, that is, when an incompetent physician is sued for malpractice, or a threat of losing accreditation occurs because of newly discovered quality problems. Trustees also may be too apprehensive to act decisively on quality issues because of self-doubt and fear. Self-doubt arises from lack of clinical experience. At an American Governance and Leadership Group Conference, a typical trustee reaction to the presentations focused on improving trustee knowledge of quality was: "These clinical quality problems are the job of doctors, nurses and administrators. I wouldn't know the first thing about those issues. I'm a banker."[11] Many boards lack an adequate number of trustees who are doctors, nurses, or other health professionals who can educate nonclinical trustees on quality. As a result, trustees fear acting decisively on contentious issues such as denying a physician reappointment or disciplining an incompetent physician. They fear loss of patient referrals from aggrieved physicians who may be affiliated with several hospitals and direct future referrals to other hospitals.

Trustee Confusion about Overseeing Quality

Trustees confuse oversight of quality with peer review and clinical expertise. Many consider peer review or physicians' professional judgment of their peers' practice in hospitals to be synonymous with quality oversight. This does not take into account physicians' reluctance to take corrective action against their peers. Corrective action is critical to the integrity of the oversight process. Rigorous peer review without corrective action is of little use. Without the independent authority of board trustees, it is hard to take corrective action against medical staff members. Ultimately, any quality control system is about standards, surveillance, and action. The oversight of such a system does not require medical knowledge. Yet many trustees confuse oversight of quality with possessing medical knowledge.

Financial Focus at Quality's Expense

Many health care boards have not treated quality as a priority agenda item, nor have they mandated an adequate level of education for lay board members on quality matters. Trustees have focused on what they know best—finance and strategies for achieving financial goals without recognizing that finance should be a means for funding high-quality care for the community. A prominent medical director commented on this issue by stating, "On the surface, health care senior management appears to be engaged supporters of quality. Strong statements find their way into annual reports and corporate documents. They are often in contrast to the situation most medical directors experience as they present a 'Quality Report' at a board meeting. As the medical directors start handing out the presentation, people begin looking at their watches and walls— on the one hand, quality is supported as a corporate value and is suspected to have a probable (but unknown) return on investment. On the other hand, frequent comments often suggest that it represents an irritating, sunk cost, a necessary evil of unknown value."[12] The national pay-for-performance agenda links finance with quality and is reshaping how the industry deals with these items, which have a place on every board agenda.

Inadequate Quality Reports Make Assessment Difficult

Quality reports received by many boards contain more data than information. Reports are often collated from multiple departments, lack a standardized reporting format, and lack comparative benchmarks. If a quality indicator goes down by 4%, for example, how should the board interpret this? What is used for comparison? Reports often contain more quality indicators than necessary and lack an executive summary of key trends and issues. All this makes it virtually impossible for the board to effectively evaluate hospital quality, and therefore to monitor and improve it.

Challenge to Board Authority

The board's inability to lead the quality agenda is also caused by their authority being challenged by the medical staff. A cultural assumption shared by trustees, administrators, and physicians is that hospital governance is an equal partnership among the three groups as reflected as a triad or three-legged stool. Yet such terms actually are a challenge to board authority that can undermine a board's confidence. For example, the medical staff often claims it is a self-governing body with exclusive authority over quality-related issues, yet by law, the medical staff can only self-govern in consonance with policies and purposes promulgated by the board. The medical staff organization is part of the hospital organization, and its quality-related activities fall within the board's purview—a fact upheld in several court cases. Yet lawsuits and assertions by the medical staff continue to present challenges to board authority, hindering the board's adoption of leadership roles.

Not Visiting the Patient Floors

Most trustees are outsiders, not hospital employees, and are generally unknown to the rank and file in hospitals. Trustees tend to be confined to the administrative wing of the hospital while participating in board meetings with the CEO. They seldom visit patient floors or take an active interest in quality issues, which creates the perception that trustees are only interested in financial issues and not quality. Lack of trustee visibility strengthens a self-established barrier between the board and clinical activities of the hospital.

How Boards Can Assume a Leadership Role on Quality

The board faces significant challenges in attempting to lead quality initiatives related to its lack of clinical knowledge, challenges to its authority, and general unease in dealing with quality. Yet there are environmental, legal, practical, and ethical imperatives for board adoption of a leadership role. Six steps are laid out to help boards assume a leadership role:

- Learn about quality
- Visit patient floors
- Promote board activism
- Define the board's role on quality and reports required by the board
- Establish quality standards and benchmarks
- Establish or reform the board quality committee

Learn about Quality

First, the board must recognize that providing high-quality care is the core mission of the hospital, and quality is too important in today's environment to be left to the medical staff alone. Recognizing this is essential because trustees will not devote time and effort to activities that seem insignificant. Second, the board must recognize that monitoring quality is a new capability that must be developed. Boards must educate themselves about legal responsibilities for quality and learn about indicators and processes through mandated trustee orientation and continuing education programs. Third, the nominating committee must recruit more trustees with backgrounds in quality to raise the board's knowledge in this area. Apart from external trustees with backgrounds in industrial quality, there is a need for health care professionals to assume roles on health care boards to educate fellow trustees and to increase board knowledge and comfort in making decisions about quality of care. Finally, there are several collaborative projects on quality managed by organizations like IHI and HQA that can help trustees learn the complexities and tactics for implementing large-scale quality improvement initiatives. Boards should also make available educational programming for trustees created by IHI, National Quality Forum, and others. Boards can acquire the confidence to lead only through learning about quality.

As providers are being recruited to take a role on a board, they must understand the imperative to represent the interests of the institution and not the interests of a particular department or profession. A trustee who serves only personal or parochial interests has no regard for the governance model and does not understand the inherent responsibility of being a trustee.

Visit Patient Floors

To provide legitimate leadership, trustees should be visibly involved in quality activities. Trustees need to spend time on the hospital floor talking to patients, when appropriate, in order to understand quality-related problems and demonstrate their commitment to quality. Care giving is physically and emotionally draining, especially with increases in disease severity and reduced staffing. Trustees need to acknowledge the stress clinical staff face in their jobs and be visible in celebrations of quality-related achievements. By being on the patient floors, trustees indicate that they are serious about improving quality and do not fit the stereotype of being concerned about financial issues alone. This will enhance their comfort level and provide a real chance to learn about barriers and problems facing care givers. Trustees who are health care providers can take the lead in raising the visibility of the board throughout all areas of the hospital.

Promote Board Activism

Reinertsen and Gosfield describe the fundamental source of the board's power in quality matters: "When boards ask medical staff leaders probing questions about the risks of harm in their hospital, when they insist on useful, timely data on quality and safety, when they uphold key hospital safety policies even when some prominent physicians may disagree, and when they set bold aims for improvement, boards send powerful signals that can drive change."[11] Board power for overseeing quality is derived from board activism, yet many boards limit themselves to policy making while avoiding an activist stance. Boards should be proactive by inviting experts and regulators to address the board on the subject, holding quality retreats with the medical staff, and asking significant and challenging questions about quality issues. This is essential for building a culture that supports quality improvement and creates the impetus for change. Board members who are health care providers should lead by example in promoting board activism on quality issues.

Define the Board's Role on Quality and Reports Required by the Board

A Governance Institute survey of U.S. hospitals found that less than half of the hospitals surveyed had developed a formal statement on quality. Given that the medical staff tends to contest board authority on quality matters, boards need to develop a written statement that distinguishes its role from that of the medical staff. Methods of board oversight, such as whether the board will supervise and direct individual quality programs by monitoring specific information regarding these programs' effectiveness, should be specified. Through its statement, the board can affirm its authority and send a message that it is going to lead the quality agenda. Boards must also specify the type of quality reports they wish to receive. Conventional reports to the board frequently are overly detailed, without comparative benchmarks and lacking executive summaries, thus, preventing boards from adequately understanding and evaluating hospital quality. Therefore, the board should describe what kind of report it wants in terms of level of detail, format, and frequency. Trustees with clinical backgrounds are invaluable in making such decisions and in raising their fellow board members' understanding of clinical quality matters.

Establish Quality Standards and Benchmarks

You get what you *inspect*, not what you *expect*. After choosing a quality reporting format, the board should oversee establishment of appropriate quality standards and peer benchmarks for the hospital. Physicians and nurses on the board can play an important role in providing technical expertise and explaining strengths and weaknesses of various standards. The board should aim high in setting standards. If patients are dying unnecessarily every year, incremental improvement is hardly an appropriate goal.[13] Rev. Dennis Brodeur, former senior vice president for stewardship, SSM Health Care in St. Louis, stated, "When trustees see that the national average for repeat Caesarean sections is 18% and find that their organization's average is 14%, they can say, 'That's wonderful,' or they can say, 'Even though 14% is below the average, it's unacceptable to me.'"[13] High but achievable goals are important for establishing priority and motivating the organization to greater efforts.

Establish or Reform the Board Quality Committee

Most hospital boards have a quality committee that sets goals, assesses care processes and outcomes, and appoints and credentials physicians. Some boards lack a quality committee. In such hospitals, the board's main work is perceived to be financial, and quality is left to the medical staff organization's quality committee. The board must reform the existing board quality committee or establish one if it does not exist. Best practices for the quality committee include clearly defining the committee's responsibilities, choosing an appropriate chair and committee members (i.e., with backgrounds in medicine, industrial quality, and appropriate nonquality areas), avoiding dominance of the committee by members from the medical staff, charging the committee with educating other members and the board on quality issues, and having a working relationship with the primary staff person on the committee. Therefore, if a chair or committee member has a clinical background, he or she must be educated about representing the board's interest as a trustee. Many hospitals prevent a member of the medical staff from chairing the quality committee out of concern for dominance by the medical staff. Further, a collaborative partnership between the quality committee and officers such as the hospital's chief medical officer or chief quality officer should be maintained so the committee is aware of ongoing quality projects that focus on quality and safety priorities, such as reducing medication errors and infection rates.[14] The quality committee provides recommendations to the board to advance the quality agenda.

Operational Problems Encountered by the Board

Staking out the board's role, establishing benchmarks and a quality committee, visiting patient floors, and asking significant and challenging questions demonstrate board leadership to advance quality. However, board recognition of quality problems and alignment with the organization's quality agenda is often a lengthy process and does not solve all problems. Successfully handling board issues, including operational problems, is essential for sustained board leadership of quality.

Resistance from Medical Staff

Several reasons may exist for medical staff resistance to the board's quality initiatives. A familiar reason is the medical staff seeing trustees as laypersons lacking expertise in quality, and believing that overseeing quality is the responsibility of the medical staff. Characteristics of medical staff and the hospital environment relate to medical staff resistance and are important issues the board must understand and address. Today, Gosfield and Reinertsen maintain that the extent to which physicians are independent contractors, admit patients to other facilities, or are affiliated with the hospital through a recent merger, they are likely to lack loyalty with the hospital and resist board initiatives.[15] Second, physicians are seeing their incomes decline from reduced reimbursement and competition and are sensitive to demands on their time that interfere with income-generating activities. Quality initiatives may be resisted for this reason. Third, physicians differ in their clinical and business interests, and quality projects sanctioned by the board may not be attractive to them. For example, a project requiring process improvement in the emergency room to increase patient flow is likely to increase admissions for cardiologists, but may not benefit physicians primarily focused on their ambulatory practice. Fourth, outdated medical staff bylaws (promoting a change-resistant medical staff) are often an impediment. Commentators on medical staff reform[16,17] criticize medical staff organizations' emphasis on bureaucratic rules and checks and balances that prevent meaningful changes on the grounds that it impinges on physician autonomy, for example, medical staff officials are elected as representatives rather than for their expertise in improving quality. They have short tenures, lack the mandate for change,[18] and peer review laws protect (and require) confidentiality of some medical staff and board committee proceedings. Finally, there is absence of an informal dialog between boards and medical staff today that acts as a serious communication barrier. There is much formal communication between boards and medical staff today, but there is often lack of a dialog. The conversation in medical staff committees and board committees where both are represented is on contentious issues, for example, increasing capital allocations, deciding who controls an ambulatory practice, or issues related to expanding physician privilege and practice autonomy. As Bujak comments, "Today, very little dialog takes place between the board, administration, and physicians, and as a result, untested assumptions, biases, and prejudices abound. Furthermore, because so little is known, the default assumption is that all relationships center around money and control. Doing the deal then becomes the basis for all relationship building."[19] Cooperation through dialog with medical staff is essential to long-term change in quality.

Fragmented Structure and Lack of Accountability for Quality

In addition to medical staff resistance, another problem is the fragmented structure for managing quality in hospitals that leads to lack of accountability. As Feazell and Marren describe, "Quality data and information are developed in a wide variety of contexts, using different methodologies to collect different data for different purposes by a variety of different professionals frequently reporting to different senior managers." A typical hospital may at any time have the following quality projects in progress: clinical peer review, performance measures, core measures, continuous quality improvement (CQI), patient safety programs, root causes and sentinel analyses, special studies, and utilization management/resource use analyses.[19] Each quality project is a disconnected "silo." The result is fragmented information that leads to information overload, duplication of reporting, and poor prioritization of problems.

A related problem is the disjointed hospital committee structure related to quality.[17] Unlike boards of businesses, health care boards have two groups reporting to them: hospital employees under the CEO and medical staff members led by a president. Similarly, there are frequently two committee structures related to quality: hospital committees and medical staff committees. Medical staff committees such as morbidity and mortality, utilization review, or pharmaceutical and therapeutics committees are dominated by physicians and deal with medical and surgical outcomes, mortality statistics, and medication errors. Quality improvement committees on the hospital side are dominated by nursing and ancillary services staff and generally deal with patient satisfaction and utilization issues such as admissions delays, testing delays, and excessive patient wait time. Though patient care quality is affected by physician services and services provided by nonphysician staff, the dual-committee structure creates an artificial barrier between the two sides, making it difficult for them to jointly solve problems. Fragmented structure and lack of accountability hinder advancement of the quality agenda.

Reluctance to Act against Physician Incompetence

Another major problem, in addition to fragmented structure, is physicians' reluctance to act against their peers in cases of demonstrated professional incompetence during peer review. A major contributor is the lack of documentation of physician infractions. Often this occurs because of the peer review committees' fear of litigation by the physician in question, loss of referrals, or the belief that these matters should be settled internally. In such situations, a personal approach is adopted by speaking to the physician in question. This provides no assurance that the incompetent physician will change his or her behavior. Often, trustees learn about the problem physician much later, through informal channels. Such information is difficult to verify without documentation, and often the problem is too far advanced by the time it is considered by the board. Dealing appropriately with professional incompetence must be a high priority for boards.

Low Financial Appropriation for Quality Projects

Apart from problems with the medical staff, low financial appropriations remain a difficulty. Many hospitals lack advanced information systems and the latest technology for improving patient safety and clinical outcomes. For example, most hospitals have quality assurance or quality improvement systems, but many lack audit systems to identify whether appropriate data are being collected by these systems. Also, many institutions have not invested in state-of-the-art equipment needed for upgrading the measurement and provision of quality. Sometimes boards are so concerned about the primacy of cost-efficiency for institutional survival that they devalue the importance of investing in quality-related infrastructure. It is difficult to transform quality with an inadequate technical infrastructure.

CEO Reluctance to Address Quality-Related Issues

Another problem is CEO reluctance to bring quality problems to the attention of the board. Most trustees are outsiders and depend on the CEO for communication with the medical staff on important quality issues. For example, the CEO must determine when the medical staff needs to communicate with the board on sensitive issues of quality such as physician competency, patient safety, violations of hospital policies, and disciplinary matters. Many administrators may keep communication channels flowing on these aspects only if their own survival is not at stake. This deprives boards of the information needed to take action. Boards must also share some of the blame. For example, significant improvement in quality requires change in structure, resources, procedures, and incentives that may elicit resistance from employees or the medical staff. Implementing these changes requires support from the board, but many boards lack a well-conceived plan for quality improvement that can be used as the basis for supporting the CEO.

Inadequate Quality Assessment Systems and Resources

Finally, in some institutions, quality assessment systems are outdated and ineffective. There is a lack of a systematic and consistent approach to credentialing and disciplining physicians. Often, there is no audit of the accuracy for coding, data entry, and surveillance of sentinel events. Also, inaccuracies in data input, analysis, or reporting, when identified, are not acted upon effectively. Lack of accurate data can undermine quality improvement efforts.

Dealing with Operational Problems

The operational problems discussed in this chapter relate to lack of cooperation, action, and resources. These problems should be approached using both flexibility and firmness. In matters where lack of cooperation stems from genuine quality concerns, utilizing a flexible approach will advance the quality agenda in the long-term. As a key characteristic of governance, the board is responsible for making decisions and standing behind them to demonstrate credibility.

Conduct Situational Assessment and Engage Physicians

The first step in reducing resistance by the medical staff is conducting a realistic assessment of hospital-physician relations, taking into account history, physician loyalty, economic interests, and turf battles. As Gosfield and Reinertsen assert, if process improvements in the ER give internists and cardiologists precious recaptured time but mean little to surgeons who wish to build an outpatient surgery center in the community, it may be appropriate to consider a joint venture with surgeons to assist in meeting community needs. If primary care physicians are suffering from a failed managed care strategy, offering them a staffing agency that leases nurse practitioners may be of value.[17] However, this strategy is not to support appeasement of resistant physicians; instead, it offers solutions. While a universal solution does not currently exist, boards and administrators need to be aware of the economic stress that physicians face and that threatens economic survival. This underlying anxiety can impede a rational discussion about quality.

Another challenge is to integrate providers in decision-making bodies. A Governance Institute survey[21] demonstrates that boards in high-performing hospitals set meeting agendas focusing on quality in collaboration with the medical staff. Today's boards need to recruit forward-thinking leaders from the medical staff who challenge physicians unwilling to change. To this end, the board needs to assess adequacy of physician integration measures. Are there adequate physicians on the board and its committees? Are there physician representatives other than medical staff officers? Are innovative physicians being recruited? Integrating physicians in various committees and bodies is essential for maintaining channels of communication with the medical staff. In integrating physicians, they must be educated on representing board interests, not those of their department or profession.

Promoting informal communication with physicians is equally important. Bujak suggests that trustees must informally interact with medical staff to create a dialog based on shared purpose around quality of patient care and questions like "What are we about?" and "What should our future look like?"[19] Despite financial problems, most physicians remain passionate about patient care. They are likely to find a common purpose centered on quality if the board engages them on this issue. Informal mechanisms such as retreats, educational activities, and social events can be used to accomplish this. Informal interactions help bypass formal decision structures and may lower defenses and help find common ground on matters of quality.

Aside from informal communication, asking the right questions can help. Indirectly inquiring about physician engagement is an important component of the quality agenda.[15] Gosfield and Reinertsen state that while physicians tend to be committed to their patients' welfare, they face economic pressures to avoid wasting time needed for income generation. For this reason, boards need to propose quality projects that relate to outcomes improvement while being relatively time-efficient.[15] Asking the board questions about quality often falls into two categories: "How good are we compared with others?" and

"Are we getting better?" Physicians are more likely to quarrel with measures in the "How good are we?" column than in the "Are we getting better?" column. The former creates defensiveness by attacking physicians' sense of self-worth. In the latter case, there is no comparative referent, and therefore there may be less defensiveness.

Discuss Medical Staff Reform

While engaging the medical staff, boards can raise the issue of medical staff reform. Responsibility for reform may be delegated to the medical staff after mentioning various suggested reforms in the literature,[16,17] such as increasing clarity of medical staff duties, establishing goals and accountability for medical staff officers, reducing unnecessary committees, integrating medical staff and hospital committees, and changing bylaws to initiate corrective action against practitioners if the medical staff fails to investigate a case satisfactorily. Medical staff reform should be presented as a means for promoting quality rather than an indictment of the medical staff organization. If there is resistance from the medical staff, the board must reiterate the organization's commitment to quality and the need for reform to achieve quality goals. Where resistance is strong, underlying reasons should be identified and addressed. Medical staff reform is essential for medical staff accountability and rationalizing the decision-making structure related to quality.

Develop Credentialing Criteria and Deal Effectively with Physician Incompetence

While being flexible in engaging physicians, the board must deal firmly with cases of incompetent physicians. Boards should ensure that actions related to physician incompetence are based on formal documentary evidence and well-laid-out processes. An informal system provides no assurance that a problem is being addressed. All such matters must be handled in accordance with formal channels provided in the bylaws, with communications to the physician in question to be in writing and copies kept on file. Regarding reappointment of physicians, the board's role is to ensure that a fair and effective reappointment process and criteria are in place. It must compare the results of criteria-based review with the medical staff's recommendation regarding each applicant. When all indicators are consistent, the board approves the recommendation. When indicators appear inconsistent, the board should request additional information, send the application back to the medical staff for further review, or reject the recommendation.

Create Integrated, Accountable Structure for Managing Quality

Long-term resolution of the quality problem requires an integrated, accountable structure to manage quality. This involves two related actions: establishing professional management of quality and reforming the ineffective dual-committee structure. For effective management of quality, the board should advocate establishing a professional quality management department under a chief quality officer, preferably a physician, who can monitor environmental trends regarding quality and advise the medical staff and administration; serve on and assist in integrating various quality committees; support accurate and timely data collection and analysis; and provide ongoing policy guidance.[22]

As part of structural reform, the board must also discuss integration of the dual-quality committee structure.[17] Having separate hospital and medical staff committees with two reporting mechanisms makes it difficult for the two groups to collaborate on improving quality and services. Voss provides the example of the pharmacy and therapeutics (P&T) committee, which is a medical staff committee.[17] A more effective P&T committee would be a multidisciplinary committee that is neither a hospital nor a medical staff committee, cochaired by a member of the medical staff, as well as by a hospital employee. A unified committee serving one organization—the hospital—by drawing members from multiple disciplines, would be best suited to addressing quality issues meaningfully.

Develop a Strategic Plan and Invest in Quality

Boards should adopt strategic goals regarding quality that are responsive to trends in the regulatory and competitive environment. Boards must then invest adequate resources in strategic quality initiatives, including staff, facilities, information technology (IT) systems, and safety-related technology such as computer-based medication review systems or computerized physician-order-entry systems. As a starting point, one can compare staffing and IT resources of the finance department with those of the quality and safety departments to see if the latter are appropriately resourced. Adjusting for workload, are the full-time equivalent (FTE) counts comparable? Does the quality department staff have access to adequate database and business intelligence tools? Can the quality department report on the outcomes and error rates for all departments and the majority of patients served?[23] Analogous to the annual financial budget, there should be a quality budget outlining major quality initiatives with year-end goals in terms of outcome and process indicators, and reporting periodic variance from target.

Institute a Quality Audit Process

Increases in public reporting on quality have intensified concern about the accuracy of quality data, and a rigorous audit process is needed that can be delegated to the quality management department. Lister suggests an audit of the hospital's quality assessment process should address the following: Has the board specified its approach to physician credentialing? What is the coding accuracy? Are sentinel events logged and studied? Are trends (e.g., infections, injury, medication errors, equipment failure, return to operating room, adverse outcomes, unscheduled readmissions) reviewed regularly?[24] The audit system should be validated annually by an external quality group to reassure the trustees who implemented the quality processes that they are effective, and to demonstrate to the public that the hospital has a commitment to quality.[25]

Establish Quality-Related Incentive Compensation

Well-designed external incentives are needed to create a climate in which safety and quality improvement are priorities and ultimately become a matter of routine performance. According to a survey of 4200 U.S. nonprofit hospitals and health systems by the Governance Institute, Solucient Top 100 Hospitals were more likely to have their CEO's performance evaluation linked to achieving quality improvement goals.[26] The case of Cincinnati Children's Hospital is instructive. Ten years ago, Cincinnati Children's Hospital's senior management compensation was based on attaining financial results. Ultimately, the board realized the hospital was not a financially driven institution but earned profits to provide quality care to patients. As a result, Cincinnati Children's Hospital participated in the IHI's 5 Million Lives Campaign that included educating and involving the board and linking executive compensation to quality outcomes. Today, only 30% of executives' bonus compensation is based on financial measures. Of the remaining 70% based on quality, 40% is shared by all senior management, including pediatrics, surgery, finance, and personnel.[13]

Demonstrate Courage When Tested

As the ultimate authority on quality within hospitals, the board has the power to sanction unpopular but effective quality initiatives. How this power is exercised can make or break the organizational culture related to quality. For example, if a hospital hopes to improve its mortality rate, the board may need to implement controversial issues such as how intensive care units are organized and staffed or how staff levels are determined.[13] Boards are severely tested when confronted with approving such controversial practice opposed by a few prominent members of the medical staff. If the board relents, it can undermine the hard work of physicians and nurses trying to create a safer environment for patients. Standing by unpopular but effective policies, on the other hand, can send a strong signal that the board is resolute about advancing patient safety.[27] Board decisions affect the health care organization it governs, the administration and the staff that run the organization, as well as the patients that seek care there. Board oversight of quality is essential for success.

Conclusion

Boards have spent years saddled with a passive responsibility for quality. The altered health care environment now requires trustees to play a leadership role in quality. To be leaders, trustees must learn the language of quality, visit patient floors, affirm their authority in quality matters, define quality reporting specifications, establish or reform the quality committee, and set challenging quality standards and benchmarks. For long-term success in their quality leadership role, they should engage the medical staff, address medical staff reform, manage physician incompetence, create a rational quality management structure, institute a quality audit process, establish incentive compensation, and take credible action on critical issues. Boards must realize they are mandated to lead the quality agenda. Board members who are health care providers have an opportunity to be the vanguards of this leadership movement.

Case Study

Excel Health Care System in Illinois has had AA credit ratings since 1998, thanks to strong board governance. Current chairman Roger Whetten, a retired savings and loans industry executive, became chairman of the health system in 2001 and helped raise its financial and quality performance. Whetten has served on the board for 6 years and previously served on the board of DeNobili Hospital in Chicago. Whetten graduated with degrees in sociology and worked in various savings and loans banks for 35 years before retiring in 2000. He is a tireless civic leader and has served on the boards of several nonprofit organizations.

Whetten says he learned a lot about quality during the deregulation of the savings and loans industry. Companies had to change the definition of quality from a customer standpoint, and improve employee responsiveness to customers. He finds a lot of similarities with health care today, where hospitals have to be efficient but also focus on the customer. One of Whetten's accomplishments is starting a board quality committee at the request of some system executives. The committee created system-wide quality measures and an internal benchmark to compare hospitals within each of its six regions. Comparative results of all hospitals are discussed in the board quality committee every quarter. Another accomplishment is working with the finance committee to invest in new IT systems.

Whetten believes in centralization and standardization of best clinical practices. He has tried to promote standardization of high-efficacy drugs to decrease cost while improving medical outcomes but is facing resistance from the medical staff. He believes that allowing physicians to have too much individual choice prevents optimal decisions about the best drug or medical test to use.

Study and Discussion Questions

1. Unlike many trustees with business backgrounds, Whetten is not intimidated in overseeing quality. Why?
2. What can hospitals learn from Whetten's background and qualities about the type of trustee to recruit?
3. Whetten established a quality committee of the board. How would absence of a quality committee have impacted the board at Excel Health Care System? How will its presence help the board?
4. Whetten believes in reducing individual choices for physicians in drug selection and standardizing high-efficacy drugs. Why are physicians likely to resist drug standardization? Should Whetten be firm or flexible in dealing with medical staff resistance?

Suggested Readings and Web Sites

Readings

Bujak, J. S. 2003. How to improve hospital-physician relationships. *Frontiers of Health Services Management* 20:3–21.

Dennis, D. D. and J. E. Orlikoff. 2002. *The high-performance board: Principles of nonprofit organization governance.* San Francisco: Jossey-Bass.

Marren, J. P., G. L. Feazell, and M. W. Paddock. 2003. The hospital board at risk and the need to restructure the relationship with the medical staff: Bylaws, peer review and related solutions. *Annals of Health Law* 12:179–234.

Orlikoff, J. and M. Totten. 1991. *The board's role in quality care: A practical guide for hospital trustees.* Chicago: American Hospital Publishers.

Web Site

Great Boards. *Promoting excellence in healthcare governance.* Baader & Associates: www.GreatBoards.org

References

1. Institute of Medicine. 2000. *To err is human: Building a safer health system,* ed. L. T. Kohn, J. M. Corrigan, and M. S. Donaldson. Washington, DC: National Academy Press.
2. *Pepke v. Grace Hospital,* 130 Mich. 493 (1902).
3. *Schloendorff v. Society of New York Hospital,* 211 N.Y. 125 (1914).
4. *Darling v. Charleston Community Hospital,* 33 Ill. 2d 326 (1965).
5. *Johnson v. Misericordia Hospital,* 97 Wis. 2d 521 (1980).
6. Institute of Medicine, 2001. *Crossing the Quality Chasm: A New Health System for the 21ˢᵗ Century.* Washington, DC: National Academy Press.
7. Marren, J. The smoldering issue for trustee liability for poor hospital quality: A firestorm whose time has come, pp. 1–7. http://www.hmltd.com/hc_topics.htm (accessed October 15, 2004).
8. Weiner, B., S. Shortell, and J. Alexander. 1997. Promoting clinical involvement in hospital quality improvement efforts: The effects of the top management, board and medical physician leadership. *Health Services Research* 32:491–510.
9. Arrington, B., K. Gautam, and W. J. McCabe. 1995. Continually improving governance. *Hospital and Health Services Administration* 40:95–110.
10. Shortell, S. M. 2001. A time for concerted action. *Frontiers of Health Services Management* 18:33–39.
11. Reinertsen, J. L. 2003. Understanding and improving clinical quality: The role of trustees. *Trustee* 56:17–20.
12. Fetterolf, D. E. 2003. Commentary: Presenting the value of medical quality to non-clinical senior management and boards of directors. *American Journal of Medical Quality* 18:10–14.
13. Sandrick, K. 2000. Be all that you can be. Information technology and quality care go hand in hand. *Trustee* 53:6–10.
14. Bader, B. Best Practices for board quality committees. *Great Boards* 3, no. 2. www.GreatBoards.org (accessed March 10, 2008).
15. Gosfield, A. G. and J. L. Reinertsen. 2007. Sharing the quality agenda with physicians. *Trustee* 60:12–14.
16. Marren, J. P., G. L. Feazell, and M. W. Paddock. 2003. The hospital board at risk and the need to restructure the relationship with the medical staff: Bylaws, peer review and related solutions. *Annals of Health Law* 12:179–234.

17. Voss, C. B. 2002. Improving quality through committee structure. *Healthcare Executive* 17:62–63.
18. Classen, D. 2000. Patient safety, thy name is quality. *Trustee* 53:12–15.
19. Bujak, J. S. 2003. How to improve hospital-physician relationships. *Frontiers of Health Services Management* 20:3–21.
20. Feazell, G. L. and J. P. Marren. 2003. The quality-value proposition in health care. *Journal of Health Care Finance* 30:1–29.
21. Knecht, P. R. 2007. Engaging the board: The missing ingredient in improving healthcare quality. *Healthcare Executive* 22:64.
22. Wilson, L. L. 2000. The quality manager. *Journal of Quality in Clinical Practice* 20:127–30.
23. Brynes, J. 2007. Seven tactics for hardwiring quality cost savings into hospital operations. *Hospitals and Health Networks* 81:34–35.
24. Lister, E. 2003. How can the board fulfill their quality oversight role? *Trustee* May 22–23.
25. Glazebrook, S. G. and J. G. Buchanan. 2001. Clinical governance and external audit. *Journal of Quality in Clinical Practice* 21:30–33.
26. Becker, C. 2006. Board, quality linked: Study. *Modern Healthcare* 36:18.
27. Larson, L. 2007. Physician autonomy vs. accountability: Making quality standards and medical style mesh. *Trustee* 60:14–16.

Chapter 5

The Board's Role in Building Healthy Environments

Blair L. Sadler, Jennifer DuBose, and Craig Zimring

Contents

Executive Summary

Hospitals and their boards are facing a new reality. They can no longer tolerate preventable hospital-acquired patient conditions such as infections and falls, avoidable injuries to staff, unnecessary intrahospital patient transfers that can increase errors, or having patients and families subjected to noisy, confusing environments that increase anxiety and stress. Hospitals must effectively deploy all reasonable quality improvement techniques available. Boards need to understand the clear connection between creating well-designed physical environments that promote healing and improved health care safety and quality for patients, families, and staff.

Boards also need to understand the compelling business case for creating a healing environment. When conducting a business case analysis for a new project, boards should include the ongoing operating savings, as well as revenue and market share impacts of evidence-based design interventions. Emerging pay-for-performance methodologies that reward hospitals for quality and refuse to pay hospitals for the harm they cause (e.g., infections and falls) will further strengthen the business case.

When planning to build a new hospital or renovate an existing facility, boards should address a key question: Will the proposed project incorporate all relevant and proven evidence-based design innovations in order to optimize patient safety, quality, and satisfaction, as well as workforce safety, satisfaction, productivity, and energy efficiency? Boards should consider taking 10 steps to ensure that an optimal cost-effective hospital environment is implemented.

Learning Objectives

1. To understand the clear connection between proven evidence-based architectural design innovations and improved safety and quality for patients,

families, and staff, as well as improved satisfaction levels that will help create market differentiation.

2. To understand the compelling business case for these innovations by analyzing multiyear operating savings and revenue impacts.
3. To understand how to address a sixth key question that ensures that all relevant evidence-based design solutions are included in the analysis.
4. To understand 10 steps needed to implement evidence-based design.
5. To understand design recommendations that hospitals should adopt in all new projects.

Key Words

- Business case
- Cost savings
- Evidence-based design
- Hospital facility environment
- Implementation steps
- Trustee and leadership involvement

Introduction

As described effectively in other chapters, hospital boards are dealing with numerous daunting and often competing demands: unpredictable reimbursement, workforce shortages, skyrocketing costs, increasing disclosure requirements, mounting consumer and employer expectations, and aggressive union tactics. Most importantly, a quality and safety revolution is sweeping the country.[1-3] Consumers, employers, and payers are demanding that hospitals dramatically reduce system-based errors that harm, even kill, thousands of patients annually.[4]

The speed of the quality revolution has accelerated dramatically, spurred by many converging forces, including the Leapfrog Group[a] on behalf of employers; the Centers for Medicare and Medicaid Services (CMS)–Premier Hospital Quality Incentive Demonstration project, also known as pay-for-performance[b] (which is being adopted in various forms by individual states and commercial payers); greater emphasis by the Joint Commission on their standards to improve safety and quality[c]; as well as two innovative nationwide campaigns coordinated by the Institute for Healthcare Improvement (IHI).[5,d] The IHI 100,000 Lives Campaign was so successful in reducing harm to patients that in late 2006, the IHI revamped its efforts into the Protecting 5 Million Lives from Harm Campaign. Over 3700 hospitals have joined this campaign.[5] In addition to clinicians and managers, hospital boards of trustees are now being encouraged to get much more involved in this project.

Many hospital facilities have simply come to the end of their useful lives, and in several states, seismic requirements are mandating major facility upgrades. As a nation, we have entered a major hospital construction boom. It is projected that the already strong health care construction sector will grow by 13% to a total of $53.8 billion in 2008, and will continue to experience a high growth rate through 2011[6] when it is projected to reach $71 billion.[7] These forces provide unprecedented opportunities to build better hospitals and renovate existing ones utilizing techniques that can measurably improve care and working conditions.

As Carolyn Clancy, MD, the director of the Agency for Healthcare Research and Quality (AHRQ), has written, "As hospital leaders continue to seek ways to improve quality and reduce errors, it is critical that they look around their own physical environment with the goal of ensuring the hospital contributes to, rather than impedes, the process of healing."[8] AHRQ has developed a video for boards and hospital leaders and has disseminated it to over 5000 hospitals in the United States.[e]

The physical environment in which people work and patients receive their care is one of the essential components in reducing the number of preventable hospital-acquired conditions. Research now shows that the physical environment in which patients receive care and caregivers work has a measurable and quantifiable impact on them.[9–13] Indeed, the environment can significantly assist or impede an organization's safety and quality improvement agenda.[14]

For example, published research tells us that single-patient rooms save lives and reduce harm through fewer infections. Wider patient bathroom doors contribute to reducing patient falls; more access to natural light reduces anxiety and depression while shortening length of stay. Variable-acuity rooms reduce costly, dangerous, and unnecessary patient transfers; high-efficiency particulate air (HEPA) filtration systems lessen airborne-caused infections in immunosuppressed patients; and providing positive distractions through music and art can improve the care experience and the perception of pain.[13] This research clearly shows the positive economic impact of evidence-based design.

With the rising pressure on hospital boards to improve quality and safety, and with mounting evidence that design of the physical environment can contribute to both, why haven't all hospitals boards rushed to demand implementation of these evidence-based design innovations? Some have. For those who have not, the barriers are often perceived to be economic.

The Business Case for Building Better Hospitals

Frequently, the biggest barriers to building optimal hospitals are the rapidly escalating costs of construction. Incorporating optimal design innovations can cost additional capital dollars initially. However, many do not realize that these interventions can also save significant operational costs over the life of the project that will far exceed the initial incremental capital costs. This lack of awareness is understandable because, until recently, we did not have the evidence upon which to develop solid financial operating impact assessments.

Lessons from a Fable Hospital

Based on published evidence and actual experience of pioneering health care organizations involved in the Pebble program, sponsored by the Center for Health Design, a multidisciplinary team analyzed the data in 2004 and designed the hypothetical Fable Hospital™. It was called Fable because it had not been built, but it could be at any time by anyone (and a few are now being designed). In 2004, Fable Hospital was a 300-bed replacement hospital costing $240 million—the average cost of building a hospital at that time. In Fable, the hospital's leaders decided to incorporate all the appropriate, evidence-based design innovations.[15]

After a detailed analysis, the multidisciplinary team estimated that an evidence-based design would require a relatively modest one-time capital cost of $12 million (or 5% of the $240 million base cost). When the team analyzed the operating cost savings resulting from reducing infections, eliminating unnecessary patient transfers, minimizing patient falls, lowering drug costs, lessening employee turnover rates, as well as improving market share and philanthropy, the results were stunning. The additional $12 million capital cost would be more than offset by the end of the second year. With effective management and monitoring, the financial operating benefits would continue year after year, making the additional innovations a sound long-term investment. In short, there was a compelling business case for building better, safer hospitals.

Additional Evidence of Cost Impacts

Since 2004, when the Fable Hospital article made such a strong business case, considerably more evidence has accumulated on the impact of facility design on operating costs. An update of the Fable article is beyond the scope of this chapter; however, it is important to highlight some of the most important changes that have occurred since its publication.

The costs of hospital construction have skyrocketed. A combination of increased costs of concrete, steel, and other building materials in a competitive global market, the cost of labor, and markedly more stringent building code requirements have driven construction and project costs to unprecedented levels. Despite the substantial construction cost increases, the business case for building better hospitals has become even stronger because of the significant impact of evidence-based design innovations on patient safety, quality of care, and workforce well-being.

In recent years, considerable new research has been published, and a comprehensive review of the English-language literature has been completed.[16] Single-patient rooms have become the standard since being included in the 2006 American Institute of Architects' minimum standards. The advantages of single-patient rooms are so well documented that they are no longer considered a luxury.[17] Because of the strong evidence on reduced infections, the clear patient preference, improved patient-centered care, and the greater efficiency and flexibility in optimal use, individual patient rooms are now a basic requirement of most hospitals being built today.

Studies show that installing ceiling lifts can significantly reduce the costs from workforce injuries.[18] Peace Health in Oregon saw a reduction in the annual cost of patient-handling injuries of 83% after the installation of ceiling lifts. The payback of the initial investment occurred in less than 2.5 years.[19]

Several detailed studies document the increased costs (ranging from $8000 to over $40,000) incurred for treating patients with hospital-acquired infections.[20–22] The Pennsylvania Council analysis of 168 hospitals shows a dramatic difference in the cost impact of patients with and without hospital-acquired infections. These studies show that it costs more to treat these patients and their length of stay is greater. Many indicators suggest that the rate of infection seems to be growing.

The evidence has become sufficiently strong that the strategic placement of hand-washing dispensers in every patient room and high-volume treatment area has become a standard and should be included in any new or existing hospital, as part of an infection reduction program.[23,24] HEPA filtration systems are effective in reducing airborne-acquired infections and are a worthwhile investment in areas that treat immunocompromised patients.[19]

Patient injuries from falls will become financially more significant as reimbursement rules change. Not considering any savings for avoiding litigation, the cost of falls with injuries is estimated to be $19,000 per event.[25] Research shows that the physical environment is one important component of a total fall reduction program. Environmental changes are not necessarily costly. For instance, larger patient bathrooms with double-door access can be accomplished for as little as $400 per room.[26] The concept of decentralizing nursing stations to improve line-of-sight visibility to patients, and increase the amount of direct patient care time, has gathered considerable momentum. Many believe that there is no additional cost to this concept because it results in the same amount of overall square footage, though in a different configuration.[27] For a 300-bed hospital, reduced patient falls could result in over $1 million in annual savings.[f]

The acuity-adaptable room is one of the most powerful innovations to improve care by reducing unnecessary intra-hospital transfers, having a threefold benefit of reduced errors and falls, significantly increased patient satisfaction, and reduction in nonproductive staff time. As acuity-adaptable rooms are being adopted, more data on their impact will become available. Dublin Methodist Hospital in Columbus, Ohio, has calculated that the incremental costs of including additional oxygen and vacuum systems in room headwalls is about $5700 per room. The possibility of dramatically reducing costly transfers is enormous.[27,28] Significant work in nurse training and culture support is required to realize the benefits made possible by acuity-adaptable rooms.

Noise reduction innovations—acoustical ceiling tiles in patient rooms, corridors, and nursing stations—are effective economical features. Carpet is also effective in reducing noise and can actually cost less than other floor coverings, such as vinyl.[27] All hospitals should undertake a simple sound audit to identify the noisiest areas and put additional innovations in place, such as eliminating overhead paging and moving noisy equipment—these have significant benefits in patient satisfaction.[29]

It is increasingly recognized that appropriately selected music can also reduce patient anxiety and increase their satisfaction with their health care experience. "Carefully selected music can reduce stress, enhance a sense of comfort and relaxation, offer distraction from pain, and enhance clinical performance."[30] Music can also reduce the need for anesthesia in certain circumstances. "On the day of surgery, patients exposed to music in combination with therapeutic suggestions required less rescue analgesic compared with the controls. Patients in the music group experienced more effective analgesia the first day after surgery and could be mobilized earlier after the operation."[31]

Many well-designed innovations involving music and the arts have a measurably positive impact in reducing anxiety, stress, and sleep deprivation, and in improving the patient perceptions of their experience. Most of these interventions are extremely low cost and can be implemented in virtually any hospital at any time. In addition, funding for these projects can frequently be provided by philanthropy in the arts community, so they do not compete with other philanthropic needs of the hospital.

The need to reduce employee turnover and improve retention has never been greater. A recent detailed calculation of nursing turnover estimates the cost per registered nurse lost at $62,100 to $67,100. An improved, quieter work environment can reduce stress and contribute to improved nurse satisfaction scores.[32]

Going Green: Further Enhancing the Business Case

In addition to evidence-based design features that address patient and staff safety, there are a number of emerging sustainable or green building features and strategies that can improve the health care environment with little or no capital cost and should be considered for inclusion in new projects. Sustainable design is being increasingly recognized as a key component of the hospital safety agenda. In addition, incorporating proven green building features is positive for hospitals to consider as a good community partner in improving the overall environment.

At the end of 2007, a coalition of large hospital systems and nonprofit organizations created the Global Health and Safety Initiative specifically to address the triple safety agendas of patients, workers, and the environment. While a comprehensive review of sustainability features appropriate for health care design is beyond the scope of this chapter, a few are highlighted here because of their relationship to the business case. A detailed examination of sustainability in health care facilities was recently published by Robin Guenther and Gail Vittori.[33]

Similar to the evidence-based design features discussed above, sustainable design does not necessarily have a cost premium. The most widely cited study of green building, conducted by Gregory Kats, found that green office and school buildings, on average, had a 2% capital cost premium, and that these costs were more than recovered though operational savings—primarily energy and water savings.[34] Moreover, green buildings may provide more health and productivity benefits than standard buildings, known as brown buildings. Kats' research in the office and school sectors shows improved productivity and reduced absenteeism with green buildings, both of which translated into cost savings.

While no definitive study on the cost of green hospital buildings has yet been published, the cost-consulting firm Davis Langdon recently published *Cost of Green Revisited*, comparing the capital cost of green and brown ambulatory care facilities in California.[35] Their study found that green ambulatory care facilities are not distinguishable in capital cost from their brown counterparts.

In addition to the obvious financial benefits associated with energy and water reduction, green buildings are incorporating innovative materials and products that are proving to reduce the operational cost of buildings. Rubber flooring is an example of a product that can have benefits to the bottom line and the environment, and can make for a safer and better-performing hospital. Kaiser Permanente and Herman Miller have found that the initial cost premium when compared with standard vinyl flooring is offset by a combination of reduced maintenance costs and improved safety. The environmental benefit is that it replaces polyvinyl chloride, which relies upon components and manufacturing processes linked to detrimental health effects and must be maintained by labor-intensive waxing and stripping protocols that negatively impact indoor air quality. Additional benefits arise from improved traction (reduced slips and falls) and from its noise-dampening quality, which creates a more tranquil environment. It is also softer under foot, reducing strain on caregivers who walk miles per shift.

Another green strategy that intersects with evidence-based design to improve the quality of the environment is maximizing access to daylight. Studies have shown that access to natural light and views can improve healing outcomes, reducing the length of stay.[36,37] Studies in office and school environments have correlated access to daylight and views with improved productivity and learning (in health care, this is likely to translate to reduced medical errors). One study concluded that nurses in Alaska had twice as many errors in darker months.[38] Daylight also reduces the demand for electricity to power artificial lights and improves the resiliency of the building during extended periods of power loss.

Many green strategies that improve indoor air quality have no cost premium at all and simply require thoughtful selection and procedures. Material finishes that have low volatile organic compound emissions are readily available with little, if any, additional cost. As green buildings become more pervasive, the range of product offerings will increase, and cost premiums associated with innovation will give way to marketplace competition.

In summary, the multiyear operational cost savings of incorporating evidence-based design innovations are increasingly prevalent. These contribute to the strong business case. Equally important, a series of major new reimbursement trends are beginning to emerge that will have just as important economic implications for building better buildings. They include pay-for-performance, the National Quality Forum's recommended "Never Events," not charging for hospital-caused harm, and comparable publicly reported patient satisfaction scores.

The Impact of Pay-for-Performance

In the past few years, a fundamentally new concept has emerged in the reimbursement of hospitals and physicians. This is the most significant new reimbursement concept since the enactment of Medicare and Medicaid and the adoption of diagnostic related groups (DRGs). The approach is called value-based purchasing or pay-for-performance, and it will have a profound impact on the business case for quality improvement, including the physical environment in which people work and care is received.

Three years ago, the Centers for Medicare and Medicaid Services (CMS) and Premier, Inc., launched a major demonstration program involving over 260 hospitals who voluntarily agreed to submit data about their level of compliance with 34 well-accepted quality measures that should be performed 100% of the time in 5 high-volume clinical focus areas (acute myocardial infarction, coronary artery bypass graft surgery, heart failure, pneumonia, and hip and knee replacement surgery). Using the two core concepts of transparency and a potential financial bonus for outstanding performers, the goal was to test the impact of these concepts on hospital and physician behavior. The results were significant, with the average hospital compliance score moving up by 11.8% in the first 2 years of the program. Individual hospitals are posted on the Premier Web site, so consumers can make more informed choices to get the best quality care available.[g] The findings have caught the attention of Congress and the nation.

The National Quality Forum (NQF) has identified 27 "Never Events" that are largely preventable and should simply never occur in hospitals.[39] Building on this work, in September 2007, CMS took the pay-for-performance approach to a new level. CMS selected eight types of events that harm patients[39] and have announced that there will be no Medicare reimbursement for these events if they were caused in the hospital. One of the eight conditions specifically identified is hospital-acquired patient injuries such as those that occur with falls. Several types of hospital-acquired infections were included in the 2007 rule, and several more have been proposed for consideration in 2008.[40]

Medicaid programs and commercial payers will likely follow the CMS lead and begin to announce that they will not reimburse hospitals for harm they cause. While the details are far from clear, it seems reasonable to assume that within 3 to 5 years, virtually no payers will reimburse hospitals and physicians for serious harm that they cause. Further, these hospitals will be less likely to be included in payer networks, thus, causing measurable shifts in market share to better-performing hospitals. Consumers will have easy access to clear outcome measures and will make choices about where to go for their care based on this information. Increasingly, consumers will be channeled to payer-preferred networks based on quality measures.

Another New Reality: Some Hospitals No Longer Charging for Errors

In this new era of transparency and public reporting, hospitals in some states have voluntarily decided not to charge payers and patients for errors they cause. The connection to such a policy and an organization's reputation seems obvious. In addition, the connection between hospital errors and the incidence of litigation has been effectively described.[41]

Indeed, a "no charge" policy for hospital-caused errors may soon become standard practice. The hospital associations of Minnesota and Massachusetts have adopted a "no charge for errors" policy in advance of the CMS policy. Change is taking effect and many other states will likely follow.[42] We are entering a new era—one where patients and payers will no longer pay for poor performance.

Patient Satisfaction and Transparency: HCAHPS Raises the Bar

Another significant emerging trend is the increasing transparency about reporting patient experiences in hospitals. With support from CMS and the Agency for Health Research and Quality, the Hospital Consumer Assessment of Health Providers and Systems (HCAHPS) survey was developed to: (1) produce comparable data on patients' perspectives of care on topics that are important to consumers; (2) create incentives, through public reporting, for hospitals to improve care; and (3) increase public accountability through increased transparency of quality of care. The survey is composed of 27 items, 18 of which encompass critical aspects of the hospital experience, including cleanliness and quietness of the hospital environment and overall rating of the hospital.

HCAHPS is endorsed by the NQF and the federal Office of Management and Budget. Those hospitals subject to the inpatient prospective payment system (IPPS) provisions as of July 2007 must collect and submit HCAHPS data in order to receive their full IPPS annual payment update (APU) for fiscal year 2008. CMS is connecting data submission with payment and indicated that hospitals that fail to submit their HCAHPS data may receive an APU that is reduced by 2%.[43] While there are no data yet to report from this new trend, it seems reasonable to predict that those hospitals that have more comfortable, safe, and patient-centered physical environments will be rated higher by patients in the HCAHPS survey, and this could have significant influence on patient choice of hospitals, with a resulting impact on a hospital's market share and their financial bottom line.

A Challenge: Converting "Light Green" to "Dark Green" Dollars

To fully realize any of the financial benefits of the above analysis, it is also essential to make critical cultural and operational changes in tandem with the changes to the physical environment. For example, reducing intra-hospital transfers through variable-acuity rooms will not occur by the physical environment changes alone; a significant investment in culture and training must be made and the changes must be implemented. Reduction of transfers will have significant patient satisfaction benefits and reduce errors, but they will not produce efficiency savings that are seen in the bottom line, unless staffing levels are adjusted downwards and labor costs are reduced.

To fully document the business case, the impact of the costs avoided by reducing infections or patient falls must be estimated, captured, and reflected in the organization's financial statements. Similarly, the costs of reduced nursing turnover, which requires less recruiting and training expenditures, must be captured as well.

The movement of theoretical savings (light green dollars) to actual savings for the hospital as reflected in its financial statements (dark green dollars) is a key success factor to make the business case and to accomplish the organization's objectives. This is true of any quality improvement innovation whether or not connected to environmental changes, and it was first described by an interdisciplinary team at IHI.[44] Documenting actual cost savings is invaluable in convincing boards of trustees that evidence-based design investments are cost-effective.

Making It Happen: Ask Question 6

Traditionally, hospital leaders have asked five questions when considering a major building project:

1. *Urgency*: Is the expansion or replacement necessary to fulfill the hospital's mission? What is the cost strategically of not proceeding?
2. *Appropriateness*: Is the proposed plan the most reasonable and prudent in light of other alternatives?
3. *Cost*: Is the cost per square foot appropriate in light of other projects being built in the region?
4. *Financial impact*: Has the financial impact of additional volume, depreciation expense, and revenue assumptions been reasonably analyzed and projected?
5. *Sources of funds*: Is the anticipated combination of additional operating income, reserves, borrowing, and philanthropy reasonable and enough to support the project?

In addition to the compelling business case analysis described, hospital leaders must also address a sixth question:

6. *Evidence-based design*: Will the proposed project incorporate all the relevant and proven evidence-based design innovations in order to optimize patient safety, quality, and satisfaction as well as workforce safety, satisfaction, productivity, and energy efficiency?

As hospital leaders undertake building projects, it is imperative that the ongoing operating savings mentioned above are an integral part of the analysis.[45] Hospital boards must hold management accountable to new levels of environmental excellence and efficiency. Building a new hospital or undertaking a major renovation is likely to be the biggest financial decision that a board will ever make. It also provides a unique opportunity to transform the culture and processes of the overall organizational enterprise.[46]

From Ideas to Action: Creating Your Own Business Case

As stated earlier, hospitals typically conduct a comprehensive financial analysis before undertaking a major project, including asking the five basic questions. To address the sixth question effectively, financial impact assumptions of evidence-based design interventions should be developed with a commitment from the board and management to measure and oversee them. Chief financial officers must play a leadership role in this effort.

Effectively incorporating evidence-based design will require boards and management to carry out, at minimum, the following 10 steps:

1. *Create a multidisciplinary team*: Board, management, and medical staff leaders must work as a team to develop a common vision, including specific goals (volume and patient care quality improvements) that they wish to achieve in the new project.

2. *Choose the right architects*: Select architects with a proven understanding of and experience in evidence-based design. Look for actual examples of evidence-based design innovations that they have helped to incorporate in completed or planned projects. Ask for evidence of completion of the Evidence-Based Design Assessment and Certification (EDAC) program developed by the Center for Health Design.

3. *Identify evidence-based design interventions*: Architects, management, medical staff, and board leadership must collaborate to determine which cost-effective evidence-based design interventions will support the vision that they hope to achieve in the new project.

4. *Evaluate current practice and develop a baseline for each practice*: For example, determine the current rates of transfers, employee turnover, and patient falls (institutionally and at the patient unit level). Identify the baseline operating costs associated with these outcomes.

5. *Set measurable postoccupancy improvement targets*: For example, reduction in hospital-acquired infections from x to y; increase in patient satisfaction rates from a to b; decrease in workforce lift injuries from c to d; and reduction in patient transfers from e to f. These measurable improvement targets must be agreed upon by all key stakeholders and must be well communicated throughout the organization. To be successful, it is essential to build an organizational culture of support for these changes, including developing enthusiastic staff leaders who are strong advocates.[46]

6. *Incorporate design innovations into capital and operating budgets*: Management and medical leadership must incorporate the financial impact of these improvements into the hospital's annual capital and operating budgets, which are reviewed and approved by the board of trustees.

7. *Widely communicate improvement targets*: The performance improvement targets, including the methods used to collect data, should be included in all appropriate internal and external communications. This can provide public awareness and recognition that can differentiate the organization in the marketplace and increase market share.

8. *Track and report progress*: Upon opening of the new or renovated facility, the metrics of impact (including financial impact) at the overall institutional level and the unit level should be regularly reported to all key stakeholders, including the board of trustees.

9. *Continually incorporate new evidence-based design*: Regularly review internal experience and new developments in evidence-based design. Where appropriate, incorporate new evidence-based design interventions into the organization's facility maintenance activities, process, and culture. While tracking of impact should continue for at least 2 years postoccupancy, environmental design and process improvements that emerge should be systematically incorporated.

10. *Publish the results*: The organization should commit to sharing lessons learned and publishing their results (including financial impacts) with the rest of the health care and design communities. In so doing, they will contribute to needed knowledge about the financial impact of evidence-based design.

The effectiveness of any evidence-based design intervention does not occur in isolation from other important proven process improvements that must be implemented concurrently. Similar to the experience of IHI in the 100,000 Lives and 5 Million Lives Campaigns, effective change packages are a bundle of improvements that must be implemented together. The key point is that the environmental design innovations included here are essential ingredients to optimally improving safety and quality.

Priority Design Recommendations

The following design recommendations have been developed based on the strength of the evidence available and their impact on safety, quality, or cost. Some recommendations can be implemented in any facility at relatively low cost without significant modification (Table 5.1). Any facility could implement them at any time. Other strategies require greater financial investment and significant physical modifications and are best incorporated as part of a major renovation or a new construction project (Table 5.2). Health care leaders should seriously consider including these cost-effective design strategies as part of their quality improvement efforts.

Table 5.1   Design Interventions That Any Hospital Can Undertake

	Design Interventions	*Quality and Business Case Benefits*
1	Install hand-washing dispensers at each bedside and in all high-patient-volume areas.	Reduced infections.
2	Where structurally feasible, install high-efficiency particulate air filters in areas housing immunosuppressed patients.	Reduced airborne-caused infections.
3	Where feasible, install ceiling-mounted lifts.	Reduced staff back injuries.
4	Conduct a noise audit and implement a noise reduction plan.	Reduced patient and staff stress; reduced patient sleep deprivation; increased patient satisfaction.
5	Install high-performance sound-absorbing ceiling tiles.	Reduced patient and staff stress; reduced patient sleep deprivation; increased patient satisfaction.
6	Use music as a positive distraction during procedures.	Reduced patient stress; reduced patient pain and medication use.
7	Use artwork and virtual reality images to provide positive distractions.	Reduced patient and staff stress; reduced patient pain and medication use.
8	Improve wayfinding through enhanced signage.	Reduced staff time spent giving directions; reduced patient and family stress.

Table 5.2   Design Interventions as Part of Construction or Major Renovation

	Design Interventions	*Quality and Business Case Benefits*
1	Build single-family patient rooms.	Reduced infections; increased privacy; increased functional capacity; increased patient satisfaction.
2	Provide adequate space for families to stay overnight in patient room.	Increased patient and family satisfaction; reduced patient and family stress.
3	Build acuity-adaptable rooms.	Reduced intra-hospital transfers; reduced errors; increased patient satisfaction; reduced unproductive staff time.
4	Build larger patient bathrooms with double-door access.	Reduced patient falls; reduced staff back injuries.
5	Install high-efficiency particulate air filtration throughout patient care areas.	Reduced airborne-caused infections.
6	Install hand-washing dispensers at each bedside and in all high-patient-volume areas.	Reduced infections.
7	Install ceiling-mounted lifts in majority of patient rooms.	Reduced staff back injuries.
8	Meet established noise-level standards throughout the facility.	Reduced patient and staff stress; reduced patient sleep deprivation; increased patient satisfaction.
9	Use music as a positive distraction during procedures.	Reduced patient stress; reduced patient pain and medication use.
10	Provide access to natural light in patient and staff areas.	Reduced patient anxiety and depression; reduced length of stay.

Table 5.2   Design Interventions as Part of Construction or Major Renovation (*Continued*)

	Design Interventions	*Quality and Business Case Benefits*
11	Use artwork and virtual reality images to provide positive distractions.	Reduced patient and staff stress; reduced patient pain and medication use.
12	Build decentralized nursing stations.	Increased staff time spent on direct patient care.
13	Include effective wayfinding systems.	Reduced staff time spent giving directions; reduced patient and family stress.

Conclusion

The business case for implementing proven evidence-based design interventions was strong in 2004, when the first Fable Hospital analysis was undertaken. In 2008, the business case is even stronger. The costs of unnecessary patient harm are greater. Public and employer expectations and demands are much higher. The importance to customer satisfaction is greater. Emerging benefits of green strategies are highly promising, and the reimbursement implications, as a result of the emerging pay-for-performance methodologies, are profound. As part of their management and fiduciary responsibilities, boards and hospital leaders must include cost-effective, evidence-based design interventions in all their programs or suffer the economic consequences in an increasingly competitive and transparent environment. Done successfully, responsible use of evidence-based design will improve patient safety and quality, will enhance workforce recruitment and retention, and will produce a significant multiyear return on investment.

When planning to build a new hospital or renovate an existing facility, hospital leaders should address a key question (question 6): Will the proposed project incorporate all relevant and proven evidence-based design innovations in order to optimize patient safety, quality, and satisfaction as well as workforce safety, satisfaction, productivity, and energy efficiency? When conducting a business case analysis for a new project, hospital leaders should include ongoing operating savings and market share impacts of evidence-based design interventions as well as initial capital costs. To effectively implement a business case analysis, they should consider taking the 10 suggested steps to ensure that an optimal cost-effective hospital environment is achieved, and that the potential financial benefits are realized.

Case Study

The following case study demonstrates how an organization has successfully incorporated evidence-based design into their capital project. It describes how specific design innovations have a significant economic impact on completed projects.

Methodist Hospital, Clarian Health Partners, Inc., Indianapolis, Indiana

Clarian recognized that delayed transfers of patients between nursing units and lack of available beds are significant problems that increase costs and decrease quality of care and satisfaction among patients and staff. Patients are transferred as often as three to six times during their stay to receive care that matches their level of acuity. In a pioneering project, the team led by Ann Hendrich replaced a cardiac care intensive care unit and step-down unit with a combined unit of acuity-adaptable rooms. In the new 56-bed ICU (28 rooms on two floors) design, each single room was built with acuity-adaptable headwalls, which included the gases and equipment needed to provide care as patient acuity changed without necessitating moving the patient to another room.

Twelve outcome-based questions were formulated. Two years of baseline data were collected before the unit was moved and were compared with 3 years of data collected after the move.

The findings documented significant improvement after the move in many key areas: patient transfers decreased by 90%, medication errors by 70%, and there was a drastic reduction in the number of falls. Run charts are included in the published article.[47] The cost savings are significant, which makes a very strong business case for this approach.

Study and Discussion Questions

1. What evidence-based design innovations did the hospital in the case study utilize?
2. What were the problems that the hospital was trying to solve?
3. How was the impact of the design innovations measured?
4. Based on the results of this case study, what should hospitals do to create a safe environment for patients?

Notes

[a] The Leapfrog Group is a coalition of employers that have combined their health care purchasing power to reward hospitals that meet certain quality measures. More information is available at http://www.leapfroggroup.org/home.

[b] In 2003 the Centers for Medicare and Medicaid Services (CMS) and the Premier, Inc., hospital alliance partnered to create an innovative quality improvement initiative that provides financial incentives to top-performing hospitals based on self-reported quality improvement measures. More information is available at http://www.premierinc.com/quality-safety/tools-services/p4p/hqi/index.jsp.

[c] The Joint Commission creates standards for safety and quality of patient care through extensive dialog with experts in the field. More information is available at http://www.jointcommission.org/.

[d] In late 2006 the Institute for Healthcare Improvement (IHI) launched the national 5 Million Lives Campaign aimed at improving the quality of care and reducing injuries to patients by having hospitals commit to 12 changes: deploy rapid-response teams; deliver reliable, evidence-based care for acute myocardial infarction; prevent adverse drug events (ADEs); prevent central-line infections; prevent surgical site infections; prevent ventilator-associated pneumonia; prevent harm from high-alert medications; reduce surgical complications; prevent pressure ulcers; reduce methicillin-resistant *Staphylococcus aureus* (MRSA) infection; deliver reliable, evidence-based care for congestive heart failure; and get boards on board. For more information on these programs, see http://www.ihi.org.

[e] To obtain a copy of the DVD titled "Transforming Hospitals: Designing for Safety and Quality," call AHRQ's Publications Clearinghouse at 1-800-358-9295 or send an e-mail to AHRQPubs@ahrq.hhs.gov.

[f] An analysis of NDNQI data from fourth quarter 2002 found the mean number of falls per 1000 patient days to be 3.73, and the mean number of injury falls per patient day was 0.99 (Dunton, N., B. Gajewski, R. L. Taunton, and J. Moore. 2004. Nurse staffing and patient falls on acute care hospital units. *Nursing Outlook* 52(1):53–59). Assume a baseline injury fall rate of 1/1000 patient days and a reduction of 80% for the new facility based on the experience of Clarian Health Partners.

[g] The composite quality scores for the hospitals performing in the top 50th percentile in each clinical focus area are available at http://www.premierinc.com/quality-safety/tools-services/p4p/hqi/results/index.jsp.

Suggested Readings and Web Sites

Readings

Hamilton, D. K., R. D. Orr, and W. E. Raboin. 2008. Organizational transformation: A model for joint optimization of culture change and evidence-based design. *Health Environments Research and Design Journal* 1(3).

Henriksen, K., S. Isaacson, B. L. Sadler, and C. M. Zimring. 2007. The role of the physical environment in crossing the quality chasm. *Joint Commission Journal on Quality and Patient Safety* 33:68–80.

Joseph, A. 2008. Transforming children's health through the physical environment. In *Evidence for innovation: Transforming care in children's hospitals through environmental design*, ed. S. C. Strang. Alexandria, VA: National Association of Children's Hospitals and Related Institutions.

Sadler, B. 2006. The business case for building better hospitals. *Trustee* 59(9):35–36.

Sadler, B. L., J. R. DuBose, and C. Zimring. 2008. The business case for building better hospitals through evidence-based design. *Health Environments Research and Design Journal* 1(3).

Ulrich, R. S., C. Zimring, X. Zhu, J. R. DuBose, H.-B. Seo, Y.-S. Choi, A. Joseph, and X. Quan. 2008. A review of the research literature on evidence-based healthcare design. *Health Environments Research and Design Journal* 1(3).

Zimring, C., G. L. Augenbroe, E. B. Malone, and B. L. Sadler. 2008. Implementing healthcare excellence: The vital role of the CEO in evidence-based design. *Health Environments Research and Design Journal* 1(3).

Web Sites

Center for Health Design: http://healthdesign.org/

HCAHPS: http://www.cms.hhs.gov/HospitalQualityInits/30_HospitalHCAHPS.asp#TopOfPage

IHI's 100,000 Lives Campaign and 5 Million Lives Campaign: http://www.ihi.org/IHI/Programs/Campaign/

Pay-for-Performance: http://www.cms.hhs.gov/hospitalqualityinits/35_hospitalpremier.asp

References

1. Institute of Medicine. 2000. *To err is human: Building a safer health system*, ed. L. T. Kohn, J. M. Corrigan, and M. S. Donaldson. Washington, DC: National Academy Press.

2. Institute of Medicine. 2001. *Crossing the quality chasm: A new health system for the 21st century*. Washington, DC: National Academy Press.

3. Reiling, J. 2008. *Safe by design: Designing Safety in Healthcare Facilities, Processes and Culture*. Oak Brook, IL: Joint Commission Resources.

4. Sadler, B. L. 2006. To the class of 2005: Will you be ready for the quality revolution? *Joint Commission Journal on Quality and Patient Safety* 32:51–55.

5. Institute for Healthcare Improvement. 2008. *Reaping the harvest: A review of the 5 Million Lives Campaign's first year ... and a preview of what's to come.* Cambridge, MA. http://www.ihi.org/NR/rdonlyres/A528208C-8B71-4559-BFF3-F1FBDC4CD11C/0/ReapingtheHarvestBrochureFINALwebedition.pdf.

6. Jones, H. 2008 industry forecast: Keeping pace in '08. http://www.construction-today.com/content/view/615/ (accessed April 23, 2008).

7. FMI. 2008. *FMI construction outlook—Fourth quarter.* 2007. Raleigh, NC: FMI.

8. Clancy, C. M. 2008. Designing for safety: Evidence-based design and hospitals. *American Journal of Medical Quality* 23:66–69.

9. Joseph, A. 2006. *The impact of light on outcomes in healthcare settings.* Concord, CA: Center for Health Design.

10. *The impact of design on infections in healthcare facilities.* 2006. Concord, CA: Center for Health Design.

11. *The role of the physical environment in promoting health, safety, and effectiveness in the healthcare workplace.* 2006. Concord, CA: Center for Health Design.

12. Joseph, A. and R. Ulrich. 2007. *Sound control for improved outcomes in healthcare settings.* Concord, CA: Center for Health Design.

13. Ulrich, R. S., C. Zimring, A. Joseph, X. Quan, and R. Choudhary. 2004. *The role of the physical environment in the hospital of the 21st century: A once-in-a-lifetime opportunity.* Concord, CA: Center for Health Design.

14. Henriksen, K., S. Isaacson, B. L. Sadler, and C. M. Zimring. 2007. The role of the physical environment in crossing the quality chasm. *Joint Commission Journal on Quality and Patient Safety* 33:68–80.

15. Berry, L. L., D. Parker, R. C. Coile Jr., D. K. Hamilton, D. D. O'Neill, and B. L. Sadler. 2004. The business case for better buildings. *Frontiers of Health Services Management* 21:3–24.

16. Ulrich, R. S., C. Zimring, X. Zhu, J. R. DuBose, H.-B. Seo, Y.-S. Choi, A. Joseph, and X. Quan. 2008. A review of the research literature on evidence-based healthcare design. *Health Environments Research and Design Journal* 1(3).

17. American Institute of Architects. 2006. *Guidelines for design and construction of health care facilities.* Washington, DC: Facility Guidelines Institute.

18. Chhokar, R., C. Engst, A. Miller, D. Robinson, R. B. Tate, and A. Yassi. 2005. The three-year economic benefits of a ceiling lift intervention aimed to reduce health-care worker injuries. *Applied Ergonomics* 36:223–29.

19. Joseph, A. and L. Fritz. 2006. Ceiling lifts reduce patient-handling injuries. *Healthcare Design.*

20. Morrissey, J. 2004. Debugging hospitals. Technology helps track hospital-acquired infections, along with the often unreimbursed costs of treating them. *Modern Healthcare* 34:30–32.

21. Murphy, D. and J. Whiting. 2007. *Dispelling the myths: The true cost of healthcare-associated infections.* Washington, DC: Association for Professionals in Infection Control and Epidemiology (APIC).

22. Pennsylvania Health Care Cost Containment Council (PHC4). 2006. *Hospital-acquired infections in Pennsylvania.*

23. Bischoff, W. E., T. M. Reynolds, C. N. Sessler, M. B. Edmond, and R. P. Wenzel. 2000. Handwashing compliance by health care workers: The impact of introducing an accessible, alcohol-based hand antiseptic. *Archives of Internal Medicine* 160:1017–21.

24. Trick, W. E., M. O. Vernon, S. F. Welbel, P. Demarais, M. K. Hayden, R. A. Weinstein, and Project Chicago Antimicrobial Resistance. 2007. Multicenter intervention program to increase adherence to hand hygiene recommendations and glove use and to reduce the incidence of antimicrobial resistance. *Infection Control and Hospital Epidemiology* 28:42–49.

25. Communication with A. Hendrich.

26. Hendrich, A., P. S. Bender, and A. Nyhuis. 2003. Validation of the Hendrichs II falls risk model: A large concurrent case/control study of hospitalized patients. *Applied Nursing Research* 16:9–21.

27. Communication with D. Edwards.

28. Ulrich, R. S. and X. Zhu. 2007. Medical complications of intra-hospital patient transports: Implications for architectural design and research, *Health Environments Research & Design* 1(1).

29. Sharkey, M. 2007. Aesthetic audio systems: Designed sound environments. *Health Executive*. pp. 120–21. http://www.healthexecutive.com/content/view/1502/ (accessed January 18, 2008).

30. Kemper, K. J. and S. C. Danhauer. 2005. Music as therapy. *Southern Medical Journal* 98:282–88.

31. Nilsson, U., N. Rawal, L. E. Unestahl, C. Zetterberg, and M. Unosson. 2001. Improved recovery after music and therapeutic suggestions during general anaesthesia: A double-blind randomised controlled trial. *Acta Anaesthesiologica Scandinavica* 45:812–17.

32. University of Sheffield and Queen Margaret University College–Edinburgh, PricewaterhouseCoopers LLP. 2004. *The role of hospital design in the recruitment, retention and performance of NHS nurses in England: Commission for Architecture and the Built Environment.*

33. Guenther, R. and G. Vittori. 2008. *Sustainable healthcare architecture*. New York: Wiley & Sons.

34. Kats, G., L. Alevantis, A. Berman, E. Mills, and J. Perlman. 2003. *The costs and financial benefits of green buildings: A report to California's sustainable building task force*. Sustainable Building Task Force.

35. Matthiessen, L. F. and P. Morris. 2007. *Cost of green revisited: Reexamining the feasibility and cost impact of sustainable design in the light of increased market adoption*, 1–25. Davis Langdon.

36. Beauchemin, K. M. and P. Hays. 1998. Dying in the dark: Sunshine, gender and outcomes in myocardial infarction. *Journal of the Royal Society of Medicine* 91:352–54.

37. Federman, E. J., C. E. Drebing, C. Boisvert, W. Penk, G. Binus, and R. Rosenheck. 2000. Relationship between climate and psychiatric inpatient length of stay in Veterans Health Administration hospitals. *American Journal of Psychiatry* 157:1669–73.

38. Booker, J. M. and C. Roseman. 1995. A seasonal pattern of hospital medication errors in Alaska. *Psychiatry Research* 57:251–57.

39. National Quality Forum. 2006. Serious reportable events in healthcare: 2005–2006 update. National Quality Forum. http://www.qualityforum.org/projects/completed/sre/ (accessed January 6, 2008).

40. Revision to hospital inpatient prospective payment systems—2007 FY occupational mix adjustment to wage index; implementation, 47870–8351. Final Rule 42, CFR 2006.

41. Gosfield, A. G. and J. L. Reinertsen. 2005. The 100,000 Lives Campaign: Crystallizing standards of care for hospitals. *Health Affairs* 24:1560–70.

42. Beaudoin, J. 2007. Massachusetts hospitals make "no charge" pledge for adverse events. *Healthcare Finance News*, November 20.

43. Centers for Medicare and Medicaid Services. Hospital care quality information from the consumer perspective. http://www.hcahpsonline.org/default.aspx (accessed January 10, 2008).

44. Nolan, T. and M. Bisognano. 2006. Finding the balance between quality and cost. *Healthcare Financial Management* 60:67–72.

45. Sadler, B. L., J. R. DuBose, and C. Zimring. 2008. The business case for building better hospitals through evidence-based design. *Health Environments Research and Design Journal* 1(3).

46. Hamilton, D. K., R. D. Orr, and W. E. Raboin. 2008. Organizational transformation: A model for joint optimization of culture change and evidence-based design. *Health Environments Research and Design Journal* 1(3).

47. Hendrich, A. L., J. Fay, and A. K. Sorrells. 2004. Effects of acuity-adaptable rooms on flow of patients and delivery of care. *American Journal of Critical Care* 13:35–45.

Chapter 6

Professional Affairs

William L. Thomas, Barbara R. Heller,
and Molly K. King

Contents

Executive Summary

Members of boards of directors of health care organizations are
intricately responsible for understanding and balancing governing
decisions potentially ranging from organizational sustainability

and long-term directional strategy to the quality of an individual patient's care or an overnight change in the financial markets.

Despite their backgrounds, providers on health care boards may feel overwhelmed by the domain of professional affairs since it includes diverse yet interrelated components, highly specific to various segments of the health care industry. Governance for professional affairs could potentially encompass immediate or long-range decision making related to medical staff, graduate medical education, research, information technology, and workforce strategy. Whenever possible, a provider board member should capitalize on available resources with the ultimate goal of sustaining a high-level of awareness across all components of professional affairs and, subsequently, contributing as a knowledgeable director for a highly complex organization operating in a highly complex environment.

Learning Objectives

1. To introduce and describe the various components of professional affairs, emphasizing the aspects most pertinent to governing members of a health care organization's board.
2. To outline the roles and responsibilities of the medical staff most integral to the governing body of the health care organization, including quality of care, regulatory compliance, and credentialing.
3. To describe the strategic importance of medical education, research, and health information technology as they each relate to and influence the decisions of health care board members.
4. To increase awareness of the influence of workforce supply considerations on all other governance decisions for provider members of health care boards.

Key Words

- Accreditation
- Designated institutional official
- Institutional review board
- Institutional statement of commitment
- Medical staff credentialing
- Privileging process
- Provider-specific competencies
- Workforce supply

Introduction

As a key stakeholder in quality assurance and improvement in health care organizations, the governing board has a critically important responsibility for oversight of professional affairs. For the health care provider aspiring to serve as a member of a health care board or a current board member, this challenge may be greater than anticipated. It can be troublesome for providers who are trained to focus on medical problems affecting individual patients, one at a time, and who direct their loyalties to the care of those patients, to step back and view a situation more broadly. A provider on a health care board will be expected to maintain a laser focus on specific elements of patient care while being able to broaden that focus into a wider context as a board member—all the while acquiring the knowledge needed to provide meaningful input into board decisions. Since the fiduciary responsibility as a member of the board is to the organization, not to a practice, specialty, or profession, that role is inherently difficult.

Huge iterative changes have occurred in health care delivery over the past 20 years, with dramatic increases in complexity and expectations for accountability; yet we cannot overestimate the pace of change—witness the slow but steady introduction of standardized clinical quality metrics during the same period of time. Most lay board members will have had limited exposure to the evolution of the U.S. health care delivery system and will rely on the expertise of their clinical colleagues to question, verify, and interpret trends and issues affecting professional affairs.

The purpose of this chapter is to delineate the roles, relationships, and processes related to oversight by governing boards of professional affairs in the context of health care organizations. Topics to be considered include medical education, safety of clinical research, quality assurance, adoption of health information technology, workforce supply, as well as medical staff structure and credentialing. Much of this chapter will be devoted to the issues of workforce supply within health care organizations, principally because it is a seemingly insoluble problem that will dramatically impact the quality, availability, and access to health care in this country for the foreseeable future. The other topics, though interconnected to workforce quality and safety issues, are more reducible to the key features that clinical professionals on health care boards need to know. Some of these are covered in more detail in other chapters, particularly Chapters 3 and 4, but some will be covered in this chapter as well.

Roles and Responsibilities of the Medical Staff

Physicians appointed to health care boards are often selected because of their expertise in a clinical specialty, or secondarily because of their medical staff leadership skills, not necessarily because of demonstrated management skills or even an extensive understanding of the health care field. Such an individual, nevertheless, will wield a powerful influence on the ability of other board members to understand a wide variety of issues that touch the clinical setting. Since it is unreasonable to expect clinicians to be experts in all matters, such as research, medical education, and professional workforce issues, the clinician appointed to any health care board will need to demonstrate a balance between expert knowledge and openness to learning. He or she will be expected to opine thoughtfully on the interplay among physicians, specialties, and locations of care, among other topics, and be able to articulate reasoned positions, not ones of advocacy for a profession or specialty—all in the service of quality and patient safety.

In Chapter 3, Barry Bader outlines the seven core board responsibilities, among which are quality, patient safety, and credentialing. The Joint Commission has, for many years, guided the board, management, and medical staff by developing and revising standards for each of these areas while serving as the principal accrediting body for most major health care organizations, including hospitals and health care systems.[1] Interestingly, the Joint Commission has historically conferred the primary duty for these through the hospital and its board to the medical staff, as a self-governing body, since the physician component of care has traditionally been seen as the key determinant of quality.

Twenty-five years ago, both the credentialing and associated privileging processes were far more simple, with privileges essentially rights, once granted, unless valid peer review of exceptional cases revealed a pattern of care that required intervention. This process was generally containable within the medical staff structure, which held itself responsible for the "oversight of the quality of care, treatment and services delivered by practitioners who are credentialed and privileged through the medical staff process."[1]

In recent years, health care boards have taken an increased role in driving organizational quality through both the medical staff and management, as discussed in Chapter 4. Health care organizations differ substantially in how these tensions play out. Some still largely defer to the medical staff structure and process, which naturally are more narrowly focused on what the medical staff can effectively oversee—the individual practice of medicine and the credentials of those professionals overseen by the medical staff. The board may engage in the broader aspects of quality, those that involve teams, complex services, and processes of care, not limiting their scope to the qualifications of certain providers.

A clinician member of a health care board, then, needs to inherently understand how the organization operates in this regard, and must help board and management mitigate their approaches to accommodate the new realities, while at the same time protecting the rights of individual practitioners.

Such an approach requires the professional on the board, especially if a physician, to understand the Joint Commission's standards covering the organized medical staff found in the MS-1 section of the *Comprehensive Accreditation Manual for Hospitals*. The provider must also understand the particular ways in which the organization has adapted and complied with standards, and must understand the nuances of the medical staff bylaws. Finally, lay board members will reasonably expect provider board members to grasp the operating styles of peer review committees and other standing and *ad hoc* committees of the medical staff.

The complex interaction of the board, management, and medical staff's respective and complementary roles in quality and patient safety have been more rapidly evolving over the past 10 years. For example, it was only between 1997 and 2002 that specific hospital quality standards with widely agreed upon definitions were developed and tested. A requirement for reporting the results on a specific set to the Joint Commission was established as recently as 2004. Mandatory public reporting of standardized quality data has emerged even more recently.[1] Thus, the board, management, and medical staff have fairly rapidly evolving relationships, with changing sets of accountabilities to each other and to their communities within this emerging era of transparency.

With all of this comes the relatively new expectations of the public, payers, and others for collective accountabilities and performance, little of which existed 10 years ago.[1] The provider member of a health care board has a role in advising, guiding, and responding to these new realities.

Finally, any provider on a health care board will need to help the board understand and interpret another new reality, the emergence of provider-specific measured competencies that are becoming mandated by the Joint Commission. The impact will be felt not just at the medical staff level of the credentialing and privileging process, but also at the board level. While this trend may parallel the national movement for institutional measurement on quality and safety, it lags by a decade[1] and promises to be more provocative, since it deals with individual, not just institutional performance.

Disciplinary Procedures and Adverse Actions

The roles of the board and those of the organized medical staff are well outlined in the Joint Commission's *Standards for Hospitals*, Section MS-1: 20 and within the organizational bylaws and medical staff bylaws. The biggest hurdle to overcome for the physician board member is the need to take on a new perspective. The role of a board member trumps the provider's role as a medical staff member (unless appointed *ex officio* as medical staff president) or as a professional colleague. It demands that he or she put the organization ahead of any individual.

This is a difficult, frequently awkward position with many attendant risks, including the loss of referrals and trust from some colleagues. Yet who better to interpret the complexities for a board than an informed, thoughtful, courageous colleague. A board physician needs to be familiar with the medical staff bylaws, rules, and regulations regarding corrective actions and the fair hearing and appeals process.[1]

To be sure, boards can get drawn into the controversial details of many adverse actions taken by the medical executive committee. The board's responsibility, however, is not to second-guess the clinical details on peer judgments, but to ensure the encoded processes are appropriately followed.

Medical Education

Health care institutions, especially major hospitals and health care systems, have both a huge dependence on the professional workforce supply, and a major role in the production of certain professionals, especially physicians. The provider board member will be expected to have a working knowledge of the educational process and its underpinnings in the role. This would be true even in an organization that may have a minor teaching affiliation or, conversely, is wholly dependent on others that produce the physician workforce.

The finance leadership of a health care organization may be most expert on the federal, state, and local funding streams in support of medical education. The institution's educational leadership may be most knowledgeable about the intricate details of medical student and resident training. It is only through a true working collaborative of both the finance and education leadership that optimal reimbursement and funding of graduate medical education (GME) can be realized. Yet it is certain that the board will be expected to understand and deliberate on the strategic value and performance of the programs of medical education.[2] The financing of GME relative to the mission and strategy is a complex topic, one minimally understood by most physicians while they were in training and which has evolved dramatically over the last 25 years and will continue to evolve with each approaching year.[3]

Years ago, residents and fellows trained in "apprentice model" programs that often had relatively informal structures, curricula, and evaluation processes in exchange for massive exposure and responsibilities for patient care. The structure and performance of these programs are now far more tightly regulated. They are more critically reviewed by the major accrediting body for graduate medical education, the Accreditation Council for Graduate Medical Education (ACGME), and by the respective 27 (Residency) Review Committees representing each specialty.

Any board physician will be asked about changes in medical education—for better or for worse. It probably should not suffice that they pass off the present (generation X) as inferior to the old ("See one, do one, teach one"). The story is far more complex. The issues of effective oversight, regulation, patient safety, ACGME competencies, duty hour restrictions, and human resource realities (the student–employee relationship) need to be balanced against the memories of wide-open opportunities in training with faculty who were perceived to have been more available to teach. Aside from standardized tests, the formal assessment of core competencies and the impact of the residents on quality are informal at best.

In a teaching hospital setting, a provider board member may be expected to understand differences between undergraduate medical education (UGME) and GME, as well the common threads that bind them.[4] Having formal medical student rotations and sponsoring residency programs influences the aims and vision of a health care organization. The oversight of these activities is within the purview of the medical staff structure, and for GME, under the oversight of the designated institutional official (DIO) and a GME Committee. Today's institutional requirements of the ACGME specifically address two governance-related oversight requirements. First, the governance body must be a signatory to an institutional statement of commitment, which details the institution's support—specifically addressing "the educational, financial and human resources support of the GME programs."[4] Second, the DIO is required annually to provide a written report to both the organized medical staff (OMS) and the governing bodies of the sponsoring institution and any major participating sites. This report is required to include information on resident supervision, resident responsibilities, evaluation, duty hour compliance, and resident participation in quality and safety of patient care activities.[4] Since dabbling in medical education is not a good option, the whole board must understand the benefits and obligations that attend this educational commitment, as well as support the allocation of resources required to be a participant in formal medical education programs. The positive impact of the presence of teaching programs on the culture of any health care setting is significant.

It would be reasonable to expect a physician board member of an organization either sponsoring or otherwise participating in GME to be familiar with some major details about institutional programs and performance. The ACGME has become increasingly specific about what are termed common program requirements (CPRs).[5] These specify the common requirements that all residency programs, regardless of specialty, are required to meet. Key among these are the specific resources an institution must provide the program directors, faculty, and house staff to be successful, and the most recent revisions transition from process-based orientation to an outcomes-based assessment.[6]

Table 6.1 Program Director Turnover, Accredited Programs, and Resident Position Data

	Program Director Turnover			Programs and Residents	
Year	Turnover Rate (%)	Total Program Directors	Number of Turnover	Total Accredited Programs	Resident Positions Filled
2007–2008	—	—	—	8485	109,325
2006–2007	13.35	8354	1115	8355	107,245
2005–2006	13.35	8186	1093	8186	104,472
2004–2005	13.85	8037	1113	8037	102,511
2003–2004	13.35	7968	1064	7968	100,390
2002–2003	14.34	7878	1130	7878	98,569
2001–2002	14.57	7838	1142	7838	96,976
2000–2001	—	—	—	7820	98,197

Source: All data obtained from the ACGME Web Accreditation Data System (WebADS), www.acgme.org/webads/public/ (accessed April 20, 2008).

Parenthetically, the annual turnover of residency program directors is quite high, averaging 13% to 14% nationally each year between 2001 and 2007,[7] reflecting the rigors of the job[8] and the relative lack of influence program directors wield to garner resources to be effective within their institutions. In the same time period, the number of programs and residents enrolled in accredited positions rose by 8% and 13%, respectively (Table 6.1).

The ranks of program directors are filled with excellent, often junior, teacher-clinicians, who in many cases have little or no management or leadership training in their organizations. Knowledgeable provider board members can balance discussions about institutional commitment, program resources, and program performance by helping interpret the deliberations and decisions made at the GME Committee level.

Specific issues within programs, such as resident and faculty evaluations, resident promotion and disciplinary actions, curriculum development, and scholarly activities, certainly reside within the GME operations and the GME Committee, but some regulations and their metrics, like adherence to duty hour rules and educational performance outcomes, should attract the attention of the board. The evidence is substantial regarding the impact of excessive hours of duty on the safety of patients and trainees alike. Yet violations continue to occur at this intersection between training and safety.

Safety in Clinical Research

Research involving human subjects takes place in myriad health care settings, not just in major teaching hospitals or mission-driven research institutions. The demand for rapid turnaround in clinical trials for drugs and devices has driven opportunities for research involvement, even in institutions and health care organizations that have not previously participated.[9] It is incumbent on the institution to understand research risks and obligations, but many health care boards may be relatively inexperienced in this area. It would be natural for lay board members to conclude that physicians would have substantial experience or expertise in the subject, which may be a misplaced assumption.

While a detailed description of human subject research is beyond the scope of this chapter, there are some fundamental concepts that bear mention, and some resources that are excellent references,[10] especially concerning the institutional review board (IRB).

Over the past several decades, it has become clear that increased regulation in support of human subject safety has required health care organizations to invest proportionately more in their research infrastructures to create a critical mass of human and other resources supporting research. In a sense, this trend is similar to that in GME, where requirements for infrastructure and support have increased significantly over the years.

While health care organizations' legal and compliance departments would be expected to be knowledgeable in many aspects of research, the board provider would be expected to have a broad command of the medical research field, specific biomedical knowledge, and perhaps even experience in conducting and organizing research. Some might have served on scientific review or advisory boards, and some might be able to help in identifying external sources of research support.

At a minimum, however, the provider board member should be or become knowledgeable in a few key areas. First, and perhaps most importantly, the provider should understand the broad outline of the evolution of protection of the human subjects in research, past abuses of rights and the welfare of individual research subjects, and how and why the U.S. government agencies have come to provide oversight and regulate research activities.

In order to meaningfully participate or lead a discussion in this area, the provider board member should understand the Belmont Report[11] and its role in providing the basic framework for conducting research involving human subjects;

and the principles of respect for persons, beneficence, and justice, and how they are incorporated in the federal government regulations for the protection of research subjects, including informed consent, review for risk-benefit, and the equitable selection of subjects and protection of vulnerable populations.

All of the following would constitute background for understanding the organization and operation of the human subjects protection program within the organization: institutional review board (IRB) staffing and memberships and clinical research staff, as well as patient and subject advocacy programs, among others.

For large health care organizations with major research programs, knowledge and oversight capability may be more readily focused on the board. For smaller health care organizations with more limited research staff, it is expected that a physician or other health care provider on the board be reasonably knowledgeable about the program and the issues surrounding human subject protection.

Health Information Technology

It is clear that hospitals and physicians seeking to improve health care quality and safety will need to utilize health information technology, also known as HIT. This will require a significant investment of dollars and people. It should also be understood that for HIT to demonstrate significant value, it will require skilled implementation, significant training, workflow redesign, buy-in from physicians and staff, and a continued focus on the quality objectives of the mission. HIT in any of its forms is at best an enabling infrastructure; HIT per se is quality neutral.

With that in mind, hospital boards should consider opportunities for investment in HIT as part of an overall mission for quality and safety improvement or for participation in pay-for-performance or other quality reporting opportunities. Boards need to include in technology investment decisions an analysis of organizational and medical staff readiness for change. Provider board members should also be especially sensitive to media hype, since HIT is often portrayed as a solution unto itself, with barriers to successful implementation unfairly blamed on physician recalcitrance.

Health care providers who are hospital board members should be generally familiar with several aspects of HIT—its emerging value to patients, physicians, and the health care system, as well as some of the controversies surrounding adoption and optimal usage of HIT. There is no need, however, to develop a deep technical expertise, since the greatest value that a provider board member can add is guidance surrounding HIT purchase and usage decisions.

Health information technology has dramatically risen in visibility and importance in recent years, as it has increasingly been seen as a vehicle for improving quality, safety, and efficacy, all the while decreasing costs. Hospitals and health systems that do not have HIT in place are under strong pressure to adopt it as soon as possible—if for no other reason than to be and remain competitive. Hospitals and health systems that already have HIT in place are under significant pressure to continue to rapidly enhance the technology—since HIT is expected to serve as the vehicle for allowing the hospital or system to measure and demonstrate quality improvement—for internal as well as external purposes. In both cases there is a growing need to extend HIT programs from within the walls of the hospital and employed medical staff to affiliated staff and patients. Lastly, there is growing pressure for hospitals to share data across systems and geographic areas, using what has been termed health information exchange to make available and mobilize health information in a patient-centric approach. As health care organizations continue to adjust to changes in the external environment, including patient expectations and shifting demographics, the opportunities to enhance efficiencies through HIT will become increasingly significant considerations for boards of directors.

Adequate Workforce Supply

Perhaps the single most relevant issue affecting health care now and in the foreseeable future is the growing shortage of health care professionals. Public agencies at the federal, state, and local levels, private foundations, professional associations, and provider organizations have individually or collaboratively examined the present and future state of the health care workforce. Subsequently, the staggering projections for supply and demand across multiple health professional categories now confront health care management teams as readily accessible statistics, frequently cited strategic issues, and real organizational challenges.

In light of the timing of past or present experiences, a provider serving on the board of a health care organization may or may not have grappled with the frontline implications of workforce shortages; however, clinician board members do provide lay board members with direct perspectives on the patient care environment. Consequently, providers on health care boards serve as vital resources for connecting trends in workforce supply and related operational realities to organizational sustainability and key governance objectives, including quality of care and patient safety.

As board members with collective responsibility to ensure the comprehensive and long-term viability of the health care organization, all directors must remain generally informed of workforce supply levels across critical settings and job categories. Organizational trends in workforce supply must be monitored by the governing board in relation to projected demand for patient care services, evolving job descriptions, reasonable benchmarks, and quality of care measures. Through regular monitoring, the health care board may deduce issues from trends. Clinician board members may find themselves at an inherent advantage during such comparative discussions and, as such, may assume the responsibility of raising any pressing concerns to the board at-large.

Boards of directors of health care organizations have the responsibility of monitoring patient safety and the quality of care. For this reason, providers serving on the board must consider external trends as well as internal trends, across diverse professional categories, including all categories of medicine, nursing, and allied health, to identify areas of current and projected personnel shortages. The context for comparing internal and external workforce statistics minimally includes the evolution of roles and responsibilities for various health care professionals, the increasing prevalence of automation, and the expanding landscape for the delivery of care—each of which may be a differentiating characteristic for an organization. Yet, providers on the board maintain the responsibility to evaluate and communicate workforce statistics, with consideration of every situation or setting, but in ultimate relation to the quality of care, patient safety, and accessibility of an organization's health care services. Therefore, considering their distinct understanding of the patient care environment, providers must ensure understanding of the relationship between workforce supply and quality of care.

Various studies have examined the impact of levels of physician supply on the accessibility and quality of patient care. A 2007 report from the Association of American Medical Colleges notes at least 15 studies, since 2002, evaluating the adequacy of the current or future physician workforce. Findings across nearly all studies indicate looming specialty provider shortages, which will most likely have the greatest impact on the underserved and elderly populations.[12] A 2006 report from the Health Resources and Services Administration (HRSA) estimates the growth in demand for both primary and nonprimary patient care to outpace supply over the next 15 years.[13] For providers serving on health care boards, these statistics indicate a need to proactively monitor internal levels of physician supply, in the appropriate contexts, to ensure sufficient levels of accessibility and quality of patient care services.

Similarly, the Agency for Healthcare Research and Quality (AHRQ) has sponsored multiple studies of the association between nurse staffing and quality of care. According to a 2007 study of nurse staffing in acute care hospitals, AHRQ-sponsored investigators found positive associations between more registered nurse staffing and fewer adverse events, such as hospital-related mortality, failure to rescue, cardiac arrest, hospital-acquired pneumonia, and others.[14]

Similarly, a 2004 AHRQ study found that lower nurse-to-patient ratios were associated with higher rates of nonfatal adverse outcomes.[15] The same study also cites the increasing amounts of nursing time spent managing new medical technologies during a shorter average length of stay per patient. Therefore, today's nurses find themselves balancing the latest demands of evolving health care operations with the need to spend dedicated time with fewer patients to ensure high-quality care. These statistics, considered in isolation or combination, indicate multiple arguments for additional nurse staffing—ignoring these arguments may result in serious negative consequences for patients.

In addition to these considerations, the nursing workforce continues to decline with a projected U.S. shortage of 340,000 registered nurses by 2020.[16] The probabilities of adverse patient outcomes associated with low nurse staffing levels, coupled with the projected nursing shortage, have drawn large-scale attention from multiple organizations, including, but not limited to, the American Hospital Association, the Joint Commission, and the Institute of Medicine.[15] Similarly, and on the immediate scale, providers on health care boards, who may bear the responsibility of monitoring, interpreting, and discussing organizational trends in the context of quality of care, must dedicate sufficient time and effort to understanding the quality of care implications of the nursing shortage.

Finally, shortages across allied health fields, such as pharmacy and diagnostic imaging technology, also present quality of care implications for health care organizations. In a 2000 report to Congress, HRSA cited the broadening responsibilities of pharmacists to improve patient safety through the reduction of medication errors and the provision of patient education related to an increasing array of new medications—all in the face of a pharmacist shortage, including increasing vacancy rates and difficulties in hiring.[13] Shortages persist in diagnostic imaging technology as well, according to a 2002 survey released from the American Hospital Association. At the time of the hospital survey, vacancy rates for imaging technicians were the highest among any health profession,[9] potentially inhibiting reductions in unnecessary invasive surgical procedures and increases in the early detection of life-threatening diseases, possible through diagnostic imaging.[17] Providers serving on health care boards retain responsibility for monitoring trends in the internal allied health workforce that might threaten the sustainability of provider functions that play a vital role in quality and safety initiatives.

The issue of workforce supply will persist across organizations as demographics shift and provider roles change. Throughout these transitions and all related organizational challenges, providers on health care boards must rise above day-to-day operational considerations to interpret trends in workforce supply, which may ultimately impact organizational sustainability and the quality of patient care services.

Conclusion

Given the enormous challenges facing the health care professional who is in active practice and who is nominated to serve on a board of directors, it is easy to understand why one would pause before accepting the appointment. Nevertheless, these challenges also present the opportunity to significantly impact the delivery of safe, effective care to a much larger population than one could serve acting alone. As a corporate body, the board is composed of people with differing backgrounds and varying skills. The danger for the individual board member is to give in to the temptation to try to manage the organization rather than to set the policies by which the organization will be managed. Thus, the insurance executive on the board wants to get directly involved in risk management, the real estate entrepreneur wants to get involved in real estate transactions, and so on. The challenge for health professionals is obvious—to bring their expertise to the board to help the board make intelligent policy decisions for the benefit of the patients and the continued viability of the organization, and to remember that those two objectives are inextricably intertwined.

Case Study

Dr. Joseph Powell was a fifth-year resident, looking forward to graduating and practicing surgery in the summer. He had struggled throughout his residency, having to retake his national examinations and scoring very low on his in-service examinations. His patient care and operative skills were marginal, and he had a proclivity to embellish facts to compensate for his shortcomings. In spite of his academic difficulties, Dr. Powell was affable and was well liked by his patients, and most of the faculty and his fellow residents. He was not a favorite among the nursing staff, however, because of his tendency to be hostile and autocratic in his professional interactions.

Three residency program directors had been concerned and had given Dr. Powell many warnings and remediation plans throughout his 5 years. Now, in his final year of training, it is clear that Dr. Powell should not practice independently. The residency program director has informed Dr. Powell that he will not be certified as having passed his residency training requirements.

Dr. Powell has, however, received an employment offer from Dr. Fritz Stoughton, vice chair of the hospital board of directors and the lead physician in a large general surgery practice that accounts for 20% of the hospital's operating room volume.

Questions for Consideration

- What residency program characteristics could have contributed to Dr. Powell's poor performance?
- What factors in this case caused 4½ years to pass before definitive action was taken?
- How might formal evaluation of house staff by senior nursing staff have helped avoid the current situation?
- You are a physician member of the hospital board, and Dr. Stoughton asks you to intervene to the residency program director on behalf of Dr. Powell. What is your response?

Study and Discussion Questions

1. Describe the role of the governing board in oversight of professional affairs.
2. Discuss external factors that may influence quality of patient care within an institution.
3. Describe internal processes that impact the quality of medical staff.
4. What is the responsibility of the governing board in relation to medical education?
5. Discuss the implications of workforce shortages on quality of care.
6. What is the responsibility of the governing board in relation to clinical research?
7. Discuss the impact of health information technology (HIT) on health care quality and safety.

Suggested Readings

Amdur, R. and E. Bantent. 2006. *IRB management and function*. 2nd ed. Gainesville, FL: University of Florida College of Medicine.

Coughlin, J. R., D. C. Daley, T. Ibrahim, and Alliance for Academic Internal Medicine Task Force on Financing Medical Education. 2000. Why Medicare supports graduate medical education. *American Journal of Medicine* 109:516–21.

Freburger, J. K. and R. E. Hurley. 1999. Academic health centers and the changing health care market. *Medical Care Research and Review* 56:277–306.

Rich, E. C., M. Liebow, M. Srinivasan, D. Parish, J. O. Wolliscroft, O. Fein, and R. Blaser. 2002. Medicare financing of GME. *Journal of General Internal Medicine* 17:283–92.

Whitman, N. 1997. *Essential hyperteaching: Supervising medical students and residents.* Salt Lake City, UT: University of Utah School of Medicine.

References

1. The Joint Commission Standards, MS 4.50. 2008. Oakbrook Terrace, IL: The Joint Commission.
2. Taskforce on Academic Health Centers. 1997. *Leveling the playing field: Financing the missions of academic health centers.* New York: The Commonwealth Fund.
3. U.S. Department of Health and Human Services. 2000. *COGME fifteenth report: Financing GME in a Changing health care environment.*
4. Institutional Requirements I.B.2–I.B.4.b. Chicago: Accreditation Council for Graduate Medical Education.
5. ACGME Common Program Requirements.
6. The Program Director's Guide to the Common Program Requirements.
7. ACGME WebADS (Web Accreditation Data System). http://www.acgme.org/ads-public/ (accessed April 20, 2008).
8. ACGME Common Program Requirements II.A.4.a–o. Chicago: ACGME.
9. Lader, E. W., C. P. Cannon, E. M. Ohman, L. K. Newby, D. P. Sulmasy, R. J. Barst, J. M. Fair, et al. 2004. The clinician as investigator: Participating in clinical trials in the practice setting. *Circulation* 109:2672–79.
10. Amdur, R. and E. Bantent. 2006. *IRB management and function.* 2nd ed. Gainesville, FL: University of Florida College of Medicine.
11. National Commission for the Protection of Human Subjects of Biomedical and Behavioral Research. 1979. *The Belmont report: Ethical principles and guidelines for the protection of human subjects of research.*
12. Association of American Medical Colleges. 2007. *Recent studies and reports on physician shortages in the U.S.*
13. U.S. Department of Health and Human Services, Health Resources and Service Administration, Bureau of Health Professions. 2000. *The pharmacist workforce: A study of the supply and demand for pharmacists.*
14. Kane, R. L., T. Shamliyan, C. Mueller, S. Duval, and T. J. Wilt. 2007. Nurse staffing and quality of patient care. *Evidence Report/Technology Assessment* 151:1–115.
15. Stanton, M. W. and M. K. Rutherford. 2004. *Hospital nurse staffing and quality of care.* Rockville, MD: Agency for Healthcare Research and Quality.
16. Auerbach, D. I., P. I. Buerhaus, and D. O. Staiger. 2007. Better late than never: Workforce supply implications of later entry into nursing. *Health Affairs* 26:178–85.
17. Subcommittee on Health of the House Committee on Ways and Means. Statement of Cherrill Farnsworth, Chairperson, National Coalition for Diagnostic Imaging Services. March 17, 2005.

Chapter 7

The Bottom Line

Caryl E. Carpenter and John K. Dugan

Contents

Executive Summary

The governing board of a health care organization (HCO) is responsible for oversight of the organization's finances. To exercise this responsibility, trustees must understand and monitor the HCO's financial performance. Oversight begins with an understanding of how the three primary financial statements—the statement of operations, the balance sheet, and the statement of cash flows—are constructed and what they tell about the organization's finances. Trustees also need to learn how the HCO is reimbursed for services provided. Reimbursement, in many ways, drives the organization. Utilization data such as occupancy rate, number of admissions, and average length of stay are important complements to the financial reports provided by management. Trustees should expect management to arrange for board education about financial reporting in general and health care finances in particular.

Trustees should meet with the senior management team of the HCO to determine the types of financial and operational performance reports the board and its committees need in order to make informed decisions. Agreed-upon performance indicators should be reported to the board regularly. Some of these performance indicators will be financial ratios that are used to analyze the HCO's financial statements.

Financial performance determines the organization's ability to attract long-term capital to finance its growth. Nonprofit hospitals and nursing homes typically finance some of their assets with long-term, tax-exempt bonds. Rating agencies that evaluate the creditworthiness of an HCO that proposes to issue tax-exempt debt expect that the governing board understands the organization's finances and are able to exercise their fiduciary responsibility to provide oversight of those finances.

Learning Objectives

1. To learn the role of the governing board in the oversight of an HCO's finances.
2. To understand the meaning of the accounts reported on the three primary financial statements for an HCO—the statement of operations, the balance sheet, and the statement of cash flows—and the different ways the HCO is reimbursed for services provided.
3. To understand the difference between charity care and bad debt and the use of tax-exempt bonds for long-term financing in an HCO.
4. To learn the meaning of 11 financial ratios typically used to evaluate financial performance in an HCO.

Key Words

- Accrual accounting
- Assets
- Average collection period
- Average payment period
- Bad debt
- Balance sheet
- Bond ratings
- Charity care
- Current ratio
- Days cash on hand
- Debt ratio
- Debt service coverage
- Depreciation
- Expenses
- Generally accepted accounting principles
- Growth rate in equity
- Income
- Liabilities
- Net assets
- Operating margin
- Restricted net assets
- Return on equity
- Revenues
- Statement of cash flows
- Statement of operations
- Tax-exempt bond
- Total asset turnover
- Total margin
- Unrestricted net assets

Introduction

Understanding and monitoring the financial performance of an HCO is one of the most important fiduciary responsibilities of a governing board. Board members must be able to understand and interpret the financial statements and other financial reports prepared by management, and what drives the finances of a provider organization. It has been argued that the answer to every question in health care is *reimbursement.* If a particular policy or practice in a hospital, for example, seems to be a bit mysterious, the explanation is often reimbursement related. The way a provider is paid determines many of its operating practices. Reimbursement for services delivered is one of the unique aspects of financial management in a health care organization. A new trustee should expect the HCO to provide some board education about the basics of health care reimbursement.

This chapter will present and explain the types of financial information a trustee should expect to receive from management and discuss how to interpret financial performance based on that information. Throughout this section, we refer to a sample set of financial statements for Memorial Hospital that appear at the end of the chapter. These statements are included as an example of the kinds of financial information typically shared with board members to help them make decisions. (Please note that all numbers on these statements are in thousands.)

Financial Statements of Nonprofit Organizations

The financial statements of a nonprofit HCO are very similar to those in the for-profit world. The purpose of financial statements is the same in both settings; however, there are some differences in the accounting language, which will be explained. The most important statements are the balance sheet, the statement of operations, and the statement of cash flows.

Financial statements are prepared using a set of guidelines called *generally accepted accounting principles* (GAAP). The American Institute of Certified Public Accountants (AICPA) publishes accounting guides for different industries; the guide specific to the health care industry is *Health Care Organizations—AICPA Audit and Accounting Guide.*[1]

Financial statements are prepared using *accrual basis accounting.* This is an important concept for trustees to understand. Put simply, the revenues and expenses reported on a financial statement are not the same as cash received or cash paid. Revenues are recognized and recorded when they are earned, that is, when the service is provided, not when the cash payment is received. In most cases, HCOs are not paid at the time of service. Expenses are also recognized and recorded when they are incurred, rather than when they are paid. For example, employee salaries are recorded as an accrued expense when the work is done, not when they are actually paid.

Balance Sheet

The balance sheet is also called a statement of financial position. It is a snapshot of the organization's financial condition at a specific point in time. There are three major components of a balance sheet: (1) *assets* or what the HCO owns; (2) *liabilities* or what the HCO owes; and (3) *net assets* or the HCO's net worth, the difference between assets and liabilities. For the statement to be in balance, assets must equal liabilities plus net assets. In the sample statements, Memorial Hospital had total assets of $115,600 on December 31, 2007, and total liabilities of $40,000 (Table 7.1).

The assets on the balance sheet are divided between current and long term. *Current assets* include cash and other assets that can be expected to be converted into cash within a year. The most important current assets for an HCO are *cash* and *accounts receivable*. Receivables represent money owed to the HCO. The largest category of receivables is net patient accounts receivable, the payments owed to the HCO by third-party payers and individual patients. Any time a patient, who is not eligible for charity care, receives services and does not pay at the time of service, a receivable is recorded. The receivables on the balance sheet are recorded *net* of any third-party payer contractual allowances, discounts, or charity care.

Many hospitals incur a significant amount of uncompensated care, which can be divided into two categories: charity care and bad debt. *Charity care* represents services provided for which payment was never expected. In most cases, patient qualification for charity care is determined before services are provided. Nonprofit hospitals are required, as part of their tax-exempt status, to provide emergency room treatment for all patients without regard for ability to pay. Hospitals have established policies for determining eligibility for charity care, usually based upon multiples of the federal poverty level. However, there are no national criteria for determining charity care eligibility, so policies vary considerably across hospitals. Nonprofit HCOs are expected to post their policies so that patients are aware of the option to apply for charity care. Charity care appears in the notes to the audited financial statements.

In contrast to charity care, the hospital incurs *bad debt* when a patient who is not deemed indigent and is able to pay for services is billed for them but does not pay. Usually HCOs go through an established process that may result in a collection effort using internal or external agencies before an account is written off as bad debt. Bad debt appears on the statement of operations.

Long-term assets have a life greater than a year. The most significant long-term assets are *plant, property, and equipment*, also called fixed assets. These include land, buildings, and equipment with a long-term useful life. These long-term assets are recorded at their cost when acquired. The HCO records an expense on the statement of operations that represents the use of these long-term assets over time; it is called *depreciation expense*. The accumulation of depreciation expense over time is shown on the balance sheet as *accumulated depreciation* and is subtracted from the historical costs of these assets. The account on the Memorial Hospital balance sheet is called *property and equipment, net*, and for 2007, the

Table 7.1   Sample Hospital Balance Sheet

Memorial Hospital Balance Sheets *December 31, 2007 and 2006* *(in thousands)*		
	2007	*2006*
Assets		
Current assets:		
Cash and cash equivalents	$4800	$5800
Short-term investments	15,900	10,700
Assets limited as to use	900	1300
Patient accounts receivable (net of allowance)	15,100	14,200
Other current assets	2700	2900
Total current assets	$39,400	$34,900
Long-term investments	4700	4700
Property and equipment, net	51,000	50,500
Other assets	20,500	19,700
Total Assets	$115,600	$109,800
Liabilities and Net Assets		
Current liabilities:		
Current portion of long-term debt	$3000	$1800
Accounts payable and accrued expenses	5900	5400
Estimated third-party payor settlements	2200	1900
Other current liabilities	1900	2100
Total current liabilities	$11,500	$11,200
Long-term debt, net of current portion	23,100	24,000
Other long-term liabilities	3900	3200
Total liabilities	$40,000	$38,400

Table 7.1   Sample Hospital Balance Sheet (*Continued*)

	2007	2006
Memorial Hospital Balance Sheets *December 31, 2007 and 2006* *(in thousands)*		
Net assets:		
Unrestricted	69,900	65,400
Temporarily restricted	2100	2500
Permanently restricted	3600	3500
Total net assets	$75,600	$71,400
Total liabilities and net assets	**$115,600**	**$109,800**

amount was $51,000. Other long-term assets include investments that are held for more than a year.

Liabilities are also divided into current and long term. *Current liabilities* are debts or obligations of the HCO that must be paid within a year. The largest of these liabilities in a typical HCO is *accounts payable*, money owed to suppliers and other vendors, and *accrued expenses*, expenses incurred but not yet paid. Accrued salaries would be an example of accrued expenses. Memorial Hospital had $5900 in accounts payable and accrued expenses in 2007. The sample statement also has a current liability account called current portion of long-term debt, which is the value of any principal payments due in the current year.

Long-term liabilities are those that are due in more than a year. The largest of these would be various forms of long-term debt—a mortgage, a bond, or other long-term loan. (Debt financing is discussed below.) A long-term debt is recorded as the amount of money borrowed, the principal. The account decreases as principal payments are paid over time, just like for a home mortgage. In 2007, Memorial Hospital had $23,100 in outstanding long-term debt plus $3900 in other long-term liabilities.

Net assets are the equity accounts for a nonprofit organization. In the for-profit world the equity accounts would be stock and the accumulated profits and losses over time, called retained earnings. On a nonprofit balance sheet, the HCO's equity is called net assets, the assets of the corporation net of its liabilities.

The Memorial Hospital balance sheet has three categories of net assets. *Unrestricted net assets* are the nonprofit equivalent of retained earnings. They are the accumulation of profits and losses over time. In some instances, unrestricted net assets may include charitable contributions that have not been restricted by the donor. It is important to understand that unrestricted net assets are not the equivalent of cash, because of the use of accrual accounting. In most cases, the actual cash holdings of an HCO will be less than its unrestricted net assets ($4800 in cash and $69,900 in unrestricted net assets for 2007 for Memorial Hospital).

Temporarily restricted assets are usually charitable contributions or grants that are held for a specific purpose but will eventually be spent. *Permanently restricted assets* represent the investments held as an endowment for the HCO. Only the earnings on those investments may be used.

Statement of Operations

The statement of operations is also called an income statement, or a profit and loss statement. Unlike the balance sheet, which represents financial position at a point in time, the statement of operations is a summary of financial activity over a period of time—a month, a quarter, a year. The statement of operations for Memorial Hospital is for a fiscal year. Put simply, the statement reports the revenues, expenses, and profits of the HCO.

Revenues include those earned from providing patient care or from other HCO activities. In the sample hospital, the primary source of revenue is patient care, reported as *net patient revenue*. This number reflects the revenues the HCO has collected as cash or can reasonably expect to collect from third parties and individual patients. A hospital, for example, has a long, itemized list of charges for every service provided, which is summarized on an itemized bill submitted to third-party payers or directly to patients. The revenue reported is net of contractual allowances (deductions from charges that some insurance companies make), discounts offered to some patients, and allowances for charity care.

It is important for trustees to understand that hospitals and other HCOs are rarely paid their charges. Insurance companies today typically set reimbursement rates independent of the hospital's charges, often prospectively on a per-day, per-admission, or per-outpatient-encounter basis, or on a fee schedule rate negotiated directly with each provider. For this reason, the *net patient revenue* number is more important to assess than total charges. Net patient revenue reflects the amount of money the hospital is likely to collect.

Other revenues may appear on an HCO's statement of operations. These may be revenues from nonpatient care activities such as a gift shop, cafeteria, parking garage, or rental property, or income earned on the HCO's investments. Memorial Hospital reported $6500 in investment income in 2007 (Table 7.2).

Revenues represent funds paid to the HCO; expenses represent funds paid out by the HCO. *Operating expenses* include salaries, fringe benefits, supplies, and insurance. *Depreciation expense* represents use of the HCO's fixed assets over the time period of the statement. *Interest expense* is the amount of interest paid in the statement's time period. The *allowance for bad debt* represents the HCO's recognition of charges net of discounts it does not expect to collect. Expenses are subtracted from revenue to get excess of revenues (plus gains and other support) over expenses. This is the HCO's profit or loss. The bottom line of the statement of operations would be called *net income* on a for-profit statement. On nonprofit statements, it is called the *increase (decrease) in unrestricted net assets.* Increases or decreases in unrestricted net assets result in increases or decreases in the unrestricted net assets account on the balance sheet (Table 7.1).

Table 7.2   Sample Hospital Income Statement

Memorial Hospital Income Statement Years Ended December 31, 2007 and 2006 (in thousands)		
	2007	*2006*
Unrestricted revenues, gains, and other support:		
Net patient service revenue	$96,300	$89,900
Investment income	6500	8300
Total revenues, gains, and other support	**$102,800**	**$98,200**
Expenses:		
Salaries and benefits	53,900	50,000
Medical supplies and drugs	26,500	22,100
Insurance	8000	8500
Depreciation and amortization	4700	4300
Interest	1700	1800
Allowance for bad debts	1000	1300
Other	2500	1300
Total expenses	**$98,300**	**$89,300**
Excess of revenues, gains, and other support over expenses	$4500	$8900
Increase in unrestricted net assets	$4500	$8900

Statement of Cash Flows

The statement of operations and balance sheet are constructed using accrual accounting. In accrual accounting, revenues are not the same thing as cash collected, and expenses are not the same thing as cash paid out. Therefore, the statement of operations and balance sheet do not provide a clear picture of the actual flow of funds into and out of the HCO. The *statement of cash flows* is designed to provide this important information (Table 7.3).

The first section of the statement lists *cash flows from operating activities*, the sources and uses of cash that can be tied directly to operations (patient care). Changes in net assets (or net income) are listed first since it is the primary source of cash. However, since the change in net assets is derived from accrual numbers, the value must be adjusted to reflect actual cash flow. Depreciation (a noncash expense) is added back first. Increases in current assets are subtracted, or decreases in current assets are added. For example, a decrease in accounts receivable means cash has been collected and that amount must be added to net income. Conversely, an increase in inventory means cash was used to purchase supplies and that amount must be subtracted from net income. Next, increases in current liabilities are added and decreases in current liabilities are subtracted. The net effect of these adjustments is called *net cash from operations*.

The next section of the statement lists *cash flows from investment activities*. Here, any expenditures for long-term assets are subtracted. The final section lists *cash flows from financing activities*. Increases in investments such as marketable securities or long-term investments are subtracted (because cash was spent to purchase them); decreases in these accounts are added (because cash was collected when they were sold). Increases in debt, either short-term or long-term, are added; decreases in debt are subtracted.

The bottom line of the statement represents the net effect of the various increases and decreases in cash listed above. The net increase (or decrease) in cash for the year reconciles the difference in the cash balance from one period to the next.

A financially healthy HCO should be increasing cash by providing services (operations) and earning returns on its investments. An HCO that must sell off its fixed assets to generate cash is not in good financial health.

Monitoring Financial Performance

Board members, as part of their oversight responsibility, should meet with members of the senior leadership team (i.e., the chief executive officer and chief financial officer) to determine the types of financial and operational performance

Table 7.3 Sample Hospital Statement of Cash Flows

Memorial Hospital *Statement of Cash Flows* *Year Ended December 31, 2007*	
Cash flows from operating activities:	
Change in net assets	$4200
Depreciation	4700
Allowance for bad debt	1000
Increase in net patient accounts receivable	(1900)
Decrease in other current assets	(600)
Increase in accounts payable and other accrued expenses	500
Increase in other current liabilities	800
Net cash from operations	$8700
Cash flows from investment activities:	
Capital expenditures	(3971)
Increase in other long-term assets	(3769)
Net cash from investment	(7740)
Cash flows from financing activities:	
Increase in short-term investments	(150)
Change in long-term investments	0
Decrease in long-term debt	(2100)
Increase in other long-term liabilities	290
Net cash from financing	(1960)
Net increase (decrease) in cash	($1000)
Cash, beginning of the year	$5800
Cash, end of the year	$4800

information the board and various committees need to make informed decisions. The board also should determine the types of management reports (e.g., statement of operations, balance sheet, key performance indicators) and the timeframe for report generation (i.e., monthly, quarterly, annually) needed to perform ongoing evaluation. It is not uncommon for larger health care providers to have the board meet on a quarterly basis to review operational and financial results, and also distribute monthly financial reports as a courtesy.

Financial Reports

Typically, HCOs produce monthly internal financial statements and management reports. These financial statements and supplementary management reports summarize the performance of the organization for the month completed and year to date. Often the reports provide comparisons of actual results to the budget and to the results from the previous year. Monthly internal financial statements may be more detailed than what is required under external reporting requirements.

The board should expect management to produce a balance sheet and statement of operations at least on a quarterly basis for evaluation. The board should assess whether management has appropriately accrued expenses in accordance with generally accepted accounting principles, and that management believes that information being reported to the board represents their best estimates at the time of reporting.

In addition to presenting the balance sheet and statement of operations on a quarterly basis, health care organizations are required to annually produce a statement of cash flows, which the board may also periodically request. This statement is useful when evaluating net revenue within the statement of operations.

Utilization Data

The board should meet with the senior leadership team to determine the key performance indicators that will be reported to the board on a regular basis. Examples of utilization and statistical information that management evaluates may be different, depending on the type of HCO (e.g., hospital, home health agency, skilled nursing facility). It is important for the board to understand what the relevant performance indicators are associated with each type of HCO. Some examples of financial and utilization statistics typically reported by hospitals are:

■ Inpatient (IP) discharges
■ IP patient days
■ Case mix index
■ IP charges

- IP contractual allowances
- Outpatient (OP) visits
- Emergency department visits
- OP charges
- OP contractual allowances
- Nursing hours
- Benefits expense
- Supply expense
- Gross revenue per discharge (charges/IP discharges)
- Gross revenue per patient day (IP charges/IP days)
- Net revenue per discharge (IP charges – contractuals)/discharges
- Net revenue per day (IP charges – contractuals)/days
- Nursing hours per day (nursing hours/patient days)
- Benefit cost per full-time equivalent (FTE) (benefits expense/FTEs)

These statistics can be further evaluated by service line (e.g., cardiac, orthopedic, or oncology) or payer mix (e.g., Medicare, Medicaid, or Blue Cross).

The board is responsible for providing oversight of financial performance as part of its fiduciary responsibility. One of the most effective ways a board can carry out its responsibilities is to have management provide the board with ongoing education concerning factors that impact the HCO's performance. These factors could include federal and state regulations, trends in uncompensated care, changes in reimbursement policies, market competition, and medical staff composition.

Financial Ratio Analysis

A common method for evaluating financial performance is *financial ratio analysis*.[2] Financial ratios utilize information from financial statements to compare performance over time, to compare one HCO to another, or to compare one HCO to industry averages. There are no universal definitions for most financial ratios, which can make comparisons across organizations difficult. It is important for board members to know how various ratios are calculated and to confirm that the same definitions are being used when comparing one HCO to others.

Financial ratios fall into four broad categories: profitability, liquidity, capital, and activity. Examples of each category of financial ratios are presented here.

Profitability Ratios

The profitability of an HCO is a function of many managerial policies and decisions. Profitability ratios help the board and management evaluate the impact of policies and decisions on overall financial performance. Higher values of these ratios are better than lower. The following are a few examples of the profitability ratios typically utilized by hospitals and many other HCOs.

Total margin:

$$\frac{\text{Excess Revenues over Expenses}}{\text{Total Revenue}} \times 100$$

This ratio compares the bottom line of the statement of operations (excess of revenues over expenses) to total revenues. Excess of revenues over expenses is the measure of profits; total revenues are from all sources, not just patient care. The 2007 total margin for Memorial Hospital was:

$$(\$4,500/\$102,800) \times 100 = 4.4\%$$

For every $1 of revenue, the hospital earned 4.4 cents of profit. The industry average in 2005 was 5.0%, so Memorial Hospital was slightly less profitable than the average acute care hospital in the United States.

Operating margin:

$$\frac{(\text{Net Patient Revenue} - \text{Total Expenses})}{\text{Net Patient Revenue}} \times 100$$

This ratio measures profitability on the HCO's primary line of business, patient care. Investment income is not included in the calculation. Net patient revenue less total expenses is the measure of operating profits; net patient revenue is the revenue from patient care. The 2007 operating margin for Memorial Hospital was:

$$(\$96,300 - \$98,300)/\$96,300 \times 100 = -2.1\%$$

For every $1 of net patient revenue, the hospital lost 2.1 cents. Memorial Hospital did not make a profit on patient care in 2007. Its overall profitability was positive because of the income from investments. This is not a good sign of financial health. An HCO should be able to earn a positive bottom line from its fundamental purpose, patient care. In 2005, the average operating margin for an acute care hospital was 1.2%.

Return on equity:

$$\frac{(\text{Excess Revenue over Expenses})}{\text{Net Assets}} \times 100$$

The return on equity ratio compares profits or losses (excess of revenue over expenses) to the HCO's equity base (net assets). The 2007 return on equity for Memorial Hospital was:

$$(\$4,500/\$75,600) \times 100 = 6.0\%$$

For every $1 of net assets, Memorial Hospital earned 6 cents. The industry average in 2005 was 8.0%, considerably more than the value for Memorial.

Growth rate in equity (net assets):

$$\frac{(\text{Net Assets Yr 2} - \text{Net Assets Yr 1})}{\text{Net Assets Yr 1}} \times 100$$

Growth rate in equity is the primary test of an HCO's ability to survive and grow over a long period of time. A hospital that expects to add new assets at a rate of 8% per year, for example, must generate new equity capital at a rate equal to or greater than 8%. New equity for a nonprofit would include profits (increase in net assets), contributions, and grants. If a hospital fails to grow its equity base, it will need to either increase its debt financing or reduce its asset growth rate. The 2007 growth in equity ratio for Memorial Hospital was:

$$(\$75,600 - 71,400)/\$71,400 \times 100 = 5.9\%$$

For every $1 of net assets, the hospital increased total net assets by 5.9 cents. If Memorial Hospital had a target growth rate in assets of 8%, the increase in equity in 2007 would be insufficient to finance that growth.

Liquidity Ratios

Liquidity ratios measure short-term creditworthiness, that is, how easily the HCO can meet its short-term obligations (liabilities) with short-term assets. These ratios utilize the short-term or current accounts on the balance sheet, current assets, and current liabilities.

Current ratio:

$$\frac{\text{Current Assets}}{\text{Current Liabilities}}$$

The current ratio is the most widely used measure of liquidity in the health care industry. The ratio compares current assets to current liabilities. High values for the current ratio (i.e., between 2.0 and 2.5) indicate strength in ability to pay short-term obligations and a lower probability of insolvency in the short-term. Many lenders expect to see a value of at least 2.0 for this ratio. The 2007 current ratio for Memorial Hospital was:

$$\$39,400/\$13,000 = 3.0$$

For every $1 of current liabilities, Memorial Hospital has $3 worth of current assets to cover them. This is a good liquidity position for the hospital and better than the industry average in 2005 of 2.3.

Average collection period:

$$\frac{\text{Net Patient Accounts Receivable}}{(\text{Net Patient Revenue}/365)}$$

The average collection period ratio measures the average time it takes the HCO to collect its revenues. Decreasing values of this ratio are favorable. High values for this ratio imply longer collection periods, thus, a need for the HCO to finance its investment in accounts receivable. The typical value for this ratio will vary by type of HCO; that is, collection periods are longer in some industry segments than others. The 2007 average collection period for Memorial Hospital was:

$$\$15,100/(\$96,300/365) = 57.2 \text{ days}$$

On average, it took Memorial Hospital 57.2 days to collect the revenues earned when services were provided, which is much better than the 2005 industry average of 73.4 days.

Average payment period:

$$\frac{\text{Current Liabilities}}{[(\text{Total Expenses} - \text{Depreciation Expense})/365]}$$

The average payment period ratio may be thought of as the counterpart to the average collection period ratio. The average payment period measures the average time it takes the HCO to pay its expenses. The denominator in the ratio is an estimate of the hospital's average daily expenses minus depreciation (which is a noncash expense). Creditors regard high values for this ratio as an indication of potential liquidity problems. The 2007 value for the average payment period for Memorial Hospital was:

$$\$13,000/[(98,300 - 4,700)/365] = 50.7 \text{ days}$$

On average, it takes the hospital 50.7 days to pay its expenses from the time they are accrued. This means that cash flows out of the hospital at a faster rate than it comes in. This is a typical pattern for any business that extends credit, and is typical of HCOs that are reimbursed after they provide services. The difference between the collection period and the payment period creates a financing need for Memorial Hospital.

Days cash on hand:

$$\frac{(\text{Cash} + \text{Short-Term Investments})}{[(\text{Total Expenses} - \text{Depreciation Expense})/365]}$$

The days cash on hand ratio measures the number of days of cash expenses the hospital can cover with cash and short-term investments, their most liquid assets. High values for this ratio usually imply a greater ability to meet short-term obligations and are viewed favorably by creditors. The 2007 days cash on hand ratio for Memorial Hospital was:

$$(\$4,800 + \$15,900)/[(\$98,300 - 4,700)/365] = 80.7 \text{ days}$$

On average, the hospital had enough cash and short-term investments to cover 80.7 days of expenses. This is also much better than the 2005 average of 30.6 days; however, the average was unusually low that year.[2]

Capital Ratios

Capital ratios may also be called capital structure ratios or leverage ratios. There are two types of capital ratios—capitalization ratios and coverage ratios. Capitalization ratios measure the mix of debt and equity on a firm's balance sheet. Coverage ratios measure the firm's ability to make interest and principal payments on its outstanding debt.

Debt ratio:

$$\frac{\text{Total Debt or Liabilities}}{\text{Total Assets}} \times 100$$

The debt ratio measures the proportion of the firm's assets that are financed with debt, both long-term and short-term. The 2007 debt ratio for Memorial Hospital was:

$$(\$40,000/\$115,600) \times 100 = 34.6\%$$

The hospital financed 34.6% of its assets with debt—both short-term and long-term. That is a fairly low value for the debt ratio, which suggests the hospital may be able to borrow in the future. The industry average in 2005 was 42.3%.

Debt service coverage:

$$\frac{\text{(Excess of Revenues over Expenses + Depreciation Expense + Interest Expense)}}{\text{(Current Portion of Long-Term Debt + Interest Expense)}}$$

The debt service coverage ratio is a measure of long-term creditworthiness. It evaluates the HCO's ability to meet its long-term debt obligations with current income. This is a ratio that usually appears in the documents used to sell tax-exempt bonds. Bond rating agencies and investors expect to see a value of 2.0 or better. The 2007 debt service coverage ratio for Memorial Hospital was:

$$(\$4,500 + 4,700 + 1,700)/(\$3,000 + \$1,700) = 2.3$$

For every $1 in interest and principal payments, the hospital had $2.30 in income to make those payments. This is a healthy value for the hospital and roughly equivalent to the 2005 average for all acute care hospitals.

Activity Ratios

Activity ratios are also called asset management ratios or efficiency ratios. The ratios all have revenues in the numerator and some part of assets in the denominator. They are measures of efficiency because assets are considered the inputs to the health care production process, and revenues are the outputs; that is, assets are used to produce services that are measured as revenue.

Total asset turnover:

$$\frac{\text{Total Revenues}}{\text{Total Assets}}$$

The 2007 total asset turnover ratio for Memorial Hospital was:

$102,800/$115,600 = .89

For every $1 invested in assets, the hospital generated 89 cents in revenue. This is not an unusual value for an organization with a substantial investment in fixed assets, which is typical of hospitals. The 2005 industry average was somewhat worse, at 0.78.

Overall, Memorial Hospital has good liquidity, a reasonable amount of debt, and good coverage of its long-term debt obligations. The primary financial concern for the hospital is its negative operating margin. A hospital cannot survive in the long run if it loses money on its core mission, patient care. Board members at Memorial Hospital should ask whether the loss on operations is due to under-utilization of the hospital's services, poor expense control, weak revenue management, or some combination of all three. Finally, the board should determine what management proposes to do to improve the hospital's financial condition.

Capital Financing

All businesses have a need to finance their assets. In fact, the right-hand side of the balance sheet—liabilities and equity—can be viewed as the mix of capital (either debt or equity) used to finance the assets on the left-hand side. All businesses can use a mix of short-term debt, long-term debt, and equity for capital financing. As noted above, equity in a for-profit business is the value of the company's stock when first sold plus the accumulated profits or losses over time. In a nonprofit, equity equals charitable contributions, grants from public and private sources, and the accumulated profits or losses over time.

Most hospitals and nursing homes finance their capital projects (additions or renovations to buildings or the purchase of expensive pieces of equipment) with long-term debt, and they do so for the same reason most people take out a mortgage to buy a house—they do not have enough cash to make the purchase. Some capital projects can be financed with a long-term bank loan or even a mortgage on the HCO's property. However, the most common form of long-term debt is a *tax-exempt bond.*

Tax-Exempt Bonds

All states passed legislation in the 1960s and 1970s that permitted some types of nonprofits, including health care organizations, to issue bonds through quasi-public authorities. These authorities serve as conduits for the funds raised by a tax-exempt issuance. Nonprofit hospitals and nursing homes utilize this form of capital financing, as do private universities. The interest paid to the bondholders is exempt from personal income tax at the federal level, and usually at the state level. Investors accept lower interest rates in exchange for these tax benefits.

There are many participants in the process of issuing tax-exempt debt. The HCO typically hires a consulting firm to complete a feasibility study of the proposed capital project. Bond rating agencies such as Moody's or Standard & Poor's will evaluate the bonds for creditworthiness. These ratings are major determinants of the interest rate on the bond. Attorneys called bond counsels must attest to the tax-exempt status of the bonds. Investment banking firms sell the bonds to both institutional and individual investors. The proceeds from the bond sale flow through a trustee bank to the HCO; interest and principal payments from the HCO flow through the trustee bank to bondholders.

The major advantage of issuing tax-exempt debt is the lower interest rate the HCO will pay to bondholders. Offsetting this benefit are the substantial costs of issuance (given all the participants involved) and the long period of time it takes to get to market compared to taxable debt instruments. On balance, most of the time, the difference between taxable and tax-exempt interest rates is large enough to make the tax-exempt option cheaper, even when the costs of issuance are added in. As with any form of debt, the primary risk associated with tax-exempt bonds is the fixed nature of the obligation. Interest and principal payments cannot be adjusted when revenues are down.

Some HCOs purchase bond insurance to further reduce interest rates. Companies that sell insurance to bond issuers charge a premium in exchange for the promise to meet interest and principal obligations should the HCO default on its payments. Until very recently, all insured bonds carried a AAA credit rating reflecting the creditworthiness of the insurer, not the HCO. This high rating results in lower interest rates for the HCO.

Most of the tax-exempt bonds issued by HCOs are *revenue bonds*. The revenues of the HCO are pledged as collateral on the loan. This means that the bondholders have first claim on the HCO's revenue, before the claims of other creditors or even employees. This is an example of the kind of restrictive covenants that often accompany tax-exempt financings. In this case, the hospital agrees to maintain a charge structure that ensures sufficient income to make interest and principal payments. Other bond covenants may restrict additional borrowing, the sale of assets, or the development of joint ventures.

Bond Ratings

The bond rating agencies evaluate the HCO's ability to meet the debt service requirements of the bond—interest and principal—over the life of the bond. Most HCOs issue tax-exempt bonds that mature in 20 to 30 years, so the rating agency's job is to assess the HCO's ability to make payments far into the future.

The rating agencies evaluate a variety of financial and nonfinancial parameters. They complete an extensive analysis of the HCO's financial performance, using ratios like those described above. They also evaluate the utilization of the HCO's services, including trends in admissions, length of stay, outpatient and emergency room visits, and most importantly, occupancy rates. They look at medical staff characteristics, including board certification, average age, and concentration of admissions. They are also interested in staff turnover, contracts with third-party payers, cost containment strategies, market share, and many other aspects of operations.

Rating agencies evaluate the capabilities of management and the governing board. The document used to sell a tax-exempt bond is called an official statement. This document includes the names and backgrounds of senior managers and the members of the board. The rating agencies want to determine whether the HCO is well managed and the trustees are qualified to carry out their fiduciary responsibilities.

Recently, rating agencies have become interested in the quality of patient care at a bond-issuing organization. HCOs that have a record of poor quality are not likely to attract or retain the patients who generate the organization's revenues. If occupancy rates and revenues decline as the result of poor quality, the financial condition of the HCO will also decline. Rating agencies like to see organizations with strong programs for quality measurement and process improvement, and governing boards that ensure these quality-related systems are in place.

Conclusion

Nonprofit health care organizations have complex financial structures. The board of an HCO has the ultimate responsibility for oversight of those finances. An effective board is one that has a basic understanding of the key determinants of financial performance, including reimbursement policies. Board members should have a basic understanding of the key financial statements, what they reveal about the HCO, and how to use them as a mechanism to assess the organization's activities.

Case Study

Memorial Hospital is the case study for this chapter. Readers should calculate the 2006 values for the 11 ratios presented in this chapter and evaluate whether the financial condition of the hospital improved or deteriorated between 2006 and 2007.

Study and Discussion Questions

1. How did Memorial Hospital's financial performance change from 2006 to 2007?
2. How might the change in financial performance affect the hospital's bond rating or its ability to issue new long-term debt?
3. What types of financial and operational reports should a health care governing board expect to receive from management on a regular basis?

Suggested Readings and Web Sites

Reading

Cleverley, W. O. and A. E. Cameron. 2007. *Essentials of health care finance*. Sudbury, MA: Jones and Bartlett Publishers.

Web Sites

Cain Brothers & Co.: www.cainbrothers.com
Healthcare Financial Management Association: www.hfma.org
Moody's Investors Service: www.moodys.com
Standard & Poor's: www.standardandpoors.com

References

1. American Institute of Certified Public Accountants. 2006. *Health care organizations—AICPA audit and accounting guide*. New York.
2. Gapenski, L. C. 2005. *Healthcare finance—An introduction to accounting and financial management*. Chicago: Health Administration Press.

Case Study Answers

Total margin (2006):

$$\$8,900/\$98,200 \times 100 = 9.1\%$$

Memorial Hospital was more profitable in 2006 than 2007 (4.4%).

Operating margin (2006):

$$(\$89,900 - 89,300)/\$89,900 \times 100 = 0.7\%$$

Memorial Hospital was more profitable in its basic line of business—patient care—in 2006 than in 2007 (–2.1%).

Return on equity (2006):

$$\$8,900/\$71,400 \times 100 = 12.5\%$$

Memorial Hospital was more profitable in 2006 than 2007 (6%).

Growth rate in equity (2006):
The growth rate in equity ratio for 2006 cannot be calculated because the case does not include the net assets value for 2005. If the 2005 value for net assets was (hypothetically) $65,000, then the ratio value for 2006 would be

$$(\$71,400 - 65,000)/\$65,000 \times 100 = 9.8\%$$

The hospital experienced a more significant growth in equity in 2006 than in 2007 (5.9%).

Current ratio (2006):

$$\$34,900/\$11,200 = 3.1$$

Memorial Hospital was slightly more liquid in 2006 than 2007 (3.0).

Average collection period (2006):

$$\$14,200/(\$89,900/365) = 57.7 \text{ days}$$

It took Memorial Hospital slightly more time to collect receivables in 2006 than in 2007 (57.2 days).

Average payment period (2006):

Current liabilities/[(total expenses – depreciation expense)/365]

$$\$11,200/[(\$89,300 - 4,300)/365] = 48.1 \text{ days}$$

It took Memorial Hospital slightly longer to pay its bills in 2007 (50.7 days) than in 2006.

Days cash on hand (2006):

$$(\$5,800 + 10,700)/[(\$89,300 - 4,300)/365] = 70.8 \text{ days}$$

Memorial Hospital had less cash on hand in 2006 than in 2007 (80.7 days).

Debt ratio (2006):

$$\$38,400/\$109,800 \times 100 = 35.0\%$$

Memorial Hospital's leverage (use of debt) increased slightly from 2006 to 2007 (34.6%).

Debt service coverage (2006):

$$(\$8,900 + 4,300 + 1,800)/(\$1,800 + 1,800) = 4.2$$

Memorial Hospital had much better coverage of its long-term debt obligations in 2006 than in 2007 (2.3).

Total asset turnover (2006):

$$\$98,200/\$109,800 = .89$$

Memorial Hospital's total asset turnover ratio remained the same in 2006 as in 2007 (.89).

The comparison of financial ratios in 2006 and 2007 demonstrates that Memorial Hospital experienced a significant decline in profitability from both operating and nonoperating sources in 2007. There was no change in operating efficiency, reflected in the total asset turnover ratio, and a small increase in long-term debt. The decrease in income did not result in a substantial decline in short-term liquidity. However, the hospital's debt service coverage ratio decreased significantly, which would be a concern to the hospital's bondholders and the rating agencies.

Chapter 8

Auditing and Compliance: The Conscience of an Enterprise

Alton F. Knight and Stephen J. Neitz

Contents

Executive Summary

Auditing, compliance, and risk management play important roles in helping the board to fulfill oversight responsibilities and management to achieve business objectives. In health care organizations, these functions are particularly important given the complex array of regulatory, financial, clinical, and operational risks that exist.

Management has the primary responsibility for establishing and guiding the direction of the organization. It identifies strategy, evaluates enterprise risks, and establishes internal controls to manage and achieve the organization's mission, goals, and objectives.

The combined roles of external and internal audit and compliance provide assurances to the board and management that the established systems of internal controls are effective and efficient, provide reliable financial reporting, and comply with applicable laws and regulations. The audit committee serves as the principal committee of the board for audit, compliance, and risk reporting. However, all committees of the board review and monitor risks associated with their chartered roles and responsibilities.

Learning Objectives

1. To gain an understanding of the roles and responsibilities for risk management, auditing, and compliance, and how these activities relate to the roles of board members.
2. To be able to better assess the organization's risk profile and strategy, quality of financial reporting, quality of internal controls, and compliance with applicable laws and regulations.

Key Words

- Annual work plan
- Audit committee
- Compliance
- Enterprise risk management
- External auditing
- Internal auditing
- Internal control

Introduction

Risk is prevalent in all organizations and must be managed for long-term success. In today's nonprofit health care environment risks and challenges are increasing on many fronts with growing public demands for more effective board oversight, improved management practices, and greater transparency in reporting. At the highest level, boards need to be concerned with challenges to the organization's nonprofit status, business ethics, and reputation, among others (see "General Nonprofit Provider Risks" box), and to ensure that appropriate board oversight activities, management systems, and internal controls are in place to meet these challenges.

GENERAL NONPROFIT PROVIDER RISKS

- Maintaining nonprofit status
- Complying with laws and regulations
- Maintaining business reputation
- Maintaining financial performance
- Maintaining business continuity
- Maintaining patient confidentiality
- Ensuring positive business ethics
- Ensuring appropriate business structures

INTERNAL CONTROL ENVIRONMENT

- ■ Vision, mission, and values
- ■ Business strategies and plans
- ■ Organization structure and design
- ■ Staffing and workforce
- ■ Policies and procedures
- ■ Financial and administrative reporting

Management has the primary responsibility for establishing and implementing direction for the organization. It identifies strategy in conjunction with enterprise risks and establishes internal controls to manage processes. Primary internal controls are critical management activities and are the foundation for effective and efficient business operations (see "Internal Control Environment" box). The absence of or weakness of internal controls generally reflects greater risks to the organization, while the existence and execution of appropriate controls at each level of the organization reduces risks and improves performance.

In combination, the roles of external and internal audit and compliance help provide reasonable assurances that management's systems of internal controls are effective and efficient, provide reliable financial reporting, and comply with applicable laws and regulations. The principal activities of external and internal audit and compliance are to audit and attest to the annual financial statements prepared by management, to review and report on the effectiveness of internal controls established and implemented by management, and to review and report on management's compliance with regulatory requirements. Key to these roles is the separation and independence of the auditors from management and business decision making.

In recent years, a number of high-profile business scandals have led government, corporate boards, and other interested entities to seek greater assurances from the public accounting profession and business management for auditing, financial reporting, and risk management practices. In this regard, the government enacted Sarbanes-Oxley (SOX) legislation in 2002 to strengthen public accounting and for-profit business reporting requirements, and in 2004, the accounting industry, through the Committee of Sponsoring Organizations (COSO) of the Treadway Commission, introduced the concept of enterprise risk management (ERM) to help guide management in assessing risk. With increased government and public scrutiny of nonprofit health care organizations, the industry has taken lessons from these events and is now beginning to implement elements of SOX and ERM.

**BOARD COMMITTEE RISK MANAGEMENT
RESPONSIBILITIES**

- Parent board—All risks
- Governance—Membership, ethics, and board management risks
- Strategic planning—Mission strategy risks
- Finance and investment—Finance and performance risks
- Audit and compliance—Compliance, accountability, and operating risks
- Quality—Clinical strategy and program risks
- Compensation—Executive compensation risks

In terms of board activities, the board has ultimate oversight responsibility for risk and often delegates it through its committee structure (see "Board Committee Risk Management Responsibilities" box). Audit committees have traditionally served an oversight role for audit, compliance, and risk-related activities and, more recently, have taken a leadership role in addressing ERM requirements; however, the scope and demands of ERM extend beyond the traditional focus of the audit committee, and the board must ensure that all committees review and monitor risks associated with chartered roles and responsibilities. This chapter will explore these important concepts, functions, and activities as they relate to board oversight.

Enterprise Risk Management

Definition

Enterprise risk management (ERM) is an activity carried out by management to identify, assess, prioritize, and strategize risks affecting the current and future performance of an organization. ERM considers an organization's mission, goals and objectives, business environment, systems of internal controls, as well as external and internal risks impacting the organization, its business units, and operating functions.

Background of Enterprise Risk Management

Enterprise risk management is a recent development. Boards, government, and regulatory bodies have demanded greater accountability and transparency from corporations following Enron and other high-profile scandals in recent years.

In this regard, the federal government implemented SOX legislation in 2002 and, through the Securities and Exchange Commission (SEC) and the Public Company Accounting Oversight Board (PCAOB), instituted major changes in audit standards and for-profit reporting requirements.[1] Following the issuance of the ERM guideline in 2004, the SEC further recommended that ERM be implemented by all businesses. With growing public scrutiny of nonprofit organizations and the health care industry, elements of SOX and ERM are now being adopted by nonprofit health care providers.[2]

Guidance

The Committee of Sponsoring Organizations (COSO) of the Treadway Commission has, over the years, provided authoritative guidance on the roles and responsibilities of auditors, management, and the board for internal controls and, more recently, enterprise risk management. In 1992, COSO issued "Internal Controls—Integrated Framework."[3] It made clear the roles and responsibilities of management, external and internal auditors, and the board of directors for the establishment, monitoring, and reporting of internal controls and best practices. In response to the Enron scandal and the need to strengthen management of enterprise risks, COSO issued "Enterprise Risk Management—Integrated Framework" in 2004.[4] This guidance builds upon COSO's internal control framework with a common approach to risk management that has been adopted by the accounting and auditing profession, management and audit committees of for-profit enterprises, and more recently, nonprofit health care providers.

Framework

"Enterprise Risk Management—Integrated Framework" provides guidance for improved risk assessment in business settings. Its framework reflects business objectives, elements, and ERM review processes (Figure 8.1).[4] The framework establishes four categories of business objectives consistent with an effective internal control environment:

- *Strategic*: Objectives relating to and aligned with the organization's mission.
- *Operating*: Objectives relating to the effective and efficient use of the organization's resources.
- *Reporting*: Objectives relating to the reliability of the organization's reporting.
- *Compliance*: Objectives relating to the organization's compliance with laws and regulations.[4]

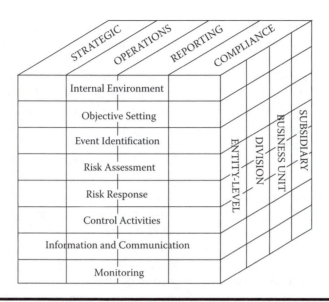

Figure 8.1 Enterprise risk management integrated framework.[4]

RISK REVIEW PROCESS

- Understand control environment.
- Identify external and internal risks.
- Assess risks for likelihood of occurring.
- Assess risks for impact on mission.
- Determine organization risk appetite.
- Develop and coordinate action plans.
- Communicate and monitor plans.

The framework depicts the enterprise and its operating parts, and describes eight components for risk review (see "Risk Review Process" box). Combined, the framework provides ERM review processes for each operating unit or function of an enterprise, with the sum results determining overall enterprise risk and level at which risks should be managed.

Review Components

The ERM review process begins with an understanding of the organization's mission, internal control environment, and strategic objectives. It includes people, their individual attributes, ethical values and competence, the business environment they work in, and the internal control processes that set and align business strategy and objectives.

With this understanding, external and internal events with potential to impact and influence mission, goals, and objectives are identified. These include events that represent both risk and opportunity to the organization and their impact on business plans and objectives. Regulation, competition, innovation, technology, stock market fluctuations, and natural disasters are examples of external risks and events to be considered. The lack or failure of internal controls, services, and processes are examples of internal risks and events.

Once identified, risks and events are then assessed for their likelihood of occurring and impact on objectives, management's options for avoiding, accepting, reducing, or sharing with others, and management's risk tolerance—how much risk management is willing to take to achieve the business strategies. Management's action plans should then align with the organization's mission, goals, and objectives and provide assigned accountability.

Finally, ERM requires that information be communicated at all levels of the organization in order to identify and respond to risk, and that mechanisms be established to monitor the ever-changing risk environment. Ideally, management will report on its risk management program on an annual basis and incorporate risk strategies in its short-term and long-term plans.

Roles and Responsibilities

Enterprise risk management is the responsibility of many parties with various levels of authority. The board of directors and its committees exercise oversight responsibility of management and its actions. The board sets expectations with regard to organizational philosophy, integrity, and ethics, approves key elements of business strategy, and oversees management performance. The board maintains and carries out its responsibilities through delegation of authority to committees. As part of their chartered roles and responsibilities, each committee has oversight for some aspect of enterprise risk. Audit committees have taken a leadership role in audit, compliance, and ERM developments. However, the scope and demands of ERM extend beyond the audit committee, where all committees review and monitor risks associated with their chartered roles and responsibilities. Ultimately, the board has overall oversight responsibility. Boards and their committees need to stay current on best board practices, the industry they operate within, organization risks, management's risk strategies and plans, as well as committee oversight. The absence of effective oversight is a risk in itself.

Management, through the chief executive officer (CEO) and executive team, has the primary responsibility for establishing and implementing direction for the organization. It identifies strategy considering enterprise risks and establishes internal controls to manage and achieve mission, goals, and objectives. The CEO and executive team promote risk management, compliance with laws and regulations, and assure transparent reporting. Through the organization's chain of command, employees are responsible for complying with management direction and its systems of internal controls.

The combined efforts of external and internal audit and compliance provide assurances to the board and management that management's systems of internal controls are effective and efficient, provide reliable financial reporting, and comply with applicable laws and regulations. The principal activities of external and internal audit and compliance are to audit and attest to the annual financial statements prepared by management, to review and report on the effectiveness of internal controls established and implemented by management, and to review and report on management's compliance with regulatory requirements. As part of these processes, external and internal audit and compliance activities consider risks in audit and review processes and coordinate with management overall risks as part of the annual and long-term audit and review programs.

Focus on Risk Management

Businesses are evolving entities constantly at risk from the business environment and internal business practices. Many once prominent companies no longer exist because of their inability to address the risks of the changing business environment or to effectively manage their internal operations. In terms of health care and nonprofit providers, the business environment and internal business practices are influenced by a complex array of political, business, and operating activities that make board oversight an ongoing challenge. Business risks and opportunities are mitigated by knowledge of the industry, the business environment, the organization's mission, vision, and values, and its system of internal controls. Among the latter are business strategies, organization structure, workforce requirements, policies and procedures, and reporting and monitoring activities. The absence of or weaknesses in any of these basic business requirements increase risk, while effective management and board oversight decrease risk and improve competitive advantage. From the board's perspective, it has ultimate responsibility for risk oversight through its own actions and those of its committees. As a result, a clear and well-functioning governance structure is essential to risk management and oversight.

External Auditing

Services Provided by External Auditors

External auditing is typically performed by a certified public accountant or public accounting firm. Most corporations with a board of directors consisting of outside (i.e., nonmanagement or nonfamily) directors tend to hire a regional or global public accounting firm as opposed to a small firm or an individual practitioner. For purposes of this discussion, we will define external auditors as medium (i.e., second tier) and large (i.e., Big Four) public accounting firms. The external auditor provides a number of valuable services to the board of directors, including attestation and various permitted advisory services.

The external auditor's attestation function typically involves reviewing and evaluating the financial statements and corporate tax returns prepared by management and expressing an opinion on the quality and fairness of the presentation of the financial results of the organization. The primary responsibility of the external auditor in carrying out the attestation function is to plan and perform the audit to obtain reasonable—not absolute—assurance about whether the financial statements are free of material misstatement, whether caused by error or fraud. The scope of work performed on tax returns is generally more limited than the financial statements. This attestation is typically performed on an annual basis coincident with the end of the organization's fiscal accounting year. However, it is not uncommon for the board to engage an external auditor to provide attestation on a more frequent basis, such as semiannually or quarterly, depending on the specific business needs of the organization. For example, a requirement may be in place to provide audited quarterly financial statements to certain creditors or bondholders to maintain favorable terms.

External auditors can also provide consultative services to the board of directors or to management, although there are some types of consulting that they should not engage in with an organization if they are also responsible for the audit of the organization's financial statements. In particular, since the advent of SOX requirements in 2002, the audit committee of the board of directors is typically required to preapprove any services provided by the external auditor, particularly when not related to the financial statement audit. In general, the nature of consulting services provided by external auditors involves financial, tax, accounting treatment, and agreed-upon procedures, which may relate to major transactions or events (including financing or tax structures), performed in accordance with the certain professional standards.

Professional Standards of External Auditors

The public accounting profession is regulated by several governing bodies, depending on the type of client for whom services are provided—primarily nonpublic and public companies. External auditors who work with nonpublic companies are subject to the professional standards established by the American Institute of Certified Public Accountants (AICPA) and the state boards of accountancy, which pertain to the legal entity domicile. Established in 1887, the AICPA mission is to "provide members with the resources, information, and leadership that enable them to provide valuable services in the highest professional manner to benefit the public as well as employers and clients."[5] The AICPA Code of Professional Conduct specifies the members' responsibilities to the public, their clients, and to their colleagues. The code specifically outlines certain principles that define responsibility, the public interest, integrity, objectivity and independence, due care, and scope and nature of services. The state boards of accountancy typically have codes of professional conduct that are consistent with the AICPA. Also, the Government Accountability Office (GAO) standards are typically followed by most nonprofits because they receive federal funds.

The external auditors for public companies must conform to the professional standards required by the Public Company Accounting Oversight Board (PCAOB), which is governed by the Securities and Exchange Commission (SEC). The SEC was created in 1934 to protect the users of financial information for publicly traded companies and to restore confidence in the capital markets of the United States. The PCAOB was created in 2003 in the advent of the Sarbanes-Oxley Act of 2002, which also sought to enhance the level of public confidence in the way financial results for publicly traded companies are developed, audited, and monitored. While consistent with the AICPA guidelines on professional standards, the PCAOB's rules for professional standards also delineate more requirements with respect to auditor independence and the types of nonaudit services that external auditors can provide to their audit clients.

Key Processes

External auditors typically engage in a substantive planning process to delineate the scope and timing of their audits. There are a number of factors to consider, such as the desire or need of the board or management to have audited statements at a certain point in time following the conclusion of the organization's fiscal accounting year. The nature of the audit also impacts the level of coordination necessary to ensure that the auditors bring to bear the most appropriate resources to conduct an effective audit, and that management can provide adequate information in a timely manner in response to questions that arise during the course of the audit.

One of the most important considerations is the cutoff period used to determine the final estimates that are incorporated into the year-end financial results. The closer to the end of the fiscal year these cutoffs occur will determine the extent to which certain auditing procedures need to be performed to provide the requisite level of assurance sought by the audit. Another consideration for the external auditors is to what extent there are significant postclosing events that may impact the financial statement presentation. The auditors need to assess the materiality of these events to determine if changes or adjustments are needed in the financial statements, or if there needs to be a footnote to the financial statements describing the event and any conclusion with respect to its materiality.

Reporting

External auditors usually provide a written report related to their attestation work (i.e., audit activities). The primary audiences for these reports are the board of directors (via the audit committee), the applicable external regulators, and the public. In addition to the audit opinion, which is always in writing, there are required communications in accordance with audit standards that are generally in writing to the audit committee.

The board of directors typically delegates the review and acceptance of the external auditor's reports to a committee of the board—either the audit committee or the finance committee. The audit committee will receive the final report on the organization's consolidated financial results for the year. The report will typically include the income statement, balance sheet, and a statement in change in cash position for the period reviewed (Table 8.1). The external auditor also typically provides to the audit committee the results of any tax work performed, and the results of any audits of other organizational entities that require separate audited financial statements.

In addition to the report, the external auditor will render an opinion on the reliability of financial statements based on his or her professional judgment. A nonqualified audit opinion is seen as the highest (that is, best) level of attestation from the external auditor. In addition, another form of attestation provided by the external auditor is a document called a "No Material Weakness Letter," which expresses the auditor's judgment that there are no material weaknesses in

Table 8.1 Components of an External Auditor's Report to the Board

Income Statement	The income statement shows the relationship of the organization's revenues and expenses and denotes whether the organization made or lost money during the period. The income statement is also known as the profit and loss statement or the statement of operations and changes in net assets.
Balance Sheet	The balance sheet shows the amount and type of assets and liabilities the organization has at the end of the accounting period under review (i.e., point in time).
Change in Cash Position	The statement on changes in cash position reflects the way in which cash flowed into and out of the organization during the year. It is sometimes referred to as the source and use of cash statement.

the internal control environment that management has developed within the organization. The basis for all of these judgments and attestations is predicated on the proper application of accounting and auditing standards that guide the profession.

In general, the same audited financial statements reported to the audit committee are used to fulfill the requirement for information by various regulatory bodies, as well as the general public. It should be noted that the actual reporting to these outside parties is performed by management of the organization—not by the external auditor.

Focus on External Audit

One of the most important duties of the board is its fiduciary responsibility to the organization. Therefore, having an understanding of the external auditor's written report of the organization's financial statements is paramount. To this end, the board member ought to pay careful attention to the opinion rendered by the external auditors in their report. To the extent that anything other than an unqualified (i.e., clean) opinion is noted, the board should ask the external auditors to explain the reasons for the qualified opinion.

Similarly, the board (or audit committee) member ought to have the external auditor elaborate on whether any material weaknesses or significant deficiencies were noted in the conduct of the audit. Finally, the board should explore any circumstances for which a "No Material Weakness Letter" could not be written by the external auditor following the annual audit.

Internal Auditing

Internal auditing is, by definition, "an independent, objective assurance and consulting activity designed to add value and improve an organization's operations."[6] Further, internal auditing "helps an organization accomplish its objectives by bringing a systematic, disciplined approach to evaluate and improve the effectiveness of risk management, control, and governance processes."[6]

Internal auditing is typically performed by members of the organization's management team, and as such, the internal auditors serve as the eyes and ears of the board of directors, either directly or via a reporting relationship to the audit committee or similar board-authorized oversight body. The internal auditor's scope of work focuses on reviewing the effectiveness of the organization's risk management, control, and governance processes and is not exclusively focused on activities associated with the organization's financial statement preparation.

Independence and Structure of Internal Audit

Most internal audit functions are headed by a person who is often referred to as the general auditor or chief audit executive (CAE). This person typically has an extensive background in auditing, accounting, finance, business operations, management, and risk management. The CAE has overall authority and responsibility for the internal audit department and its activities and typically reports functionally and administratively to the organization's chief executive officer, chief operating officer, or chief financial officer. The CAE also reports to the audit committee in the manner prescribed in the committee's charter. The audit committee charter is a governance document that delineates the role of the committee, particularly with respect to the CAE and the types of reporting, analysis, and monitoring performed by the internal audit function that support the committee in fulfilling its fiduciary responsibilities.

This dual-reporting relationship helps establish the independence of the internal audit function, which is essential to the effectiveness of internal auditing. All internal audit activities must remain free of influence by any element in the organization, including matters of audit selection, scope, procedures, frequency, timing, or report content, to permit maintenance of an independent and objective approach necessary in rendering reports. In addition, the CAE has a right and obligation to report directly to the audit committee on any matter where the normal procedures for resolution of internal audit issues are either inappropriate or have failed.

One of the most important components of an internal auditor is independence and objectivity. In order to fulfill this role, it is generally accepted that internal auditors should not develop and install procedures, prepare records, or engage in any other activity that they would normally review and appraise or which might otherwise compromise independence and objectivity.

Role of Internal Audit versus Management

Internal control is the responsibility of management. It is a process designed to provide reasonable assurance of effective and efficient operations, reliable financial data, and compliance with applicable laws and regulations.

The required reasonable assurance exists when all components of management control (the control environment, risk assessment process, control activities, information and communication systems, and monitoring activities) are present and operate effectively.

The role of the internal audit department is to provide, through objective periodic review, assurance that management's control systems are sound, in place, and operating as intended.

Scope of Work for Internal Audit

The scope of internal auditing encompasses the examination and evaluation of the adequacy and effectiveness of the organization's system of internal control and the quality of performance in carrying out assigned responsibilities. This includes, but is not limited to:

- Reviewing the reliability and integrity of financial and operating information, and the means used to identify, measure, classify, and report such information.
- Reviewing the systems established to ensure compliance with those policies, plans, procedures, laws, or regulations that could have a significant impact on operations.

- ■ Reviewing the means of safeguarding assets and, as appropriate, verifying the existence of such assets in order to provide management with reasonable assurance that assets are protected against loss that could result from fire, theft, other improper or illegal activities, or exposure to the elements.
- ■ Reviewing and appraising the economy and efficiency with which resources are employed. In this regard, internal auditing evaluates whether operating standards have been established for measuring economy and efficiency; whether operating standards are understood and are being met; whether deviations from operating standards are identified, analyzed, and communicated to those responsible for corrective action; and whether effective corrective action has been taken.
- ■ Reviewing operations to ascertain whether results are consistent with established objectives and goals, and whether the operations or programs are being carried out as planned.
- ■ Providing consultation and other services to management as needed with forensic audit services, IT auditing services, and risk management services.

Management does not place any restrictions on the scope of the audits. However, it is recognized that management and the audit committee provide general direction as to the scope of work and the activities to be audited, and may request that internal audit carry out special reviews or audits.

Services Provided by Internal Audit

The CAE and the staff of the internal audit department typically perform activities for management and the audit committee. Table 8.2 is an example of the key responsibilities performed by most, if not all, internal audit functions. There may be other responsibilities performed by internal audit departments in organizations that are unique to a given company or specific industry.

Relationship with External Auditors

The internal audit function typically coordinates its activities with those of the external auditors. Both groups evaluate internal control and examine financial and other records. Appraisal of those systems in which both have an interest is most effective when shared.

Specifically, coordination includes developing common techniques, establishing common files, exchanging audit working papers, conducting joint audits where appropriate, mutually participating in on-site reviews of audit work, and coordinated and common seminars and training.

Table 8.2   Tasks Performed by Chief Audit Executive and Staff

Develop a flexible annual audit plan using appropriate risk-based methodology, including any risks or control concerns identified by management, and submit that plan to the audit committee for review and approval.
Implement the annual audit plan, as approved, including, and as appropriate, any special tasks or projects requested by management and the audit committee.
Maintain a professional audit staff with sufficient knowledge, skills, experience, and professional certifications to meet the requirements of the office.
Establish a quality assurance program by which the CAE assures the operation of internal auditing activities.
Perform consulting services, beyond internal auditing's assurance services, to assist management in meeting its objectives.
Issue periodic reports to the audit and compliance committee and management summarizing results of audit activities.
Keep the audit committee informed of emerging trends and successful practices in internal auditing.
Assist in the investigation of significant suspected fraudulent activities within the organization and notify management and the audit committee of the results.
Consider the scope of work of the external auditors and regulators, as appropriate, for the purpose of providing optimal audit coverage to the organization at a reasonable overall cost.

Professional Standards of Internal Auditors

The internal audit function is practiced in most organizations in the United States within the guidelines promulgated by the Institute of Internal Auditors (IIA). Founded in 1941, the IIA strives "to cultivate, promote, and disseminate knowledge and information concerning internal auditing and subjects related thereto; to establish and maintain high standards of integrity, honor, and character among internal auditors; to furnish information regarding internal auditing and the practice and methods thereof to its members, and of other persons interested therein, and to the general public."[7] The IIA also has a Code of Ethics to promote an ethical culture in the profession of internal auditing. This code extends beyond the definition of internal auditing and includes the following two essential components: (1) principles that are relevant to the profession and practice of internal auditing; and (2) rules of conduct that describe behavior norms expected of internal auditors. These rules are an aid to turn the principles into practical applications and are intended to guide the ethical conduct of internal auditors.[6]

The key principles that all internal auditors are expected to apply and uphold include integrity, objectivity, confidentiality, and competency. Furthermore, to ensure that internal auditing activities are performed in accordance with these underlying principles, the IIA promulgates the *International Standards for the Professional Practice of Internal Auditing* (hereafter *Standards*), which are designed to:

1. Delineate basic principles that represent the practice of internal auditing as it should be.
2. Provide a framework for performing and promoting a broad range of value-added internal audit activities.
3. Establish the basis for the evaluation of internal audit performance.
4. Foster improved organizational processes and operations.

The *Standards* are further broken down into attribute, professional, and implementation standards. The attribute standards pertain to the attributes of organizations and individuals performing internal audit services. The professional standards relate to the nature of internal audit services and the quality criteria to be applied when measuring performance. The implementation standards apply to the attribute and professional standards and provide additional guidance on when and how to apply the standard in certain types of engagements.

Reporting

The CAE typically develops an annual audit plan that is designed to provide some assurance on the design and effectiveness of the internal control environment related to key areas of business risks to the organization. The annual plan is prepared in accordance with an enterprise risk assessment process, which seeks to take into account the critical risks to the organization as seen from the vantage point of multiple stakeholders (i.e., senior management, board members, regulators, etc.). An assessment is made of the likelihood and potential impact should any of the key risks materialize or are not adequately addressed. This information, along with other areas of known risks (i.e., risks inherent in the nature of the business the organization is in), is used to develop a prioritized list of areas for the internal audit function to consider in developing its annual audit plan. In addition to the risk areas, the CAE must allocate resources at his or her disposal to ensure that the audit coverage afforded by the plan is adequate to satisfy the risk appetite of the audit committee.

The annual plan is submitted to the audit committee for its review and approval. Once the plan is approved, the internal auditors provide periodic written reports to the audit committee on the results of their activities. Included in the report are results of both planned and unplanned audits and investigations. The committee usually focuses on the outcomes of the audit and the planned corrective actions taken by management when issues arise from the audit process. It is important that issues noted in audit reports are addressed in an appropriate and timely manner.

Focus on Internal Audit

The audit committee typically oversees the chief audit executive (CAE) and relies on the internal audit function to review the effectiveness of the organization's risk management, control, and governance processes. The audit committee should ensure that the objectivity and independence of the internal audit effort, particularly the role of the CAE, is not unduly influenced by management. One way to gain reasonable assurances with respect to this independence issue is to conduct an executive session periodically, wherein the audit committee meets exclusively with the CAE to ascertain if there are any matters of concern that should be brought to the attention of the committee. Having an executive session provides the opportunity for the CAE to discuss issues in an open and straightforward manner, particularly those that might have had a detrimental impact on the performance of the audit function. Alternatively, these sessions can be used to validate and reassure the committee about the cooperation received by management, as well as the absence of any undue influences.

Compliance

History of Compliance

The history of compliance goes back to the 1860s, when the False Claims Act (FCA) was enacted during the Civil War. The FCA sought to prevent individuals from profiting by selling bogus goods to the Union Army. Since that time, the FCA has evolved through amendments, and it currently mandates fines and penalties at double and triple the amount of damages of each false claim made against government agencies. The mandates are now a major weapon in preventing fraudulent claims issued by health care providers.[8]

Role and Structure of Compliance in Health Care Organizations

The compliance function is typically led by a person in a high-level position with direct access to senior management and to the board in a health care organization. Based on the size of the organization, there are different ways to structure the role of the chief compliance officer. For example, in a single hospital or other type of health care organization, there may be one person who fulfills this role. In a large, multihospital health care system, on the other hand, there may be a chief compliance officer at the main facility or corporate location, with local compliance officers or compliance directors who operate within the other hospitals and affiliated health care businesses. These local compliance officers often report directly to the chief compliance officer or, minimally, have a dotted-line reporting relationship to the chief compliance officer. The chief compliance officer is usually charged with the responsibility of operating and monitoring the compliance program and will report to the CEO and the governing body or designated committee.

Office of Inspector General (OIG) Guidance for Compliance Programs

The U.S. government is the biggest purchaser of health care services in the nation. Purchasing services through Medicare, Medicaid, TRICARE, and various other programs led to this designation. In 1976, the government established the Office of Inspector General (OIG) for the Department of Health, Education, and Welfare (HEW), the predecessor organization to the Department of Health and Human Services (HHS). With the ever-increasing amount of money being spent on health care and the common belief that fraud and abuse was occurring in many of the government-sponsored health care programs, the OIG was established as a central office dedicated to fighting fraud, waste, and abuse in HEW.

The OIG has promulgated a number of guidelines on how health care organizations such as hospitals, physician offices, and nursing homes, among others, should model their compliance programs. In general, the OIG guidance identifies several elements as starting points for health care providers to consider when developing an effective compliance program. These key elements can be found in Table 8.3.

Table 8.3   Elements of an Effective Compliance Program

• Standards and procedures
• Designation of a compliance officer
• Appropriate training and education
• Open lines of communication
• Response to detected problems
• Internal auditing and monitoring
• Enforcement of disciplinary standards

These elements of a compliance program, when developed and implemented in accordance with the unique circumstances of each health care provider, provide a framework for structuring and aligning resources within the organization to help address key risks as seen by the OIG. Table 8.4 outlines the key risks.

It is expected that the compliance officer will develop programs and align resources to ensure the organization's management and board is well informed of the compliance implications of these regulations, statutes, and laws.

Table 8.4   Key Compliance Risks for Health Care Providers

• Billing for items or services not actually rendered
• Providing medically unnecessary services
• Upcoding
• Diagnostic related group (DRG) creep
• Outpatient services rendered in connection with inpatient stays
• Teaching physician and resident requirements for teaching hospitals
• False cost reports
• Unbundling
• Billing for discharge in lieu of transfer
• Credit balances—failure to refund
• Stark physician self-referral law

Risk Assessment and Reporting

The organization's chief compliance officer will typically develop an annual work plan to ensure that the compliance program continues to remain effective in light of the changing nature of the business and the corresponding impact of both regulatory and compliance risks that the organization faces. In this regard, the compliance function is usually a key participant in the enterprise risk assessment process if one exists. Minimally, the chief compliance officer will coordinate its risk assessment efforts with those that occur elsewhere in the organization, such as the internal audit department. The chief compliance officer makes periodic reports to the organization's governing body to keep them abreast of the progress being made and discusses the impact and plans to address emerging compliance issues.

Focus on Compliance

The board of a health care provider organization must be concerned with a host of compliance and regulatory issues. Therefore, the board must initially approve and be involved with ongoing oversight of the organization's compliance program. The myriad government regulations and the increasing number of enforcement actions that occur when these regulations are violated make this one of the biggest risks faced by health care organizations and their boards. Consequently, the board must be fully informed of the nature of the organization's compliance program and its efforts to provide effective training, education, and monitoring of the key aspects of the compliance program. The board should receive periodic reports from the chief compliance officer or appropriate senior management personnel to gain assurance about the compliance risks faced by the organization and how the compliance program is structured to address these risks.

Conclusion

Given the increasing regulatory scrutiny and financial pressures with which organizations must cope, the board of directors faces a tremendous challenge in fulfilling its fiduciary responsibility. A higher level of engagement is required to be an effective board member. In order to be relevant, board members must have appropriate information to exercise sound judgment and to provide sufficient oversight. Management needs to clearly articulate the organization's mission, its strategies to achieve the mission, the risks facing the enterprise, as well as the risk mitigation activities in place that directly relate to the organization's risk appetite. Further, the board must receive periodic reports on all of these activities.

Understanding the roles of enterprise risk management, external audit, internal audit, and compliance within the organization will help board members to be proactive in asking questions of management, as well as in providing direction that is consistent with the board's sense of stewardship of the organization's assets and preservation of its mission.

Case Study

The executive team is asked to sign a document certifying that they are not aware of any ethics or compliance issues in the organization, which they have not already discussed with the compliance officer. Recently, one senior executive has been made aware, albeit with only sketchy details, of a situation that could have compliance implications. This executive is reluctant to discuss it with the compliance officer because the executive is fearful that the compliance officer will make a big deal out of the situation. The situation may not amount to anything, but then again, it may. The executive feels he needs to investigate the matter further, to get more information, before deciding whether to talk to the compliance officer. So he decides not to talk to her for the time being. And he signs the management certification stating that he is not aware of any issues. Did this executive betray the purpose behind the certification?

Study and Discussion Questions

1. Does the organization have an enterprise risk management program? Does the board understand its fiduciary responsibilities and roles with respect to the organization's enterprise risk management program?
2. Do all board members understand the roles of the external auditors, internal auditors, and compliance function? Has the appropriate level of independence and objectivity been established for each of these activities?
3. Have the board members reviewed the charter of the audit and compliance committee to ensure that appropriate oversight

authority has been established? Does the committee consist of board members with the requisite expertise and background to exercise the responsibilities within its charter?

Suggested Readings and Web Sites

Readings

Carlile, R. 2008. Directors should make risk management a priority. *Executive Counsel* 5, no. 1, January/February.

Committee of Sponsoring Organizations of the Treadway Commission. 1992. *Internal controls—Integrated framework—Executive summary.* Jersey City, NJ: AICPA.

Committee of Sponsoring Organizations of the Treadway Commission. 2004. *Enterprise risk management—Integrated framework—Executive summary.* Jersey City, NJ: AICPA.

Guide to enterprise risk management—Frequently asked questions. 2006. North America: Protiviti, Inc. www.protiviti.com.

Jackson, P. M. and T. E. Fogarty. 2005. *Sarbanes-Oxley for nonprofits—A guide to building competitive advantage.* New York: John Wiley & Sons. http://www.executivecounsel.info/issues/current/summaries.htm.

Sobel, P. J. 2005. *Auditor's risk managment guide—Integrating auditing and ERM.* Chicago: Commerce Clearing House.

Web Sites

American Institute of Certified Public Accountants: www.aicpa.org
Institute of Internal Auditors: www.theiia.org/guidance
Open Compliance and Ethics Group: www.oceg.org
Public Company Accounting Oversight Board: www.pcaobus.org

References

1. Royo, M. B. and D. B. Nash. 2008. Sarbanes-Oxley and not-for-profit hospitals: Current issues and future prospects. *American Journal of Medical Quality* 23:70–72.

2. Jackson, P. M. and T. E. Fogarty. 2005. *Sarbanes-Oxley for nonprofits—A guide to building competitive advantage.* New York: John Wiley & Sons.

3. *Internal controls—Integrated framework—Executive summary.* 1992. Committee of Sponsoring Organizations of the Treadway Commission.

4. *Enterprise risk management—Integrated framework—Executive summary.* 2004. Committee of Sponsoring Organizations of the Treadway Commission.

5. American Institute of Certified Public Accountants. http://www.aicpa.org/ (accessed May 9, 2008).
6. *The professional practices framework.* 2007. IIA Research Foundation.
7. History & milestones—The Institute of Internal Auditors. http://www.theiia.org/theiia/about-the-institute/history-milestones/ (accessed May 9, 2008).
8. Bissey, B. S. 2006. *The compliance officer's handbook.* Marblehead, MA: HC Pro.

Chapter 9

Gavel of Governance: Legal Considerations

Catherine C. Oetgen and Elizabeth A. Simpson

Contents

Executive Summary

Most nonprofit health care organizations are governed by a volunteer board of trustees that is charged with actively overseeing the management, operations, financial resources, and program services of the organization. Today, health care organizations must comply with diverse legal and regulatory requirements, and the board is responsible for ensuring that the organization is operating in accordance with the wide variety of applicable state and federal laws. Organizations and their volunteer trustees face the risk of liability as a consequence of noncompliance in many of these areas. This chapter identifies important areas of legal responsibility and addresses ways in which potential liability can be avoided.

Learning Objectives

1. To understand general areas of liability facing health care organizations and their volunteer trustees.
2. To recognize various ways in which volunteer trustees may be protected from personal liability.
3. To describe key statutes impacting the health care industry and to discuss the board's role in ensuring compliance.
4. To identify good governance and ethics practices that may reduce the risk of liability for the organization and board members personally.

Key Words

- Charitable immunity
- Corporate form
- Employment at will
- Federal antidiscrimination laws
- Federal antikickback statute
- Federal False Claims Act
- Federal physician self-referral (Stark) law
- Fiduciary duty
- Indemnification
- Intermediate sanctions
- Medical malpractice
- Privacy laws
- Third-party liability
- Trustees and officers liability insurance
- Vicarious liability

Introduction

Many nonprofit health care organizations rely on volunteer boards to lead and carry out important oversight responsibilities. This rewarding role is accompanied with legal obligations (and potential liabilities) that are important for trustees to understand.

Today, the traditional oversight role of health care organization leaders has grown more challenging as the health care industry increases its focus on quality of care and patient safety issues, and health care regulators make enforcement of these areas a high priority.[1] Health care boards now face more obligations and responsibilities than ever before, and with responsibility comes risk.

Organizations and volunteer trustees are exposed to the risk of litigation and legal liability in a host of areas, such as claims of impermissible conflicts of interest, self-dealing, negligence, failure to supervise the conduct of employees, and financial mismanagement, to name a few. Beyond basic corporate liability risks, there are a number of federal and state statutory and regulatory schemes, and failure to comply can lead to legal trouble for an organization and its trustees. Whether or not an organization or trustee is actually liable, lawsuits must be defended and legal costs can run high.

In the face of a complex legal and regulatory environment in the health care industry, it is essential that health care organization leaders understand their responsibilities and know how to ask the right questions to implement their oversight duties effectively. This chapter identifies the key areas of legal compliance and liability facing health care organizations and their leaders and concludes with a discussion of ways risk can be reduced by adhering to good governance and ethical practices.

The Corporate Form and Corporate Liability

The Corporate Form Generally

Most hospitals in the United States are organized as nonprofit corporations because of the special advantages that the corporate legal form offers.[2] A corporation is a legal entity created under authority of law, generally state law. In general, a corporation possesses an independent identity distinct from that of the individuals comprising its shareholders, members, trustees, or officers, and is treated as a separate legal person. Corporations possess the power to conduct most types of business, to sue and be sued, to enter into contracts, and to own property in their own name. A corporation generally has perpetual existence, a centralized governing body in its board of trustees, and perhaps most importantly, limited liability for its shareholders or members, employees, officers, and trustees. Corporate trustees are not personally liable for the corporation's obligations as long as they act on behalf of the corporation and within their authority.

A nonprofit corporation is created under state law, and as such, the laws of the particular state of incorporation control with respect to issues of corporate governance. Important considerations for nonprofits, such as the powers given to the board of trustees and the extent of permissible limitations of liability for volunteer board members, all stem from state law and vary from state to state.

Civil and Criminal Liability of Corporations

As a corporation, a nonprofit may be exposed to civil and criminal liability under various legal theories, including through a theory of vicarious liability under which the corporation is held liable, albeit indirectly, for the acts of an individual. Vicarious liability in the corporate context is commonly found by way of the doctrine of *respondeat superior*, under which a corporation is held liable to a third party for the negligent conduct of its employees when the wrongdoing occurs within the scope of employment.[3] The question of whether an employee's actions fall "within the scope of employment" typically depends on whether the behavior has been authorized by the employer, whether the behavior falls within an employee's job description, and whether the behavior is intended to benefit the employer. It should be noted that in cases where an employee's behavior is found to be intentional, as opposed to negligent, such behavior is generally considered outside the scope of employment unless the intentional misconduct is authorized by the employer, relevant to the nature of the job and motivated by a desire to serve the employer.

Liability may also extend to a corporation for contracts entered into by employees with authority. Authority to contract is manifested in different ways (either through express, implied, or apparent authority). Regardless of whether authority to contract exists, a corporation is usually held responsible when a contract is approved and the benefits are accepted.

In addition to liability based on the employer–employee relationship, a corporation may be held directly liable for its own civil or criminal wrongdoings. A corporation's civil liability derives from its existence as an "artificial person" permitted to enter into contracts and pursue all activities permitted by its corporate charter and applicable law. It may sue or be sued, be held liable under contractual or other legal obligations it has undertaken, and be subject to civil fines and penalties. A corporation may also be held liable criminally, with or without individual criminal liability on the part of its employees, officers, or trustees. As an example, a situation could occur in which no single employee or agent is responsible for misconduct, but the net effect of several individuals' actions results in wrongdoing by the corporation.[3] In this kind of scenario, the corporation itself may be held liable without having to prove the culpability of specific individuals.

The U.S. Department of Justice (DOJ) has aggressively pursued enforcement of criminal laws against corporations. Indeed, DOJ's aggressive actions in pressuring accounting firm KPMG to cease funding its employees' defense costs if they did not cooperate with the government led one U.S. District Court to find that the DOJ's tactics violated several defendants' constitutional right to counsel.[4] In health care fraud and other corporate prosecutions, the DOJ has often required organizations to waive the attorney-client or work product privileges as part of their cooperation to avoid indictment. While a 2003 memorandum issued by then Deputy Attorney General Larry D. Thompson to U.S. attorneys (the Thompson Memorandum) set forth a "revised set of principles to guide Department prosecutors as they make the decision whether to seek charges against a business organization,"[5] it remains clear that the DOJ is willing and able to seek indictments against corporations if it deems them appropriate. Several of the factors noted in the Thompson Memorandum as appropriate factors to consider in determining whether to charge a corporation highlight the importance of board oversight; those factors include the pervasiveness of the wrongdoing and the related corporate culture, the corporation's response to the wrongdoing, and the existence of a corporate compliance program.

The Legal Role and Function of the Board

The board of trustees serves as the governing body of a corporation, with ultimate authority over the acts of that corporation. Individual trustee duties and obligations are generally derived from state corporate law. The corporation's charter and bylaws (often collectively termed its governing documents) generally specify the composition of the board, the manner in which it must act, and other requirements of the internal workings of the corporation. Statutes add specific requirements and prohibitions. In all instances, the actions of the corporation and its board must comply with the governing documents of the corporation and relevant statutes. Generally, the board does not engage in day-to-day management of the corporation, rather, it delegates authority for management to a chief executive officer and subordinate officers. A health care board typically retains authority for general oversight of the corporation; appointment of key officers, strategic direction and goal setting, quality of care, avoidance of conflicts of interest, ensuring compliance with applicable laws, the financial viability of the organization, and ensuring that policies and procedures are in place for appropriate performance of these functions. As a threshold matter, it is advisable for each board member to ensure that he or she understands the basic legal structure of the health care organization involved, his or her obligations and duties under state law, and his or her obligations under the governing documents of the organization. Further, it is advisable for the board collectively to ensure that it shares a common vision of its role vis-à-vis management, its authority, and its responsibilities.

Personal Liability of the Trustees

Although the corporate form generally protects nonprofit trustees from personal liability for the obligations of the organization, under some circumstances, trustees and officers may be held personally liable for harm to or caused by the nonprofit. This is true despite the fact that the majority of individuals serve nonprofit boards in a volunteer capacity. Even volunteers face risks associated with oversight. Four main areas of potential personal liability facing nonprofit trustees are addressed here: (1) breaches of fiduciary duty, (2) injuries to third parties, (3) federal tax penalties, and (4) other noncompliance under federal and state regulations.

Breaches of Fiduciary Duty

Nonprofit trustees and officers owe fiduciary obligations to the organization and can be held liable to the corporation or to the state or federal government for breaches of those duties. Chapter 3 of this book examines the duties and responsibilities of nonprofit trustees and takes a close look at the three fiduciary duties of obedience, loyalty, and care. Chapter 3 also focuses on the key issues trustees deal with that implicate fiduciary duties and that sometimes lead to breaches of those duties, including conflicts of interest, corporate opportunities, and trustee independence. This chapter discusses these concepts with regard to the nonprofit trustee's personal liability risks.

Arising in the context of certain legal relationships, fiduciary duties impose high standards of behavior on one party to act in the best interest of another party. These duties require fiduciaries to act unselfishly and to exercise skill, care, and diligence on behalf of a person or organization.[6] In the nonprofit context, trustees and officers are charged with fulfilling these obligations with respect to the nonprofit itself and, indeed, to the public as a whole given that many nonprofits are viewed as holding their assets in trust for public benefit. Breaches of these obligations can result in personal liability for trustees, officers, and managers.

The *duty of care* requires trustees to perform their responsibilities in good faith and with a degree of diligence, care, and skill that an ordinarily prudent person would exercise under similar circumstances. In practice, this means that every trustee is required to use his or her best judgment in making decisions for the nonprofit and overseeing its operation.[7] Breaches of the duty of care generally occur in two broad categories: when a trustee fails to adequately supervise the nonprofit, or fails to make an informed decision when required to do so.[6] Such breaches could arise from circumstances in which trustees fail to attend board meetings on a regular basis, fail to review financial statements or other meeting materials, or fail to notice clear signals of mismanagement.[7] In some jurisdictions, the duty of care may be overlooked in circumstances where the business judgment rule (also called the best judgment rule in the nonprofit context) applies. Under the business judgment rule, even if the corporation has been damaged, a trustee will not be held personally liable if, at the time of the decision, the trustee believed his or her decision was in the best interest of the nonprofit. This requires that the trustee made a decision in good faith, without a conflict of interest, and on an informed basis.[8] This rule prevents trustees from facing liability when a decision is discovered to be flawed in hindsight, but does not apply in cases of gross misconduct such as fraud or significant conflicts-of-interest.

The *duty of loyalty* requires trustees to place the interests of the nonprofit corporation above their own. A trustee may not act in a way that will harm the corporation, take advantage of opportunities belonging to the corporation, or use his or her position to obtain improper benefits.[6] Examples of a breach of the duty of loyalty include usurping a corporate opportunity and competing with the organization for private gain. The duty of loyalty is also implicated in situations involving conflicts of interest and self-dealing. Many state statutes address the issues related to conflicts and self-dealing, typically identifying impermissible transactions, such as certain loans to trustees, and requiring specific disclosures and processes for such transactions to be valid.

In general, a conflict-of-interest arises when an organization enters into a transaction or arrangement that might benefit the private interest of a trustee;

however, a transaction is not impermissible solely because there is a conflict-of-interest. There may be legitimate reasons for a commercial transaction with a trustee, such as a trustee who is a local banker or business person, or a physician affiliated with the health care organization. Several key steps are recommended to deal with such a transaction that will help protect an interested trustee from personal liability: (1) the interested trustee should disclose the conflict-of-interest to the organization as soon as it is known, (2) the interested trustee should recuse himself or herself from the discussion and decision making related to the transaction, and (3) only the remaining disinterested trustees should make the decision whether the transaction should be approved. In light of the current regulatory environment in which conflicts of interest are facing heightened scrutiny at the state and federal levels, it is strongly recommended best practice for a nonprofit board to adopt and abide by a comprehensive conflict-of-interest policy and procedures that determine how such transactions are handled.

Finally, the *duty of obedience* requires nonprofit trustees to act in furtherance of the nonprofit organization's mission and purpose as embodied in the organization's mission statement and governing documents. This duty also requires that trustees comply with state and federal laws. A trustee may be held liable for a breach of this duty if he or she approves action by the nonprofit that falls outside its purposes and powers. For example, Section 501(c)(3) of the Internal Revenue Code (IRC) of 1986, as amended, requires organizations to be organized and operated exclusively for charitable purposes, and no part of the net earnings may inure to the benefit of a private shareholder or individual. If an organization is acting outside the limitations of 501(c)(3), a trustee could be held personally liable for a breach of his or her fiduciary duty of obedience. To avoid this, measures should be taken to monitor required compliance.

Third-Party Liability

As noted above, since nonprofit corporations have an independent legal identity, trustees are not generally held personally liable for the debts or obligations of the organization. Likewise, trustees are not usually held liable for the negligent acts of the corporation or its employees. In the unlikely scenario that a trustee is found liable for negligent acts, this would require that he or she have participated or had knowledge of the activity, or be found to have negligently managed or supervised the affairs of the corporation to an extent that caused or contributed to the injury.[7] To offset the concern that exposure to liability may discourage the participation of volunteer trustees on nonprofit boards, many states have adopted laws that limit liability of third-party claims against volunteer trustees to circumstances involving gross negligence on the part of the trustee.

Federal Tax Liability

Another potential personal liability pitfall for nonprofit trustees arises under federal tax law. The Internal Revenue Service's "intermediate sanctions" rule imposes sanctions in situations where nonprofits organized under IRC Section 501(c)(3) or (c)(4) (which includes most tax-exempt hospitals) engage in transactions that bestow improper benefits to insiders. (IRC § 4958.) Intermediate sanctions are so named because they are less severe than the ultimate sanction of loss of tax-exempt status for the organization. Under the intermediate sanctions rule, the IRS may assess penalties against individual nonprofit trustees for authorizing transactions that result in so-called excess benefits to certain individuals who are in a position to exercise substantial influence over the affairs of the organization. The list of individuals covered by this rule (referred to as disqualified persons by the IRS) generally includes insiders such as trustees, officers, and their family members. These penalties commonly are enforced in the realm of executive compensation, in situations where amounts other than reasonable compensation are approved by a board to compensate executive management or trustees, but they may also arise in other instances that result in excess benefits to insiders.[9]

Under the rule, the IRS has authority to impose three levels of excise taxes in cases of excess benefit transactions. An initial penalty tax of 25% of the excess benefit must be paid by the person who benefits from the transaction. If the excess benefit has not been corrected in a certain period of time, the person is subject to an additional penalty tax equal to 200% of the excess benefit. Finally, in any case when a tax is imposed, a penalty tax of 10% of the excess benefit is imposed on one or more organization managers (including an organization's officers or trustees) who knowingly permitted the excess benefit transaction, unless such participation is not willful and is due to reasonable cause. Reliance on appropriate comparable compensation data or the reasoned written opinion of an attorney (or other professional advisor) may help contribute to a presumption of reasonableness if such a transaction were ever investigated. In egregious cases of excess benefit transactions, the IRS can go so far as to revoke an organization's tax-exempt status.

Noncompliance with Federal and State Regulations

In addition to the foregoing areas that may give rise to a trustee's personal liability, nonprofits are subject to various other federal, tax, and state laws and regulations. Trustees may face personal liability in the event that the organization fails to comply with assorted requirements, such as public disclosure laws, charitable solicitation laws, annual filing requirements, and sales, payroll, or withholding taxes. In addition, a governing body's role and responsibility for general organizational compliance with the law commends to the board an understanding of key laws applicable to health care organizations and the consequences of noncompliance. The board as a whole and trustees individually should make organizational compliance a priority and should install safeguards, such as periodic reporting from management, to ensure compliance.

Protection against Personal Liability

Federal Volunteer Protection Act

To encourage individuals who are reluctant to volunteer for fear of being sued, there are some available protections limiting the trustee's liability. In 1997, Congress enacted the Volunteer Protection Act to provide protection from liability to volunteers serving nonprofit organizations. The act was intended as an incentive to volunteers who have been deterred from offering their services because of the potential for liability, and as a way to repair the adverse effects experienced by organizations impacted by the withdrawal of volunteers from boards and service in other capacities. The act protects the liability of a volunteer only in situations where the volunteer was acting within the scope of his or her responsibilities and the harm was not caused by criminal or reckless misconduct, or conscious disregard to the rights or safety of the individual harmed. Although the act provides some protection, it is narrow and does not protect from any action brought by the nonprofit against the volunteer for wrongdoing.

Statutory Charitable Immunity on the State Level

In addition to the Federal Volunteer Protection Act, currently, a majority of states have charitable immunity laws that limit the liability of individuals involved with nonprofit or charitable organizations, although the extent of limitations vary and typically do not exempt liability for intentionally harmful or grossly negligent acts.[10] The federal act preempts state charitable immunity laws unless they provide additional protection from liability.

Indemnification

Although it is rare for a nonprofit trustee to be held personally responsible for monetary judgments for damages caused by the organization or its volunteers, the possibility exists, and it is one that discourages many volunteers from serving on nonprofit boards. Indemnification provisions serve to protect trustees from this risk under certain circumstances and are usually found in an organization's governing documents, but they may also be included in separate contracts between the organization and trustees. In general, indemnification provisions either authorize or require a nonprofit to reimburse a trustee or officer for any judgments, fines, penalties, or amounts paid in settlement and other reasonable expenses (often including attorney's fees and costs of investigations) incurred by the trustee or officer with respect to any threatened or actual legal proceeding that arises because of his or her service to the organization.

Indemnification of trustees or officers may be prohibited in certain circumstances under state law. These circumstances can vary from state to state, but generally include situations where a court establishes (or the board determines) that such person's acts were committed in bad faith, that the acts were the result of intentional dishonesty, or that he or she personally gained a financial profit or other advantage to which he or she was not legally entitled. Usually indemnification is also prohibited when a proceeding is brought against a trustee or officer by the board based on claims of misconduct by the individual.

The determination of whether a trustee or officer may be indemnified may be mandated by a court or, if not court ordered, the board may determine whether and to what extent the organization is permitted to indemnify the individual. In the event the board makes such a determination, a trustee with a personal interest in the outcome, or who is a party to such legal proceeding for which indemnification is sought, must not participate in or vote on the determination of his or her indemnification. If enough disinterested trustees are not available to make the determination, it is recommended that independent legal counsel be retained to determine whether indemnification is proper in the circumstances under applicable law and the organization's governing documents.

Insurance

Liability insurance offers protection against losses and is a crucial risk management tool for nonprofits. General liability insurance coverage protects an organization from third-party claims of personal or bodily injury or property damage due to the organization's negligence or alleged negligence. To cover gaps in general liability coverage, trustees and officers (commonly referred to as director and officer [D&O] insurance) liability insurance is an additional and imperative part of a nonprofit's risk management and enables many organizations to cover costs of required or permissible indemnification payments if and when faced with such an obligation. D&O insurance also protects volunteer board members from personal responsibility in the event that an organization becomes insolvent or in cases where the board refuses to authorize indemnification.[11] Most importantly, the insurance may cover the cost of defending actions, some of which are brought against trustees personally without merit. D&O insurance usually also offers corporate reimbursement, which provides payment on behalf of the organization for losses suffered by the trustees or officers.

Medical Malpractice

Physicians and health care organizations can be held liable for claims related to medical mistakes and quality of care under a theory of medical malpractice. A medical malpractice claim can be brought against health care providers directly and hospitals (or other medical organizations that employ health care providers) under a theory of direct liability or vicarious liability, discussed above. The cause of action is comprised of the basic elements of negligence: the patient-plaintiff must first establish a standard of care that the physician or hospital is required to meet, and then show evidence of a breach of the standard of care due to some unreasonable or careless action that is the cause of injury or damage to the patient. The standard of care applied in each case varies from state to state, but is generally defined as the level of care, skill, and treatment that a reasonably prudent health care provider or hospital would provide in similar circumstances.[12] The board's role in ensuring the provision of quality care in a health care organization, including its key role in credentialing of health care providers, is critical to minimizing the risk of professional liability claims against the organization and its providers.

Other Key Health Care Laws

Regulators' efforts to address fraud and abuse in the health care sector have steadily increased in recent decades in both scope and intensity. With total Medicare expenditures in federal fiscal year (FY) 2006 exceeding $382 billion, the government perceives significant opportunity for fraud and abuse and devotes substantial resources to combating suspect practices. The Health Insurance Portability and Accountability Act of 1996, as amended (HIPAA, better known for its privacy and security provisions, discussed below) established the national Health Care Fraud and Abuse Control (HCFAC) program to coordinate federal, state, and local law enforcement activities with respect to health care fraud and abuse under the joint direction of the U.S. Attorney General and the Secretary of the U.S. Department of Health and Human Services (DHHS), acting through the HHS Office of Inspector General (OIG). In its most recent annual report, HCFAC reported that during FY 2006, the federal government won or negotiated approximately $2.2 billion in judgments and settlements.[5] Several key laws, discussed next, create significant potential liability for health care organizations.

The Federal Antikickback Statute, Civil Monetary Provisions, and Related Fraud and Abuse Provisions

The federal antikickback statute criminalizes certain business transactions in health care. Now in its fourth decade of existence, the antikickback statute provides that whoever "knowingly and willfully" solicits, receives, offers, or pays "any remuneration," directly or indirectly, in return for or to induce the referral of an individual for services payable, in whole or in part, by a federal health care program is guilty of a felony, and may be subject to a fine of up to $25,000 or imprisonment for not more than 5 years, or both.[13] The antikickback statute may also be enforced civilly, with monetary penalties of up to $50,000 and three times the remuneration in question, as well as exclusion from participation in federal health care programs.

The statute's prohibitions possess a staggering potential breadth. Key elements required to provide a violation of the statute are (1) the act of offering, paying, soliciting, receiving, or arranging for (2) remuneration that (3) is done knowingly and willfully and (4) in return for or to induce referrals of federal health care program business. *Remuneration*, under the statute, has been interpreted both administratively—by the HHS, the chief administrative enforcement agency of the statute—and by the courts to mean "anything of value." The knowledge element derives from the general criminal law requirement of *mens rea*, or a "guilty mind," meaning that proving a criminal act generally requires proof of criminal intent. Various courts have differed in their interpretation of the knowledge requirement in the antikickback statute, some requiring that the alleged wrongdoer have specifically known that his or her actions were a violation of the antikickback statute, and others allowing a less specific intent to suffice to prove a violation of the statute (for example, that one purpose among many was to induce referrals). Taken to its logical conclusion, the antikickback statute's proscriptions mean that the offering by any person—whether an individual or a health care institution—of anything of value under circumstances from which it may be logically inferred that the intent was to encourage referrals of federal health care program business is suspect, and potentially a felony.

The statute's breadth has led to enactment of statutory exceptions and regulatory safe harbors. For example, *bona fide* employment relationships and service arrangements within very specifically detailed parameters are permissible. These exceptions and safe harbors afford some guidance, but business transactions outside the scope of the exceptions or safe harbors present risks to health care providers and those who do business with them.

In addition to the provisions of the antikickback statute described above, other federal laws provide for civil monetary penalties for additional actions related to the provision of health care services. Penalties range from $5,000 to $15,000 per prohibited act and apply to the provision of false, fraudulent, or medically unnecessary services. In addition, the Federal Health Insurance Portability and Accountability Act of 1996, as amended (HIPAA, generally best known for its privacy provisions, discussed below), also amended the U.S. Criminal Code to include several new health care offenses, including fraud specifically related to health care. Unlike the antikickback statute, which applies only if federal health care program monies are involved, these new criminal provisions apply to fraud related to both public and private plans.

Because of the knowledge element that must be proven to find a violation of the antikickback statute, trustees of a health care organization are likely to face relatively little risk of a finding of having individually violated the law. In 1995, in the *Hanlester Network v. Shalala* case, the U.S. Court of Appeals for the Ninth Circuit held that vicarious liability could not extend to individual partners in the corporate entities involved because the "knowingly and willfully" requirement of the law required specific intent to violate the law. As noted earlier, other courts have declined to require a specific intent to violate the law; nonetheless, absent clear knowledge of an impermissible arrangement, it is unlikely that a trustee could be viewed as engaging in conduct knowingly and willfully.

However, governing bodies have a clear role to play in ensuring that the health care organizations they govern comply with the antikickback statute and related fraud and abuse provisions. The statute is inherently ambiguous and implicates virtually every transaction involving the exchange of monies—or indeed, anything of value—between a referral source, such as a physician, and the recipient of those referrals, such as hospitals. Policies and procedures should be in place to ensure that all such transactions are appropriately reviewed and have a legitimate purpose unrelated to a desire to induce referrals. Further education as to the requirements of the law is essential.

The Federal Stark Law

In the late 1980s, the federal government's General Accountability Office (GAO) produced a study indicating that physicians who owned clinical laboratories were significantly more likely to refer their patients to those laboratories, resulting in a higher number of claims being submitted to payers, including governmental payers such as Medicare. That empirical evidence—consistently borne out in subsequent reviews—led eventually to the enactment of the federal physician self-referral law, commonly called Stark's law after Congressman Fortney ("Pete") Stark (D-Cal.), who introduced it. Originally reaching only clinical laboratory services, the law eventually expanded to reach, in 1995, a host of other services.

Stark law's prohibitions appear, on their face, to be relatively straightforward. The law provides that any physician who has a "financial relationship," which may be a compensation arrangement or an ownership or investment interest, in an entity may not refer to that entity for the provision of any "designated health service" unless an exception expressly applies. Designated health services (DHSs) include clinical laboratory services, inpatient and outpatient hospital services, radiology services, physical and occupational therapy services, home health services, radiation therapy services, outpatient prescription drugs, durable medical equipment (DME), parenteral and enteral nutrients, equipment and supplies, and prosthetics and orthotics. The Stark law is a civil law only, and its penalties include denial of payment for DHS provided in violation of the law, refund of monies paid for the DHS, civil penalties of up to $15,000 for each service provided in violation of the Stark law, exclusion from the Medicare and Medicaid programs, and civil penalties of up to $100,000 for attempts to circumvent Stark law's proscriptions.

The Stark law differs from the antikickback statute in several key elements. It is not a criminal law and is what is termed a strict liability law. That is, there is no knowledge or intent requirement. Thus, an arrangement entered into without any intention whatsoever to violate the law will be illegal if it entails a referral for a DHS by a physician to an entity with which he or she has a financial relationship that does not fully meet one of the Stark law's exceptions. Unlike the antikickback statute, which applies to any person, the Stark law applies only to referrals by a physician to an entity with which the physician has a financial relationship.

The Stark law contains multiple exceptions. Nonetheless, structuring financial relationships between physicians and the entities to which they refer has become increasingly complex since each financial relationship must comply with Stark law's requirements. Enforcement actions under the Stark law by HHS's Centers for Medicare and Medicaid Services (CMS) and the HHS OIG have been somewhat limited. In recent years, however, federal regulators have taken the position that submission to a governmental health care program of a claim in violation of the federal Stark law may be a false claim in violation of the False Claims Act (FCA), discussed below. Because of the strict liability nature of the Stark law, and the FCA's status as a preferred enforcement tool, this position has significantly raised the stakes for those who may knowingly or unknowingly violate Stark law's proscriptions.

The Federal False Claims Act

The False Claims Act (FCA), a Civil War-era procurement law, has become federal prosecutors' choice in health care fraud cases. The FCA prohibits the knowing submission of a false or fraudulent claim for payment to the U.S. government. In 1986 amendments to the FCA increased penalties, reintroduced the *qui tam* relater provisions described below, and specifically defined what constitutes knowledge for purposes of the FCA. Penalties for violation of the FCA range from $5,500 to $11,000 per claim plus three times the amount of damages sustained by the federal government. The knowledge requirement is statutorily addressed to provide that a person acts knowingly and willfully if he or she (1) has actual knowledge of the information, (2) acts in deliberate ignorance of the truth or falsity of the information, or (3) acts in reckless disregard of the truth or falsity of the information.

The FCA specifically permits a claim under the FCA to be brought not only by the federal government, but also by a private individual, the so-called *qui tam* relater, who has knowledge of the false claim. The *qui tam* relater is entitled to share in any monetary recovery made by the government in disposition of the case, whether through litigation or settlement. This feature of the FCA offers the individual with knowledge of wrongdoing a powerful financial incentive to bring that knowledge forward. The *qui tam* relater is required to initially file the FCA complaint "under seal" in federal court while at the same time serving it on the U.S. Department of Justice (DOJ). The DOJ has a specified period of time in which to determine whether it wishes to intervene and prosecute the case, and if it chooses not to, the relater is free to pursue the case on his or her own. Not surprisingly, cases in which the DOJ chooses not to intervene have a slim likelihood of being successfully prosecuted.

One out of every three dollars recovered through federal false claims actions relates to health care fraud. Government prosecutors use the FCA as a preferred tool because of the threat of treble damages, the specific definition of knowledge, the ability to use *qui tam* relater information, and the generally easier evidentiary standards of the FCA. Recently, government prosecutors have set forth new theories that posit that submission of a claim for poor-quality care may violate the FCA. Thus, the board's oversight responsibilities for quality of care and for ensuring the organization's compliance with applicable laws intersect in a critical area of potential exposure for the organization.

HIPAA's Patient Privacy Protections

Health care providers have multiple sources from which obligations of confidentiality derive—professional ethics, state laws on the confidentiality of patient information, and federal laws affording specific protections for certain information, such as that dealing with mental health or HIV status. In large part, the enactment of HIPAA in 1996 responded to a perceived need for federal protection of electronic information.

Fundamentally, the privacy provisions of HIPAA provide that an individual's protected health information (PHI, essentially meaning any individually identifiable health information) may not be used or disclosed by a covered entity unless either (1) the individual has executed a HIPAA-compliant authorization or (2) HIPAA otherwise permits the use or disclosure. HHS placed enforcement of HIPAA in its Office of Civil Rights (OCR), a reflection of its view that privacy is an individual civil right. Violations of HIPAA's privacy provisions are criminally and civilly punishable, with penalties ranging from $100 (for inadvertent disclosures) to $25,000, and criminal penalties for obtaining information under false pretenses or other egregious violations.

A covered entity is any entity that uses or transmits PHI in electronic form, thus effectively encompassing the overwhelming majority of health care organizations. Covered entities are allowed to use PHI for purposes of treatment, payment, and operations, and for other expressly delineated purposes (e.g., mandated disclosures required by state law, certain law enforcement purposes), but must otherwise obtain an authorization from the individual before using or disclosing the individual's PHI.

As of January 31, 2008, the HHS OCR reported that it had received over 33,277 HIPAA privacy complaints and had resolved three-quarters of those complaints, with investigated and subsequent enforcement action of some kind in 5,653 cases. The OCR had referred 419 cases to the U.S. DOJ for potential criminal investigation, generally cases that involve the alleged knowing disclosure or obtaining of PHI in violation of the law.

Members of a covered entity's board are subject to the requirements of HIPAA's privacy provisions with respect to PHI they may receive as part of their duties as board members. Thus, information received in connection with discussion of and review of quality data, credentialing, and malpractice or other litigation is subject to confidentiality not only as a part of a board member's fiduciary obligations to the organization, but also as a separate matter of federal law.

Conclusion

No matter its size, a health care organization's most valuable asset is its good name. An organization depends on its reputation to instill confidence in the community it serves, and its governing board is charged with ensuring its success. To that end, it is crucial for health care boards to make good governance practices, accountability, transparency in decision making, and high ethical standards a priority. Prioritizing these characteristics allows trustees to fulfill their duties owed to the organizations they serve and to reduce their risks of liability for non-compliance in any of the areas that have been discussed in this chapter.

The governing body of a health care organization is ultimately responsible for directing the actions of the organization. Good governance and ethical practice at the board level drive a corporate culture of compliance and high ethical standards. It is essential that trustees understand their individual and collective obligations under state law and the governing documents of their organization. Trustees should also understand the nature and extent of protection afforded them against any personal liability in connection with their acts as a trustee, including protections available under state or federal law, indemnification from the health care organization, and insurance. Education of board members as to key sources of legal liability for the organization is also critical. Finally, the board should ensure that management clearly understands the board's expectations as to communications between management and the governing body on key areas of liability.

Case Study

You serve as a volunteer member of the board of trustees of a health care organization. Management presented a proposal to the board to open an ambulatory surgical center in a shopping center in a fast-growing area of the community served by the organization. Another board member confides in you after the meeting that he is a passive investor in the company that owns the shopping center. What should you do? What procedures could be employed to allow the board to consider the transaction?

You also serve as the chair of the organization's audit and compliance committee. The organization's general counsel calls to advise you that an investigation by the HHS OIG into the organization's contracting practices has been ongoing for several months and that the OIG has advised the organization that it is making a referral to the DOJ for possible criminal charges. What should you do? What should the board do?

Study and Discussion Questions

1. Does each board member understand the basic legal structure of the organization and his or her obligations under state law and the organization's governing documents?

2. Does each board member understand the sources of protection from individual liability for his or her acts and omissions as a board member, including sources of protection such as all applicable state and federal laws, indemnification by the organization, and insurance?
3. Does the board as a whole understand the key sources of legal liability for the organization as a whole and for individual trustees and officers? How is the board educated as to key applicable laws? What are best practices as to information to be provided by management to the board on sources of liability?

Suggested Reading and Web Sites

Reading

Panel on the Nonprofit Sector. 2007. *Principles for good governance and ethical practice: A guide for charities and foundations.* Washington, DC: Independent Sector.

Web Sites

Federal Emergency Medical Treatment and Labor Act (EMTALA): www.emtala.com
HCPro—Credentialing and Privileging: http://www.hcpro.com/credentialing-privileging/index.cfm
Health Hippo—Policy and Regulation: http://hippo.findlaw.com/hippohome.html
Hospitals and Community Benefits Interim Report by the Internal Revenue Service: www.irs.gov
National Health Law Program: http://www.healthlaw.org/about/
Thurgood Marshall Law Library at the University of Maryland: http://www.law.umaryland.edu/marshall/index.html
U.S. Department of Health and Human Services: http://healthfinder.gov/
U.S. National Library of Medicine—National Institutes of Health: http://locatorplus.gov/
Washburn University School of Law: http://www.washlaw.edu/reflaw/refresearch.html

References

1. Callender, A. N., D. A. Hastings, M. C. Hemsley, L. Morris, and M. W. Peregrine. The Office of Inspector General of the U.S. Department of Health and Human Services and The American Health Lawyers Association. 2007. *Corporate responsibility and health care quality: A resource for health care boards of directors.*
2. American Hospital Association. 2006. *Hospital statistics 2006 annual survey.* http://www.aha.org/aha/resource-center/Statistics-and-Studies/fast-facts.html (accessed on August 22, 2008).

3. Kraakman, R. 2000. Vicarious and corporate civil liability. In *Encyclopedia of law and economics*. Vol. II. *Civil law and economics*, ed. B. Bouckaert and G. De Geest, chap. 3400. Cheltenham: Edward Elgar.

4. *United States v. Stein*. F.Supp.2d, WL 1735260 (S.D.N.Y. June 26, 2006).

5. Department of Health and Human Services. 2007. *The Department of Justice health care fraud and abuse control program annual report for FY 2006*. The Department of Health and Human Services and the Department of Justice.

6. Fishman, J. and S. Schwarz. 2000. *Nonprofit organizations*. 2nd ed. New York: Foundation Press.

7. Bromberger, A., R. Hobish, and L. Yarvis. 1995. In *Advising nonprofits*, chap. 7, 234–38. 4th ed. New York: Lawyers Alliance for New York.

8. Fremont-Smith, M. 2004. *Governing nonprofit organizations: Federal and state law regulation*. Vol. 4. Cambridge, MA: Harvard University Press.

9. Internal Revenue Service, U.S. Department of Treasury. Internal Revenue Code § 4948.

10. Ott, J. S. 2000. *The nature of the nonprofit sector*. Vol. 5. Boulder, CO: Westview Press.

11. Bjorklund, V., J. Fishman, and D. Kurtz. 1997. *New York nonprofit law and practice: With tax analysis*. Vol. 12. Charlottesville, VA: Michie Law Publishers.

12. Hall, M., M. Bobinski, and D. Orentlicher. 2003. *Health care law and ethics*. 6th ed., Vol. 4. New York: Aspen Publishers.

13. The antikickback statute. 42 USC § 1320a-7b(b).

Chapter 10

The Compensation Committee

F. Kenneth Ackerman, Jr.

Contents

Executive Summary

The board is responsible for deciding how executives will be paid. Total compensation for executives typically includes salaries, incentive pay, standard and supplemental benefits, and perquisites. A total compensation philosophy approved by the board is a useful tool to ensure that compensation is administered consistently from year to year. The chief executive officer's (CEO's) compensation is typically documented in an employment contract that also states what severance will be payable following termination.

In addition to board bylaws and policies, the legal requirements for governing executive compensation in tax-exempt health care organizations are contained in Internal Revenue Code (IRC) Sections 501(c)(3) and 4958 and state laws governing nonprofit corporations and charitable trusts.

Section 4958 outlines a process for establishing a "rebuttable presumption of reasonableness" for executive compensation. Boards that follow the process are positioned to assert that pay is reasonable if challenged by regulators or the public.

Learning Objectives

1. To understand how executives are paid, and to appreciate the importance of quantifying total compensation when assessing whether pay is reasonable.
2. To be aware of legal requirements boards must meet in governing executive compensation, and the role of the Internal Revenue Service (IRS) in enforcement.
3. To understand how a good governance process can protect the board from allegations of excessive executive compensation.

Key Words

- Disqualified persons
- Excess benefit transaction
- Form 990
- Intermediate sanctions
- Private inurement
- Rebuttable presumption of reasonableness
- Tally sheets
- Taxpayer Bill of Rights II
- Total compensation
- Transparency

Introduction

Good governance of executive compensation is a matter of finding the right balance between paying enough and paying too much, structuring compensation to align executives' interests with those of stakeholders, and using a disciplined process that helps the board guide the performance of the management team.

The role of the board in governing executive compensation is embedded in the notion of governance and corporate structure. The board of a corporation is charged with overseeing management of the corporation by executives it has the authority to hire and fire. The board is accountable to govern the organization in the best interests of the public. Therefore, it must determine how to pay the organization's managers in order to recruit and retain the talent it needs and to encourage them to manage in the best interest of the stakeholders—patients, physicians, employees, and the community at large—and not in the best interest of the managers. The board has the ultimate responsibility for determining compensation for executives. Most boards delegate this responsibility to a subcommittee focused on executive compensation.

This chapter describes how executives are paid, outlines the board's accountabilities in governing executive compensation, and identifies issues it should consider while making decisions.

Table 10.1 Sample Salary Range with Midpoint of $100,000

Minimum	Midpoint	Maximum
$80,000	$100,000	$120,000

How Executives Are Paid

The standard executive compensation package in hospitals and health systems includes base salary, incentive compensation, standard and supplemental benefits, and perquisites. These may be combined in any number of ways to create total compensation packages that range from bare bones to highly competitive. Some combinations of pay elements place a heavy emphasis on pay-for-performance, while others emphasize security. Some provide more current income, while others provide less cash today but greater income after retirement. Understanding the value of the total compensation package requires understanding the value of each component individually and its contribution to the value of the package as a whole.

Base Salary

Salaries form the basis of the executive compensation package. Salaries can be thought of as the paychecks executives receive. Salary is stated as an annual amount but is paid weekly, biweekly, or monthly. The board or committee that oversees executive compensation will make decisions about salaries once a year, and salaries generally will not change during the year unless an executive's job responsibilities change significantly.

Salaries are administered by determining what the organization is willing to pay a competent and experienced executive for fully satisfactory performance. Executives are paid at or near this level based on a variety of factors, including performance and tenure.

Table 10.1 illustrates a sample salary range with a midpoint of $100,000 and a range of ±20%. An executive who has recently been promoted may be paid between the minimum and midpoint. The top of the range should be used sparingly to deal with unusual circumstances, such as recruiting needs.

Incentive Pay

Incentive pay, or pay-for-performance, is a means of tying executives' self-interests to the goals of the organization. In public companies, incentive pay or

Table 10.2 Annual Incentive Opportunity as a Percentage of Salary

Position	Target Award	Maximum Award
System CEO	25–40%	35–60%
Other System Executives	20–30%	30–45%
Hospital CEO	20–30%	30–45%
Other Hospital Executives	15–20%	20–30%

Table 10.3 Long-Term Incentive Opportunity as a Percentage of Salary

Position	Target Award	Maximum Award
CEO	15%	25%
Other Senior Executives	10%	15%

bonuses usually include stock options, restricted stock, stock appreciation rights, or stock grants that allow executives to benefit directly from increasing the value of the company's stock. In nonprofit health care, there is no stock, so boards must find another way to link executive pay to performance.

Today, more than 80% of health systems and more than 70% of independent hospitals use annual incentives to reward executives for performance.[1] Incentive opportunity typically varies by position, with the CEO having a larger portion of pay at risk than other executives. Some large organizations also use long-term incentives to reward performance over a longer period (usually 3 years). Refer to Tables 10.2 and 10.3 for typical annual and long-term incentive opportunity by position.[1] The board or compensation committee is responsible for setting goals for the incentive plan, measuring performance, and determining what incentive awards will be paid.

In tax-exempt health care, most incentive plans have a financial hurdle that must be surpassed before awards are paid. Once the hurdle is passed, awards are determined by performance on a number of measures. This approach is known as a balanced scorecard.

A typical plan uses a handful of measures covering financial performance, productivity or cost-effectiveness, clinical quality, and service quality. Some plans also use measures of growth or volume; some use employee satisfaction. Incentive plan goals are often tied to the operating or business plan and budget. They are typically based on clear performance measures that can be easily quantified.

Benefits

Benefits form the third part of the executive total compensation package. Executives, like all other employees, are participants in the organization's standard benefit plans including medical, dental, and vision benefits; disability benefits; life insurance; the qualified pension plan and 401(k) and 403(b) deferred compensation plans; and vacation, holidays, and other paid time off. Many of these plans work well for employees at all income levels. But some of the standard benefit plans have built-in restrictions that make them less valuable to executives.

Group insurance benefits include limits on how much income the carrier will insure without proof of good health. For example, a group long-term disability benefit may replace 60% of salary but limit monthly disability payments to $5000. A group term life insurance benefit may provide death benefits of two times salary, but with a maximum of $200,000. Under both of these plans, executives earning more than $100,000 have less of their salary insured than other employees. Employers typically deal with caps in insured benefits by providing executives with supplemental insurance policies.

Retirement is another area where all-employee plans fall short for many executives. Qualified pension plans are limited by law in the amount of income they may use to calculate benefits. The law sets limits on employee pretax contributions to 401(k) and 403(b) plans in a single year. Social security ties retirement income to the social security wage base, currently slightly above $100,000. Tax-exempt employers face more legal restrictions than taxable employers in providing competitive retirement benefits. Nonetheless, most hospitals and health systems have found ways to accomplish this through supplemental executive retirement plans (SERPs) and nonqualified deferred compensation.

Perquisites

Executive perquisites include all those other advantages of having an executive position, some of which are quite valuable. Perquisites tend to be highly visible, which invites negative reactions from employees and the public. Therefore, most hospitals and health systems are eliminating perquisites that do not serve a business purpose, or provide taxable benefit allowances and let executives choose from a limited menu of options.

Certain perquisites remain commonplace in health care, including cars or car allowances, but hospitals limit the number of executives who receive them. Cell phones and personal digital assistants are usually provided to executives out of business necessity. Country club or luncheon club memberships are usually provided only to those who are expected to entertain as a routine part of their work. Personal use must be reimbursed or reported as W-2 income. Memberships in professional organizations and subscriptions to professional publications are usually provided because of their value in keeping executives informed.

Severance

Severance is defined as compensation that continues for a period of time after an executive's employment is terminated. Normally, if an executive retires, leaves voluntarily, or is fired for gross misconduct, no severance is paid. But if executives are terminated for other reasons, including poor performance, they may receive severance to bridge the gap until they find new employment.

Severance payment periods are most often defined by rank or class, so that all executives of the same class receive the same benefits. Severance periods are typically 1 to 2 years for CEOs of independent organizations and 12 months for other executives. Severance periods are often extended for termination connected with a change of control. Severance payments are often offset by income earned in new employment, or may cease altogether on reemployment.

Severance payments typically include more than salary. Many organizations continue benefits for the duration of the severance period or pay their value in cash. Incentive awards at target or based on the prior 3-year average are provided by some organizations. Most provide outplacement services as part of the severance program as well. To receive severance benefits, executives are usually required to release all claims against the employer.

Other Forms of Compensation

Some health care organizations provide retention incentives to encourage executives to stay during times of organizational turmoil. Other, less common forms of compensation include signing bonuses, housing allowances, relocation expenses, and low-interest loans. These are usually individually negotiated when an executive is hired.

Adding It All Up

To understand the value of executive total compensation, it is more important to consider the sum of the parts than the value of each component by itself. The mix of pay can vary widely from one organization to the next. Some organizations emphasize salaries, while others focus more on incentive compensation or provide richer benefits and perquisites. Total compensation packages that look similar on the surface may be quite different when all elements of compensation are valued. Consider these examples:

■ One organization pays average salary and offers an average annual incentive opportunity and standard benefits, with conservative severance.

■ Another organization pays average salary and offers an average annual incentive opportunity, an average long-term incentive opportunity, standard benefits, plus average supplemental benefits and generous severance.

At first, the two packages look the same, if nothing but salary, annual incentive opportunity, and standard benefits are considered. However, with long-term incentives, supplemental benefits, and generous severance, the second package is far more attractive.

Total Compensation Philosophy

Boards or committees charged with making executive compensation decisions find it useful to have a written total compensation philosophy that states the principles upon which compensation decisions are based. Perhaps the most important reason for having a clearly articulated compensation philosophy is to help the board and compensation committee make good decisions and maintain a consistent approach to governing executive compensation year after year. Otherwise, the committee is likely to focus on the size of salary increases, instead of competitiveness with the peer group or the ability to retain talented executives.

The right compensation philosophy is one that allows the board to attract, retain, and reward executives who can lead the organization to achieve its goals, and one that reflects the organization's mission and values. A total compensation philosophy statement includes these elements:

■ A definition of the *peer group* used for comparability studies. Peers should be similar to the organization in size and complexity. Thus, community hospitals will compare themselves to other community hospitals, academic medical centers to academic medical centers, integrated delivery systems to integrated delivery systems, children's hospitals to children's hospitals, and so forth. Most organizations recruit nationally and use national data in comparability studies.

■ The *mix of compensation components* to be provided. Compensation may be limited to salary and standard benefits only, or it may include annual incentives, long-term incentives, supplemental benefits, perquisites, and severance.

■ The target *competitive positioning* of total compensation and each element of compensation in comparison to the peer group. Many organizations intend to provide salaries and benefits at the peer group median or middle, but others target another level. Many organizations offer above-average incentives as a way of positioning total cash above median for outstanding performance.

Performance Evaluation and Its Impact on Compensation

One of the board's most important responsibilities is evaluating the performance of the CEO. The annual performance evaluation is an effective tool for communicating the board's expectations to the CEO, and for determining whether those expectations are being met. Most boards take the CEO's performance evaluation into account in determining salary increases. The board or compensation committee generally evaluates the CEO's performance, but delegates the evaluation of other executives' performance to the CEO. The committee may review the CEO's assessment of executive performance in succession planning and as a part of the process of approving executive salary increases.

Executive Employment Agreements

Once rare, executive employment agreements or contracts have become the norm in hospitals and health systems, at least for the CEO, and sometimes for senior executives as well. In 2006, about 80% of freestanding hospital CEOs and 28% of the CEOs of system-owned hospitals had employment agreements.[2]

The purpose of an executive employment agreement is to define the executive's role in the organization, to convey the board's commitment to the executive, and to provide income security (see "Features of Employment Contracts" box). If termination occurs, the employment agreement specifies how the executive

---

FEATURES OF EMPLOYMENT CONTRACTS

- A contract term, often 3 or 4 years, with provisions for renewal at the end of the initial contract period.
- The executive's title, reporting relationships, duties and responsibilities, and authority.
- The initial compensation to be paid, including salary, incentive opportunity, standard and supplemental benefits, and perquisites, with provisions for annual salary review.
- Definitions of types of terminations, conditions for termination, and the severance benefits payable upon each termination type, for example, death, disability, voluntary termination, termination without cause, termination for cause, change-of-control termination, lapse of contract without renewal.
- A requirement not to compete with the organization, along with a definition of what constitutes competition.

will be notified, what recourse is available, and what severance benefits will be paid after employment ends.

The Regulatory Environment

Nonprofit hospitals and health systems operate in a different legal environment than their counterparts in corporate America. Hospitals are community assets; they exist to serve the needs of their communities. Hospital boards are accountable to their stakeholders—patients, physicians, employees, donors, the community at large—instead of being accountable to stockholders. Both state and federal governments regulate hospitals and health systems in an effort to protect the interests of these stakeholders.

Legal Framework for Governing Executive Compensation

There are four sets of legal requirements for governance of executive compensation in nonprofit health care:

IRC Section 501(c)(3) prohibits giving any individual a right to a portion of the revenues, profits, or assets of a tax-exempt organization. Violation of this prohibition is known as private inurement.[3,4] Section 501(c)(3) prohibits paying more than whatever is reasonable compensation or fair market value, which is generally defined as what a like organization would pay for like services under like circumstances.[5] A tax-exempt organization that is found to have provided unreasonable compensation may be punished with the loss of its tax exemption.[6]

IRC Section 4958 implements the Taxpayer Bill of Rights II passed by Congress in 1996. It authorizes fines when an organization engages in private inurement by paying too much, selling assets for too little, or basing pay on revenues.[7,8] The financial penalties under Section 4958 are known as intermediate sanctions because they fall short of the ultimate sanction, revocation of tax exemption. Section 4958 also defines a process for establishing a "rebuttable presumption of reasonableness" that shifts the burden of proof to the IRS and, in effect, makes it unlikely that the IRS would challenge the reasonableness of pay.[9]

State laws governing nonprofit corporations typically list the determination of pay for the CEO as one of the board's duties. The laws sometimes authorize payment of reasonable compensation, thereby prohibiting payment of unreasonable compensation, like IRC Sections 501(c)(3) and 4958.

State laws governing charitable trusts establish a principle that some states' courts and attorneys general are extending to nonprofit corporations—that the organization's resources may not be misused by diverting funds to executive compensation that should be used instead to provide services to beneficiaries. In the past, most courts have held directors of nonprofits to the far more lenient standard of making reasonable business decisions.

The organization's own bylaws and policies are not regulations or legal requirements, but corporations are required by state law to follow them. Bylaws typically say something about governance of executive compensation. They may delegate this to a compensation committee, or they may require the board as a whole to act on it. Most boards define the rules for governing executive compensation in the committee charter, a charge to the compensation committee, or a policy statement defining how decisions should be made.

Recent Regulatory Developments

Several recent regulatory initiatives are having an impact on the governance of executive compensation. In for-profit corporations, new guidelines have come from the Sarbanes-Oxley Act of 2002 (SOX), the Securities and Exchange Commission (SEC), and a host of other organizations focused on governance. While none of these apply directly to tax-exempt organizations, they influence the thinking of health system boards and tend to reinforce the governance standards contained in the Taxpayer Bill of Rights II.

More important for tax-exempt health care is the oversight exercised by the Internal Revenue Service, Congress, and state attorneys general. In 2004 and 2005, the IRS conducted abbreviated audits of executive compensation practices at roughly 1200 hospitals and health systems. These were followed in 2006 with a survey of 550 hospitals to assess compliance with its rules about compensation governance. These studies found that high compensation levels were generally substantiated based on appropriate comparability data. However, they also found that 15% of tax-exempts were not reporting executive pay correctly on Forms 990 and W-2, and half of tax-exempts were not meeting the requirements to establish the rebuttable presumption of reasonableness. The studies resulted in financial penalties in excess of $21 million. Issues were excessive compensation, vacation homes, personal legal fees, and other corporate payment of personal expenses.

The Government Accountability Office, at the request of the House Ways and Means Committee, recently surveyed 100 health care organizations, asking about their structure and basis for determining executive compensation, and about the process in place for approving and monitoring executive perquisites. The survey was designed to uncover ineffective governance, inadequate controls, and inappropriate forms of compensation. While the study found widespread indicators of good governance, it also found widespread use of supplemental benefits and perquisites and some questionable practices in reimbursement of travel and entertainment expenses.[10]

Concurrently, the IRS conducted a study of charity care and community benefits provided by nonprofit hospitals and found widely varying levels of charity care. Twenty percent of hospitals reported spending 10% or more of net revenues on uncompensated care, while 45% reported spending less than 3%, and 22% reported spending less than 1% on uncompensated care.[11]

In 2006, the Senate Finance Committee, which exercises oversight of nonprofit organizations, conducted hearings on charity care and community benefits that focused on the criteria used to grant tax-exempt status to nonprofit hospitals. The hearings followed a survey of 10 major nonprofit hospitals asking a series of questions about their care of the poor and service to the community. The committee chairman used the hearings to call attention to executive compensation and benefits practices and to express his intention to seek reforms.[12]

Attorneys general in several states have stepped up enforcement activity under state charitable trust statutes. In Minnesota, the attorney general forced the breakup of the state's largest integrated health system and replaced its board. The attorneys general of Kansas and Missouri sued over the sale of a nonprofit system to an investor-owned corporation, resulting in reduced severance for the CEO and appointment of a new foundation board to oversee proceeds of the sale. In Ohio, the attorney general sought unsuccessfully to implement limitations on executive compensation at nonprofits. In Illinois, New Hampshire, and Pennsylvania, local jurisdictions have challenged the legality of property tax exemptions for hospitals.

All of this activity suggests that executive compensation may be more strictly regulated in the future. Boards need to take seriously their responsibility for setting executive compensation and ensuring that it is reasonable, to reduce the potential for public criticism, financial penalties, and loss of tax exemption.

New Form 990 Reporting Requirements

Form 990 is an annual report to the IRS that must be filed by tax-exempt organizations. A new Form 990, the first major redesign in 30 years, will take effect in 2009 for reporting 2008 activities. The new form requires more detailed reporting of executive compensation than in the past. Questions about compensation governance, collection practices, charity care policies, and community benefit have been added. The content of the questions being asked on the new form suggests there may be increased scrutiny by regulators and the media in the future.

The general structure of Form 990 is a main form followed by 16 schedules, depending on the organization's structure and activities.

Compensation Governance

An entire section of the Form 990 is dedicated to governance. It poses 16 "yes-or-no" questions, several of which address compensation practices. Beyond conflicts of interest, keeping of minutes, and whistleblower policies, the form asks if the process for determining compensation of the CEO and other officers and key employees included a review and approval by independent persons, comparability data, and contemporaneous substantiation of the deliberation and decision. It also asks for a description of the process.

Schedule J contains other compensation governance questions, such as written reimbursement policies and the basis for determining the CEO's compensation (i.e., compensation surveys, independent consultants, or approval by the board or committee).

Compensation Reporting

All organizations must report basic compensation information in the body of Form 990 for the following listed individuals:

- Current officers, trustees, and key employees
- Current five highest-compensated employees who earned more than $100,000
- Former officers, key employees, or highest-compensated employees who received more than $100,000
- Former trustees who received more than $10,000

This main form requires reporting of three compensation amounts for each listed individual:

- W-2 or 1099 compensation paid by the organization
- W-2 or 1099 compensation paid by related organizations
- Estimated amount of other compensation from the organization and related organizations

Schedule J requires reporting of compensation in much greater detail than the main form. The reporting is both qualitative and quantitative. The organization must first check the box for any of the following that it provides:

- First class, charter, or companion travel
- Tax indemnification or gross-up payments
- Discretionary spending account

- Housing allowance or residence for personal use
- Payments for business use of personal residence
- Health or social club dues or initiation fees
- Personal services (e.g., maid, chauffeur, chef)
- Approval by the board or compensation committee

The organization must also provide, in narrative form, the details of severance or change-of-control payments, SERPs, equity-based compensation arrangements, compensation contingent on revenues or net earnings, other non-fixed payments, and any arrangement covered by an exception to intermediate sanctions for initial contracts.

Finally, Schedule J requires details about the compensation paid to each listed individual in table format, with columns for each of the following:

- W-2 compensation
- Deferred compensation
- Nontaxable benefits
- Total of all such amounts
- Compensation reported on prior Form 990

Establishing a Rebuttable Presumption of Reasonableness

Tax-exempt status has always been contingent on avoiding private inurement. Paying executives more than fair market value has always been forbidden as a form of private inurement. When the Taxpayer Bill of Rights II was passed in 1996, it did not change the prohibition on excessive compensation, but it gave the IRS new sanctions to enforce the prohibition. In addition to the ultimate sanction—revocation of tax-exempt status—the IRS can now impose civil fines on persons receiving excessive compensation, and on the decision makers who approved the arrangements.

What Is a Rebuttable Presumption of Reasonableness and Why Is It Important?

Section 4958 implementing the Taxpayer Bill of Rights II authorizes the IRS to impose financial penalties on the recipient of an "excess benefit transaction" and on any manager or board member who knowingly authorizes such a transaction.

Fortunately, the regulations under Section 4958 also outline steps a board may take to establish a "rebuttable presumption of reasonableness" for the cash compensation, benefits, and perquisites provided to influential individuals. This legal presumption is important because it shifts the burden of proof to the government. Prior to the passage of intermediate sanctions legislation, the burden was always with the organization.

An excess benefit transaction arises when a tax-exempt organization provides an economic benefit to a disqualified person if the value of the benefit provided exceeds the value of the consideration the tax-exempt organization receives in return. Types of excess benefit include:

- *Unreasonable compensation*: Paying individuals more than the value of services received.
- *Revenue-based compensation*: Paying individuals based on revenues in a manner that results in private inurement.
- *Bargain sales*: Paying more for assets than they are worth, or selling them for less than they are worth.

Failing to disclose all compensation correctly on W-2 and 990 forms, as required by law, causes undisclosed compensation to be deemed an excess benefit transaction, even if the compensation is otherwise reasonable.

Who Are Disqualified Persons?

A *disqualified person* is any person who is in a position to exercise substantial influence over the affairs of the organization, or was in such a position within the preceding 5 years, a family member of such a person, or an entity, at least 35% of which is owned by a person or family member of a person in a position to exercise substantial influence over the affairs of an organization.

A person is deemed to be in a position to exercise substantial influence over the affairs of the organization if that person holds any of these powers, responsibilities, or interests:

- Voting member of the governing board.
- Any person who, regardless of title, has ultimate responsibility for implementing the decisions of the governing body or for supervising the management, administration, or operations of the organization (i.e., president, CEO, chief operating officer [COO]).
- Any person who, regardless of title, has ultimate responsibility for managing the finances of the organization (i.e., chief financial officer [CFO], treasurer).

A person who does not fit into one of these categories may still be a disqualified person, depending on facts and circumstances indicating substantial influence. These relevant facts and circumstances tend to show substantial influence:

- Being a substantial contributor to the organization.
- Receiving compensation based on revenues derived from the organization's activities, or from a particular department or function of the organization that the person controls.
- Having or sharing authority to control or determine a substantial portion of the organization's capital expenditures, operating budget, or compensation for employees.
- Managing a discrete segment or activity of the organization that represents a substantial portion of the activities, assets, income, or expenses of the organization as a whole.

Some physicians will be deemed disqualified because they meet one of the definitions for automatic inclusion (board service or management responsibility). Others will be deemed disqualified because they meet a facts and circumstances test. Officers of medical staff, chiefs of service, medical directors, heavy admitters, and busy surgeons may be disqualified persons. Boards need to be aware of the potential for physicians to be considered disqualified persons under Section 4958, especially when considering revenue-based compensation for physicians.

Certain individuals are deemed not to be disqualified persons. These include individuals who have taken a *bona fide* vow of poverty on behalf of a religious organization, are contractors who provide professional advice, are directly supervised by persons who are not disqualified persons, do not participate in management decisions, or are not highly compensated.

Steps to Establish the Rebuttable Presumption

Tax-exempt organizations can create a rebuttable presumption of reasonableness by meeting these three criteria:

1. Compensation must be approved by an independent board. *Independence* means that no board member may be related to, or under the control of, a disqualified person. The board may delegate responsibility for approval to a committee made up entirely of independent directors, as long as the committee is duly authorized to approve such transactions.

2. Board or committee approval of compensation arrangements must be based on appropriate comparability data representing total compensation (i.e., salary, incentive compensation, benefits, and perquisites). The following types of comparability data may be used:
   - Compensation paid by comparable organizations, taxable as well as tax-exempt, for functionally comparable positions
   - Compensation patterns or norms in the organization's immediate locale
   - Compensation surveys by nationally recognized independent firms
   - Written offers of employment from other firms
3. Boards must adequately document the basis for their determinations in contemporaneous minutes.

Boards that adopt a streamlined process for reviewing and approving total compensation for all executives, paid board members, influential employees, and others who may be deemed disqualified persons will find that it is not overly burdensome. Boards that make their minutes as good as their approval processes will gain significant protection upon audit by federal or state authorities.

Transparency

The Taxpayer Bill of Rights II began a movement toward requiring greater transparency around executive compensation in hospitals and health systems. The movement gained momentum with the new SEC rules for publicly traded corporations. The new Form 990 makes it clear that transparency is no longer optional. At the same time, the Internet is making it easy for almost anyone to view and compare 990s and draw their own conclusions.

Transparency surrounding executive compensation means giving the full board enough information about how executives are paid, why they are paid as they are, and the process by which decisions have been made to exercise fiduciary responsibility. Transparency also means disclosing enough information to the general public to give them confidence that decisions are being made in the best interests of the organization and its constituents by people who know what they are doing and have no financial stake in the outcome.

What the Full Board Needs to Know

The board has the ultimate responsibility for ensuring that executive compensation is fair and reasonable and represents an appropriate use of the organization's resources, even if it has delegated the responsibility to a compensation committee. Therefore, the board should receive a complete update on executive compensation every year. Discussion with the board should focus on these issues:

- What is the total compensation philosophy guiding executive compensation decisions?
- What peer group is used for making comparisons to the market?
- Who is authorized to make compensation decisions at each executive level?
- How is the CEO's performance reflected in the annual salary increase?
- How were annual incentive awards determined? What were the goals, and how did the organization perform on those goals?

The full board should review total compensation for the CEO and the executive compensation program as a whole. Many boards will review total compensation for senior executives as well. Tally sheets, a tool for taxable corporations under the new SEC regulations, provide a useful format for communicating total compensation information to the board (Figure 10.1).

The full board should review the tables on executive compensation in Form 990 each year before it is published. The redesigned Form 990 will make it easier for the IRS to identify outliers constituting excess benefit transactions. Boards need to be prepared to offer cogent explanations of how executive pay is determined, including explanations of the compensation philosophy, the expertise and independence of the members making compensation decisions, and the process followed to establish a rebuttable presumption of reasonableness.

Responding to Media Inquiries

The annual newspaper article about executive salaries has become a tradition in most communities. Having a written explanation of how executives are paid is a good way of preparing for media inquiries. Providing logical explanations that people can understand and support helps to defuse controversy. The written statement may also be appended to Form 990, posted on the organization's Web site, and published in the employee newsletter.

Even if a board chooses not to publish a written statement, it should think through the issues and know how to present its case to the public. It should also appoint a spokesperson to answer questions from the media, and instruct all board members and executives to refer questions to the spokesperson. Choosing the board chair or chair of the compensation committee as spokesperson reinforces the principle that compensation decisions are made by the board. The CEO or other executives should not be put in the position of defending their own compensation to the press.

Executive name: _____   Executive title: _____

Program Component	Employer Annual Cost			
	2 Years Ago	Year Ago	Current Year	
	Actual	Actual	Target Potential	Maximum Potential
Total Compensation				
Salary				
Annual incentive award				
Long-term incentive award				
Statutory benefits (FICA, FUTA)				
Standard all-employee benefits				
Supplemental benefits				
- Life insurance				
- Disability insurance				
- Retirement contributions				
Perquisites				
- Auto allowance				
- Professional dues				
- Home computer				
Total Compensation				

Severance payable for termination without cause	This year	End of contract
2 years' salary		
2 years' annual incentives at target		
2 years' statutory benefits		
2 years' standard benefits		
2 years' supplemental benefits		
Total severance benefits		

Retirement benefits payable for termination now	Lump Sum	Annual Income	% Final Average Salary
Qualified pension plan			
401(k) employer match			
Social security (employer share)			
SERP			
Total			

Retirement benefits payable at age 65	Lump Sum	Annual Income	% Final Average Salary
Qualified pension plan			
401(k) employer match			
Social security (employer share)			
SERP			
Total			

Figure 10.1   Sample tally sheet.

Best Practices in Governing Executive Compensation

In the years since the Taxpayer Bill of Rights II became law, health care boards have changed the way they make decisions about executive compensation in order to establish the rebuttable presumption of reasonableness and reduce the risk of sanctions. Over time, a consensus has emerged on best practices in governance of executive compensation. While these practices are not specifically required by law, they are the most important things the board of a hospital or system can do to ensure good governance of executive compensation:

- Establish a compensation committee, give it an explicit charge, define the process to be followed, and expect it to meet at least three times a year. Do not let any insider (executive or physician) sit on this committee.
- Establish a clear and explicit compensation philosophy and a set of policies to guide decisions, and provide an internal standard for evaluating practices.
- Follow established compensation philosophy and policies in making decisions. When making exceptions, document the rationale for the decisions clearly.
- Evaluate every enhancement to executive compensation in terms of the impact on total compensation. Document the deliberation and articulate the rationale for the change in minutes.
- Require a thorough review of the executive compensation program in full every 2 or 3 years. Document the review carefully, demonstrating diligence in evaluating all details of the program with reference to competitive practices.
- Require full disclosure of all elements of compensation, including severance and retirement obligations.
- Charge the committee with reviewing compensation for all executives and employed physician leaders periodically. Do not limit its purview to CEO compensation.
- Use a consultant to gather data on competitive practices. Do not rely on corporate staff and have the board or compensation committee engage the consultant directly. Have the consultant report directly to the board or committee—not through the CEO.
- Establish clear policies on reimbursement of executives' business expenses and enforce them. Ask the auditor to report directly to the board on this.
- Charge the compensation committee with reviewing nonmonetary rewards and perquisites for executives, physicians, and board members. Consider the likelihood of public criticism for using corporate resources for these purposes.
- Have the board and committees meet regularly in executive session.
- Strengthen the board by recruiting members who have the capability of leading the compensation committee, and assign members who understand

performance metrics well enough to guide goal setting and oversee incentive compensation.

- Educate board or committee members on the legal requirements for governance of executive compensation, and make sure they have access to all the information they need to do a good job.
- Be proactive in communicating executive compensation in a positive way to the board, physicians, employees, and the community.

Whenever physicians or other providers are members of health care boards, the conversation about compensation can become a challenge. If a provider is employed by an institution and serves on its board, participating in compensation decisions could be regarded as a conflict-of-interest. Trustees with dual interests should recuse themselves from compensation discussions, just as they would if they had dual interests in quality, as discussed in Chapter 4. Maintaining board credibility and integrity is of paramount importance, making potential conflicts of interest a serious concern for boards to consider when defining trustee roles and committee assignments.

Conclusion

Boards today govern executive compensation in an environment of increasing oversight, scrutiny, and criticism from federal and state regulators and the general public. The board must hire and retain good leaders in order to fulfill the organization's mission and vision, and to operate effectively and efficiently in times when the organization is challenged to provide higher quality of care at a lower cost. This requires hospitals and health systems to pay competitively.

Health care boards need to take advantage of the protection afforded by the rebuttable presumption of reasonableness. They should follow the steps required to establish the rebuttable presumption, including carefully documenting the basis for decisions in minutes and ensuring that all forms of compensation are reported correctly on Forms 990 and W-2. Boards that fail to do so leave themselves and executives exposed to financial penalties, and leave their organizations exposed to the possible loss of tax exemption.

Fortunately, establishing and maintaining a rebuttable presumption of reasonableness is not difficult. Most boards or compensation committees are already doing most of the things they need to do to meet the requirements. Boards that adopt best practices in governing executive compensation and establish the rebuttable presumption of reasonableness will demonstrate their commitment to ongoing improvement of governance and leadership practices.

Case Study

A large integrated health care system was criticized by Minnesota's attorney general for shortcomings in governance of executive compensation. The attorney general referred to the standards for establishing a rebuttable presumption of reasonableness under Section 4958 as a safe harbor, standards that the organization did not meet. His report cited these faults:

- Inadequate oversight of executive compensation and inadequate documentation of the basis for making executive compensation decisions.
- An overly broad compensation philosophy and use of an inappropriate peer group for setting pay levels.
- Failure to consider all elements of compensation in combination when evaluating reasonableness.
- Reliance on internal management to provide comparability data.
- Highly visible perquisites, such as auto allowances, golf club memberships, retention and severance agreements, reimbursement of personal expenses as if they were business expenses, and off-site retreats that appeared to serve little business purpose.
- Payment of incentive awards even when performance did not meet standards established at the beginning of the year.

Compensation at the organization was, in fact, reasonable and well within the bounds of competitive practice among nonprofit health care systems of its size and complexity. This was not clear, however, because the documentation was inadequate and did not come close to establishing a rebuttable presumption of reasonableness. Given the size and prominence of the system, its pay levels may have looked excessive to an IRS auditor. Absent a rebuttable presumption of reasonableness, it could be difficult to avoid intermediate sanctions.

Had the compensation committee followed its own rules, insisted on getting comparability data directly from consultants, then articulated the rationale for its decisions and documented those decisions in minutes, the attorney general would have had much less to criticize.

Study and Discussion Questions

1. Discuss why using comparability data compiled by management was cited as a problem by the attorney general. Do you

believe this would be a problem in establishing a rebuttable presumption of reasonableness under Section 4958?

2. Discuss why paying incentive awards when performance did not meet standards established at the beginning of the year was cited as a problem. Do you believe the board could have approved paying awards in a manner that would have satisfied the requirements for a rebuttable presumption of reasonableness? What would this have required?

Suggested Readings and Web Sites

Readings

American College of Healthcare Executives. 2007. *Executive employment contracts and performance evaluations.* CEO White Paper. Chicago.

Bjork, D. A. 2004. *Strengthening governance in hospitals and health systems: A survey of governance reform initiatives in not-for-profit hospitals and health systems.* Board Committee Performance (American Government and Leadership Group Monograph Series), pp. 8–18. Chicago: Center for Healthcare Governance. (Originally published by American Governance and Leadership Group.)

Bjork, D. A. 2007. *Clarifying expectations: A first step in developing truly effective relationships between CEOs and trustees.* Collaborative Leadership Tools for CEOs (American Government and Leadership Group Monograph Series). Chicago: Center for Healthcare Governance.

Bjork, D. A. and D. J. Fairley. 2003. *Implications for the compensation committee: What the new corporate accountability guidelines suggest not-for-profit health care organizations should do to strengthen governance of executive compensation* (American Government and Leadership Group Monograph Series). Chicago: Center for Healthcare Governance.

Bjork, D. A. and D. J. Fairley. 2006. *Creating a culture of collaborative leadership between boards and CEOs: A practical guide for trustees* (American Government and Leadership Group Monograph Series). Chicago: Center for Healthcare Governance.

Bjork, D. A., D. J. Fairley, and K. S. McManus. 2004. *Healthcare governance in an era of reform* (American Government and Leadership Group Monograph Series). Chicago: Center for Healthcare Governance.

Flannery, T. and D. Hofrichter. 2007. What's the right incentive compensation plan? *Trustee* 60:22–26.

Justice, J. 2007. Determining executive compensation is a big responsibility. *Healthcare Executive* 22:24–26.

Peregrine, M. W. September 25, 2007. Smithsonian controversy spawns "second generation" best practices. (Vol: Tax Notes). *Tax Analysts.*

Peregrine, M. W., R. E. DeJong, T. J. Cotter, and K. Hastings. Summer 2006. Is the job getting harder? Updated guidance for the board's executive compensation committee. White paper. San Diego, CA: The Governance Institute.

Web Sites

American College of Healthcare Executives: www.ache.org
Center for Healthcare Governance: www.americangovernance.com
The Governance Institute: www.governanceinstitute.com
Integrated Healthcare Strategies: www.ihstrategies.com

References

1. Integrated Healthcare Strategies. 2007. *Healthcare executive compensation survey.* pp. 30–40. Minneapolis, MN.
2. American College of Healthcare Executives. 2007. *Executive employment contracts and performance evaluations.* p. 3. Chicago.
3. IRC § 501(c)(3).
4. Treas. Reg. § 1.501(c)(3)-1(c)(2).
5. Treas. Reg.§1.162-7(b)(3).
6. *Harding Hospital, Inc. v. United States,* 505 F.2d 1068 (6th Cir. 1974).
7. IRC § 4958(c)(1)(A), (c)(2).
8. Treas. Reg. § 53.4958-4(a).
9. Treas. Reg. § 53.4958-6.
10. Government Accountability Office. 2006. *Non-profit hospital systems: Survey on executive compensation policies and practices.*
11. Hospital Compliance Project Interim Report. July 19, 2007. *Tax Analysts.*
12. Press release by Senator Charles E. Grassley (R-Iowa), Chairman, U.S. Senate Committee on Finance. September 12, 2006.

Chapter 11

Dealing with Donors

Frederick Ruccius

Contents

Executive Summary

As hospitals face the challenge of funding programs and as reimbursements for services are decreasing, philanthropy becomes central to program enhancement. Traditionally, most boards have seen fundraising as an ancillary duty of trusteeship. Trustees have been more interested in budgets, policies, and governance issues. Fundraising is foreign to the people who are asked to serve on boards. However, board members are increasingly being asked to expand their role in the fundraising program. Not only are board members being asked for personal contributions, but they are also being asked to participate in fundraising with the development staff of the hospital or health care system.

Health care professionals who serve on boards provide a unique and valuable resource to the fundraising effort. Not only do they bring their community contacts to the table, but their understanding and knowledge of the health care system and their patients are invaluable to the development process.

Learning Objectives

1. To understand the emerging role and importance of fundraising as a trustee duty.
2. To understand the development process of identifying, qualifying, cultivating, and soliciting gifts.
3. To become conversant with the emerging types of gift arrangements that expand the opportunities for giving.
4. To learn how a trustee can support and enhance fundraising activity in cooperation with the professional staff.
5. To understand the special role that a health care professional can play in the development process, as well as the possible conflicts of interest that may arise.

Key Words

- Assignment of income
- Charitable gift annuity
- Charitable lead trust
- Charitable remainder trust

- Development process
- Gifts of appreciated securities
- Health Insurance Portability and Accountability Act (HIPAA) fundraising regulations
- Matching gift

Introduction

As a member of the fundraising team, health care providers who also serve as trustees are in a unique position to interpret and promote the goals of the institution. They can articulate the strategic plans and vision for the hospital that comes from participation on the board, while transforming the organization's goals into action. Their perspective is valuable for the prospective donor.

Recently, fundraising has emerged as a professional endeavor with its own standards and processes. Fundraising is more than asking for money; it is a process of identifying the proper prospects, researching their backgrounds, cultivating their interests, soliciting gifts, and stewarding them through the process of making a donation. In this chapter, these fundraising stages will be outlined, and the role of the provider trustee will be described. It is vital that the health care provider board member learn solicitation techniques so that he or she can be a more effective partner of the organization's fundraising professionals.

Expectations of the Health Professional as Board Member

While being appointed to a board of trustees is an honor, it also carries with it significant responsibility. Increasingly, that responsibility includes a role not only as a contributor, but also as a solicitor of funds for the institution. These two roles are not mutually exclusive but are interdependent.

The Board Member as Donor

The first question that community members and other prospects often ask, when approached about a gift, is: What is the board doing? Across America, boards of trustees have been progressively moving toward asking board members to participate fully in making an annual gift, as well as participation in any major gift program.

Expectations vary from institution to institution, but increasingly, minimum standards are being set and communicated to potential trustees. In a survey conducted by the Philanthropy Leadership Council in May 2007, 98 respondents representing both hospitals and academic medical centers reported on minimum gifts required of trustees. Both the 25th percentile and the median number of institutions required a minimum gift of $1,000. The 75th percentile required $2,500, and the maximum was $100,000.[1] The trend continues to move toward standardizing financial expectations for board members. Boards that have not demonstrated a commitment to standardizing financial expectations have a questionable commitment to fundraising, and trustees who have not made significant gifts are not good recruits for the development process.

When a trustee is a member of the team asking for a gift, the trustee should have made his or her own commitment to the campaign. A prospective donor wants to know that the person asking for a donation believes in the cause as demonstrated by a personal commitment. A donor needs to know that the trustee has a passion for the work of the hospital and its place in the community. That commitment is evident in the way the trustee speaks about the hospital and how the message is transmitted to the prospect. The forces that drive the trustee's commitment should be apparent to the potential donor. The enthusiasm goes a long way toward convincing a prospect that the trustee is sincere and that the institution is worthy of investment.[2] In the best of all scenarios, the trustee making an "ask" has made a gift at the same level that he or she is requesting. That is not always possible, but trustees should make a gift that is commensurate with their position in the community.

The Provider as Donor

While it is essential for trustees to make financial commitments to the hospital, it is doubly as important that a provider who is employed at the institution make a commitment to its mission and priorities. A prospective donor would certainly question why someone who is both a trustee and a provider does not financially support the hospital. If someone who is not an insider is asked to support the institution, it would be expected that those who know the most about the institution would support its mission with their philanthropy.

The Development Committee

While all members of the board are important to the fundraising effort, the development committee sets the direction of the program. The purpose of the development committee is not simply to set policy and approve campaigns; it can help the board identify prospects and direct the fundraising program. Too often, the development committee has not been viewed as one of the most desirable positions within the board structure. Activity on the development committee is foreign to most board members and often needs demystification. The first step in this process is fostering an understanding of the development process and the types of gifts that donors use to fulfill their commitments.

The Development Process

The development process consists of five stages: identification of prospects, qualification, cultivation, solicitation and close, and donor stewardship. The health care professional who is a trustee can participate effectively in each stage.

Identification of Prospects

There are several methods used to identify prospects that have the resources and desire to make a significant contribution to the work of the institution. Many organizations have used mail solicitation as a way to gain annual support as well as to identify prospects. Some organizations have tracked response rates to an annual fund solicitation in relation to the length of time since hospitalization. As expected, the response rate diminishes with time after discharge. A study of donor responses has recently shown that in the 30- to 90-day range, the response rate was 1.28%. After 120 days following hospitalization, the response rate fell to 0.88%. Solicitation timing as related to the date of care is essential. These findings underscore the need to respond quickly to potential donors after they have been discharged home.[3]

Much has been written about HIPAA regulations and their relationship to fundraising and patient privacy. Generally, the law provides that the development office can know contact information and dates of service, but not diagnosis. Mailings to patients that do not reference diagnosis or treatment information are acceptable. Any communication to a patient must include a statement that informs the patient of a choice to opt out of future communications by sending a written notice to the hospital. Many institutions include statements in their privacy policies that inform the patient that demographic information may be used in fundraising activity.[4] Once a gift is given, the donor can be contacted and usually is willing to discuss why he or she made the gift. The donor's motivation for giving a gift is valuable information that allows for further program cultivation.

Once a patient makes a gift through the mail campaign, it is imperative that the organization follow up on the gift soon after it arrives. A personal visit is the most effective way to assess interest and begin to gather information about personal resources. Hospital development staff may have the time to make these visits, but the ability to secure a visit is dependent on connection with the donor. Trustees and volunteers often have a personal relationship with the donor and are able to secure the meeting.

A donor who has made a gift should be moved to the next level of giving through personal interaction, and it is during this meeting that the trustee is most valuable to the process. In a recent study, which tracked the response rate to initial calls for an appointment with a prospect, a volunteer was successful 90% of the time when he or she called for an appointment. When development staff called they were successful 10% of the time in two instances and 40% of the time in another.[1]

People are at times more willing to meet with trustees than with development officers since they regard the trustee as a peer and person of importance with insider information. When people donate to nonprofit institutions (especially when they make a large gift) understanding the inner workings and being privy to information is important to them. Information is perceived to be more available in conversations with trustees than with the development officer.

An attraction to new prospects is the likelihood of learning inside information and having access to leadership. A trustee can use his or her network to bring people not previously affiliated with the institution in contact with those leaders. A technique that has had significant success in many programs is the small dinner or breakfast meeting initiated by a trustee. The trustee invites up to a dozen colleagues and people with means to support the organization to hear hospital leadership speak of their vision for the future and how they plan to accomplish their goals. Personal stories from a trustee or patient who has received care at the institution reinforce the vision better than words alone. The setting provides the prospects with an opportunity to ask questions and will help identify their area of interest. It is important that a development professional is present to meet the participants and begin to build the relationships vital to further cultivation as well as document the conversations. They will then help the trustee to plan the next steps for cultivation.

Following the meeting, the trustee should call and thank the potential donor for his or her attendance and follow up on areas of interest. A tour of the facility and witnessing providers at work can help to cement the interest. Use of the development professional can be integral in executing the plan, and the development professional should be seen as a partner to the trustee in the cultivation process.

Peer-to-peer interaction is integral to major gift fundraising. A person capable of making a major gift is more comfortable talking to someone who has both made a similar gift and may be a peer in business or in the community.

Trustees have a special kind of influence with prospects. They stand apart from development professionals and hospital administrators in that there is no tie (direct or indirect) between the finances of the institution and their paychecks.

For this reason, prospects see trustees as true "honest brokers" in the cultivation process. In addition, among all institutional representatives involved in cultivation, trustees are often top prospects' only true social or professional peers, and have particular credibility on that basis alone. Finally, trustees typically have connections with a far greater number of potential top donors than anyone else associated with the hospital. Therefore, they play a vital role in forging relationships and realizing gifts that would never happen in their absence.[5]

Health care professionals who treat members of the community can have a particularly significant role in identifying prospects. They see people during their treatment and are aware of outcomes and level of gratitude. In those circumstances, communication with development professionals at the hospital will speed the process. Participation by the health care professional as a part of the development team may raise some questions in the provider's mind. However, it is not a conflict if the provider mentions to a patient that the institution can provide better care or support research with enhanced funding. If the patient responds affirmatively, asking if he or she would be willing to meet to further discuss options is not a betrayal of trust; it allows the patient the opportunity to help the community.

Qualification

Once an individual has been identified through a gift or individual referral, most development offices use the services of a development researcher who can ascertain the background of a donor from public records (i.e., gifts to other organizations, publicly held stock, boards on which they serve, real estate values, and salary [if published]). This information, coupled with a personal visit, helps the institution begin to shape a plan for further cultivation.

Development professionals by nature tend to be optimistic and want to see future potential in donor prospects. Trustees interact with community prospects through various business and social activities. They can be essential to the development process by providing information on their interests and financial situation. They may move in similar circles and know their interests and personal information, such as:

- Is there a history of a medical condition in their family that might cause them to want to support research or patient care?
- How is their business doing and how much is it worth?
- What other interests exist and how can they be linked to the institution?
- Are there any extenuating circumstances that would preclude a gift at this time?
- Are they connected with another medical center?
- Who is the best person to cultivate the relationship?[5]

The health care professional who is a trustee may be privy to confidential health information unavailable to other trustees. Knowledge of a prospect's health issues is clearly not required for all participants in the development process, but the provider, as a trusted member of the community, adds to the credibility of the solicitation team. The provider's dual role is to protect private information and be a spokesperson for the institution who is available to answer questions about how the prospect's gift would make a difference to the community. Throughout the development process, the privacy of the prospect's personal health information must be protected. While the trustee who is a health care professional has a duty to the institution, the higher duty is to maintain the privacy of personal health information. The trustee must be aware of and avoid potential conflicts when they are engaged in development activities.

Providers sometimes think that they are imposing on patients when asking for support. The fact is that in many cases, patients want to do something that will help others with their condition. Others make gifts in gratitude for their care, and are often grateful when someone comes to them with the opportunity to make that gift. With that in mind, helping people make gifts can be seen as part of the continuum of the practice of health care delivery. Helping people make a gift can be as important as helping them deal with their medical condition.

Cultivation

The cultivation process is multifaceted and includes development professionals, administration, and trustees. While administration and development professionals can build relationships and close gifts without trustees, the involvement of trustees often leads to larger gifts and a long-term relationship. "Trustee participation in solicitation has a particularly dramatic impact on the size of gifts received. Development officers report countless cases of a gift amount increasing exponentially (or falling to a fraction of what was asked) because of a trustee's presence (or absence) at the ask."[5]

In order for the cultivation process to progress toward a significant gift and successful conclusion, trustee involvement is crucial. Cultivation can take various forms:

- Small dinner parties at trustee homes with administrators in attendance
- Briefings with the chief executive officer (CEO) and other key leaders
- Tours of the institution

If a trustee invites a person to an event or dinner, it is essential that the trustee is present and shows a commitment to the program. Before people are ready to make a gift, they need to know that their gift will make a difference, and they need to feel a connection to the institution. Knowing when to ask for a gift is more of an art than a science. It comes with years of experience, and the trustee who is new to the business of fundraising may rely on the development professional to set the timing of a solicitation.

Solicitation and Close

At the time of solicitation, the provider trustee often feels uncomfortable, since his or her relationship with the donor may overlap with a provider–patient relationship. When the solicitation takes place, the provider trustee may want to be present but not, the one to make the ask. It is important to keep in mind that while the provider or trustee may feel uncomfortable because of his or her dual role, the prospect does not see the solicitation as an imposition, rather it is a welcomed opportunity to support important projects.

In a recent study, 28 academic medical centers were asked about the process for soliciting donations, and the physician was often present but not the person asking for a gift. The academic medical centers involved asked who was present during solicitations of major gifts. In 90% of the cases the development professional was present, and half of the time the CEO was also present. In 20% to 24% of the centers, a volunteer or physician was present for the solicitation. In 69% of those solicitations the development professional made the ask for the gift, with the CEO making the ask in 26% of the meetings. The trustee or physician made the ask in 11% or less of the meetings. When those same organizations were asked who had the most influence on the decision to give, the physician's presence affected 50% of the solicitations.[6] When the health care professional is both trustee and provider, it expands the influence that he or she has on the solicitation and close. In many cases, no matter who makes the ask, a potential donor will go to a physician to ask about the project and whether they should make the gift.

A solicitation has a greater chance of success if it is planned and staged properly. Before soliciting there are several important steps that a trustee should consider:

■ Make a gift
■ Choose the team
■ Prepare for the visit
■ Practice
■ Schedule the meeting

First, the trustee should make a gift to the campaign. It does not have to be to the same program as the person being solicited, but the trustee should be able to reference his or her commitment as a trustee to the institution through a gift. It would be optimal if the gift was at the same level that is being solicited, but it should at least be in proportion to the trustee's means.

As the trustee prepares to solicit the prospect, choosing the team for the solicitation is paramount, and it is rarely a good idea for one person to solicit a donor alone. Soliciting gifts is not an everyday experience for trustees or even CEOs; therefore, it is important to the success of the endeavor that the development professional is present. They are experienced in directing the discussion, and they may be the right person to make the ask for the gift. The trustee or other members of the team can support the case and reinforce the need for the gift, as well as its significance for the mission of the hospital.

In preparation, the development office can prepare a research profile, which will include assets that are publicly available, such as real estate holdings and sales, and stock positions of publicly held companies if the person is a director or holds 5% or more of the stock of a company. Information regarding family members and relationships with other charitable institutions and board memberships is also helpful. Previous contacts and call reports can add significant insight for the solicitors. Setting the amount of the ask is often difficult. Some people are nervous that they may be asking for too much. That is not always a bad thing. Some prospects may turn down the request because it is more than they can afford, but at the same time be flattered by the amount that was requested. More than one solicitation has ended with the prospect accepting the solicitation very quickly. More often than not, a quick response means that the amount was too little. Preparation for the call, which includes reviewing the research surrounding the prospect, his or her financial resources, previous gifts to your institution and to other institutions, as well as their personal circumstances, will properly inform the ask amount.

Trustees are chosen for many reasons, but most are successful in their profession or business, which does not necessarily make them successful fundraisers. Even seasoned fundraisers need to practice and prepare for the call. Roles need to be established before the meeting. Who will start the conversation? Who will make the ask? What objections do you expect from the prospect, how will you respond to them, and who will respond? It may seem strange the first time to the trustee, but after trying it once and being successful, it will become a regular part of the process with prospective donors.

When all the preparation has been completed, the setting of the solicitation is the next big hurdle. If the cultivation has been moving along at the right pace, the prospect will not be surprised that it is leading to the solicitation. In many cases, a good strategy would be to include the spouse in any of the discussions. One would like to avoid the "I need to talk to my spouse about this before I give you an answer" problem. If appropriate, a meeting at the hospital would be

COMMON REASONS FOR NOT MAKING A GIFT

Objection 1: That is a lot of money, I know that the program is important, but I do not think I can do that right now.
   Response: You know, this campaign is being held over a few years, we are taking commitments spread out over that period of time.

Objection 2: I am in the middle of selling my business (real estate). Maybe when that is finished we can talk.
   Response: "You know there are ways that you can make a gift and save on taxes at the same time. We would be glad to talk to you about how that would work."

Objection 3: I am not sure we can do this, is there something a little less expensive?
   Response: "There are times when gifts can be structured through tax-advantaged vehicles that can allow you to make a larger gift than you thought you could. If you were willing to confidentially share some of your circumstances, we could work together to see if something could be structured for you."

optimal since they can be shown the work that they will be supporting as part of the approach. Giving is often an emotional decision, and the donor's emotional connection to the institution and its programs is a powerful motivation to give.

Once the question is asked, the work has just begun, and closing the gift can often be more challenging than making the solicitation. Preparation for the visit includes consideration of how one would respond to some common reasons people give for not making a gift (see "Common Reasons for Not Making a Gift" box).

Timing is crucial, and the trustee, as a peer or acquaintance, might know if there are personal or professional reasons why a solicitation would be welcome or unwelcome.

Donors will sometimes respond quickly, and often there may be continued negotiation around the gift agreement. The gift agreement serves as a legal document that controls the usage of the gift. It is important that both sides clearly understand expectations, including naming opportunity and recognition. The donor's children should be informed if the donor is making a large gift, especially an estate gift, so that the institution is protected from potential future contention by the estate regarding provisions for the charity.

Donor Stewardship

After the gift has been received, institutions sometimes fail to provide proper stewardship. Donors who make gifts today do so to make a difference in the institution and society. They want to hear about how their gift made that difference and often want to become more active in the institution. The increased activity is not necessarily trusteeship, but it could be membership on an advisory board. Data suggest that the more donors are involved in the institution, the more likely they will make a gift again. In a survey of hospital programs, it was found that those who made a gift had a 73% likelihood of making a similar gift again if they became a board member. The likelihood of making a similar gift was only 56% if they were not a board member. If the gift were $100,000 or more, the likelihood of a similar gift was 88% if they were a board member and 75% if they were not a board member.[1]

Gift Arrangements

Gifts to charitable organizations are more than writing a check. There are numerous tax-incentivized options that allow donors to make more significant gifts. Donors new to making significant gifts often believe that they are being asked to write a check for the gift in the full amount. Multiyear pledges alleviate some of these objections, but there are other gift arrangements that allow donors to make larger gifts than they may have thought possible. This section contains some of the more common methods used to make gifts.

Assignment of Income

Of particular interest to health professionals is the ability to direct fees from speaking engagements to a charity. The speaker should request that the fee for the engagement be made out to the charity. The fee is not counted as income to the speaker, and most institutions will treat the assignment of income as if the donor had written a check.

Gifts of Appreciated Assets

Stocks, bonds, mutual funds, and real estate that have been held for more than a year can be donated to a charity with several advantages. There are several important points to remember:

- The donor receives a tax deduction based on the value of the asset on the date of transfer.
- The donor can make a gift of an asset that cost him $100 and receive a deduction for $1000.

- It is important that the asset is transferred to the charity before the sale to receive the tax benefit.
- Transfer of real estate presents several issues, including the need for an environmental assessment.

Charitable Gift Annuity

The charitable gift annuity is a contract between the charity and donor (single or two lives) to pay the donor a fixed amount for the lifetime of the donor and one other person. The rate of return to the donor is usually determined by rates set by the American Council on Gift Annuities. In addition to the income, the donor receives a partial tax deduction based on the net present value of the gift and some of the income may be tax-free return of principal. The rate of return will increase with the ages of the donors. In many cases part of the income derived from the gift annuity will be tax-free return of principal, making it more attractive to the prospective donor. Gifts of securities to establish the annuity also provide a tax advantage to the donor.

Example[a]
- Two donors, both age 70, donate $100,000 cash.
- They will receive an annuity of $5900 per year, 5.9% (fixed), for both lives.
  - Of that total, $3345 would be treated as tax-free income and $2555 would be ordinary income.
  - After approximately 20.5 years all income would be treated as ordinary income.
- The donors receive a tax deduction of about $31,000, which may be used in the current tax year and carried over for an additional 5 years.
- At the time of the gift, the $100,000 is removed from the donor's estate.
- At the death of the second of the two donors, the funds are available for the charity to use as the donors directed at the time of their gift.

Charitable Remainder Trust

The charitable remainder trust allows an individual to donate appreciated assets into a trust and receive an income for one or more lives while receiving a tax deduction based upon the ages of the income recipients and the rate of income. Assets are donated to the trust, where they may be sold without any capital gains tax, and the assets are reinvested in a broad-based portfolio. The charitable trust is a good vehicle for someone who has a single large holding that he or she would like to diversify without tax implications. At the death of the last income recipient, the balance of the principal in the trust is transferred to the charity. When the asset is transferred to the trust, it is removed from the donor's estate.

The *charitable remainder unitrust* provides a variable income based on the principal value of the trust. After the donor's gift is made to the trust, the assets are sold (with no capital gains tax due) and reinvested. Each year the donor receives income based on the rate of return chosen by the donor (at least 5%). As the principal amount changes (valuation is usually made on December 31), the income will increase or decrease. The donors can add other gifts to the trust over time, and each time they make a gift, they receive a new tax deduction based on the value at the time.

Example

- Two donors, both age 70, donate $100,000 in appreciated securities with a cost basis of $10,000.
- No capital gains tax is due on the sale, and the funds are reinvested within the trust.
  - They will receive an income of 6% based on the principal of the trust (valued on an annual basis). All income will be treated as ordinary income.
- The donors receive a tax deduction of about $36,000, which may be used in the current tax year and carried over for an additional 5 years.
- At the time of the gift, the $100,000 is removed from the donors' estate.
- At the death of the second of the two donors, the funds are available for the charity to use as the donors directed at the time of their gift.

The *charitable remainder annuity trust* provides a fixed income based on the principal value of the trust and the percent of return. After the donor's gift is made to the trust, the assets are sold (with no capital gains tax due) and reinvested. Each year the donor receives income based on a fixed rate of return chosen by the donor (which has to be at least 5%). The income is fixed for the lives of the donors. Additions to the trust are not allowed.

Example

- Two donors, both age 70, donate $100,000 in appreciated securities with a cost basis of $10,000.

- No capital gains tax is due on the sale, and the funds are reinvested within the trust.
  - They will receive an income of $6000 per year (6% of the initial gift). All income will be treated as ordinary income.
- The donors receive a tax deduction of about $30,000, which may be used in the current tax year and carried over for an additional 5 years.
- At the time of the gift, the $100,000 is removed from the donors' estate.
- At the death of the second of the two donors, the funds are available for the charity to use as the donors directed at the time of their gift.

Tax law limits the maximum amount of return for charitable remainder trusts, which can be calculated by programs like PG Calc.[a] As the rate of return on the trust increases, the tax deduction decreases.

Charitable gift annuities are simple to set up, and charities usually set minimum amounts for each annuity. In recent years that minimum has been around $10,000. Trust documents are required for charitable trusts, and most charities are now suggesting a minimum gift of $100,000 because of the expenses of the trust, including the Internal Revenue Service (IRS) reporting requirements.

Charitable Lead Trust

When establishing a charitable lead trust, the donor contributes assets to the trust and the trust pays a percentage of the trust to a charity or charities for either a period of years or the donors' lives. At the end of that period, the principal in the trust is transferred, usually to the donors' children. This trust provides the donor with an estate tax deduction (not current income tax deduction), and with the proper term of years, percentage of payout can pass to the children with no estate tax due. This trust is of particular interest to individuals with large estate tax obligations.

Example

- A donor establishes a charitable lead trust with $100,000.
- The trust will pay the designated charity $7000 per year for a period of 22 years.
- After 22 years, the principal and all growth will pass to the beneficiary or beneficiaries free of any gift or estate tax.

Conclusion

The provider who serves as a trustee of a hospital or health care organization is uniquely able to participate in the fundraising process from the identification of a potential donor through stewardship. Fundraising is a team endeavor, and the health care provider and trustee bring their familiarity with prospects and their understanding of the health care system to the cultivation and solicitation of gifts. Understanding that cultivation and solicitation of gifts is more than just asking goes a long way to help the provider trustee learn how to effectively find support for the hospital. Working with the development professionals at the institution, the provider trustee can be both an effective and integral member of the fundraising team.

Case Study
Identifying Prospective Donors

What does the provider trustee say when confronted with prospective donors? How does one set up the relationship most effectively with patients or community members? Below are several scenarios with suggested responses.

Scenario 1

Patient: "Dr. Jones, I really appreciate all you have done for me and my family. What can I do to thank you? Or, what can I do to help your program?"

Never say: "I am just doing my job, your thanks is enough."

Say: "We have a (research project/program) that I would like to tell you more about. How about if I ask Jane Smith to call you, she can tell you more about the program and how you might be able to support it."

Scenario 2

You have been trying to make an appointment with a local businessman the trustees have known for years and run into him in a local restaurant.

Businessman: "I know you have been trying to talk to me about the hospital, but I am in the middle of selling some land we own and it has been eating up a lot of my time. Maybe when that is over we can talk."

Never say: "That's fine, I will talk to you in a month."

Say: "You know, a lot of people have been able to help themselves with taxes and help the hospital at the same time, but you need to make arrangements before you sell. John Smith, who works for the hospital, can explain how he has done this for others and how it might work for you. Can I have him call you?"

Study and Discussion Questions

1. How can a provider trustee augment the development process?
2. Can one be successful as a trustee fundraiser without making a personal commitment?
3. Describe ways, other than cash gifts, that individuals may make gifts to charitable organizations.
4. What are the peculiar issues that health care professionals face as part of the fundraising team?

Note

[a] Examples provided are only estimates based on prevailing tax laws existing in February 2008. PG Calc, Inc., provides software that makes calculations for life income gifts. Illustrations in this chapter are made with PG Calc software. Background information is available at their Web site: www.pgcalc.com.

Suggested Readings

Hubbell, G. J. and M. K. Reinders. 2007. *Lessons from benchmarking: Fast-forwarding the maturity of the fundraising operation.* Milwaukee, WI: Hubbell and Reinders.

Lord, J. G. 1983. *The raising of money: 35 essentials every trustee should know.* Cleveland, OH: Third Sector Press.

Lord, J. G. 1984. *Winning words: A volunteer's guide to asking for major gifts.* Washington, DC: Council for the Advancement and Support of Education.

Newman, H. B., A. Peckham, and R. G. Smiley. 1996. *Academic health care fund raising: Planning and operating a successful development program.* Falls Church, VA: Association for Healthcare Philanthropy.

Philanthropy Leadership Council. 2006. *Top relationships fostering and sustaining commitment from principal donors.* Washington, DC: The Advisory Board Company.

Philanthropy Leadership Council. 2007. *What no one else can do: Trustees' vital role in health care philanthropy.* Washington, DC: The Advisory Board Company.

Philanthropy Leadership Council. 2007. *Re-envisioning the alliance: Unlocking the value of boards and other volunteer groups.* Washington, DC: The Advisory Board Company.

Rhodes, F. H. T., ed. 1997. *Successful fund raising for higher education: The advancement of learning.* Phoenix, AZ: Onyx Press.

Teitell, C. 2005. *Portable planned giving manual,* 13th ed. Old Greenwich, CT: Taxwise Giving.

References

1. Philanthropy Leadership Council. 2007. *Re-envisioning the alliance: Unlocking the value of boards and other volunteer groups.* Washington, DC: The Advisory Board Company.

2. Lord, J. G. 1984. *Winning words: A volunteer's guide to asking for major gifts.* Washington, DC: Council for the Advancement and Support of Education.

3. Mason, J. August 16–17. Presentation to the Advisory Board. University of Chicago.

4. Smith, S. R. Fundraising under HIPAA—The Privacy Rule-AHP's Special Analysis. http://www.ahp.org/government-relations/hipaa/special-analysis/index. ph (accessed February 15, 2008).

5. Philanthropy Leadership Council. 2007. *What no one else can do: Trustees' vital role in health care philanthropy.* Washington, DC: The Advisory Board Company.

6. Philanthropy Leadership Council. 2006. *Top relationships fostering and sustaining commitment from principal donors.* Washington, DC: The Advisory Board Company.

Chapter 12

Successful Strategic Planning: The Board's Role

Gene J. O'Dell and John R. Combes

Contents

Executive Summary

Health care providers who serve as trustees for hospitals and health systems bring a unique perspective and set of competencies that can enrich board discussions and improve decision making. This background serves these trustees well in fulfilling their duties in relation to quality and clinical accountability, operational and executive oversight, and mission maintenance. When it comes to crafting and implementing strategy, provider trustees are less well-prepared by their professional training to make a significant contribution. This chapter is aimed at closing the gap between professional training of providers and the role of trustees in strategic planning and oversight.

The first part of the chapter will cover the basics of strategic planning, including the definitions of common terms, a description of the planning process, and the characteristics of successful plans. Next, the board's role in planning will be described, with emphasis on the unique contributions and perspectives of provider trustees. Finally, there will be a discussion of why plans fail and the role boards and provider trustees can play in identifying the common weaknesses and improving the chance of success.

Learning Objectives

1. To understand the basic elements of strategic plans and the planning process.
2. To learn about board and management's role in the strategic planning process.
3. To more fully appreciate the unique perspectives that providers bring to strategic planning.
4. To articulate the board drivers of successful implementation.

Key Words

- Accountability
- Environmental scan
- Goals, mission
- Performance measures
- Quality
- Stakeholders
- Strategic framework
- Strategic planning process
- Strategies
- Values
- Vision

Introduction

Articulating the strategic direction for the organization is one of the basic duties for a health care board. In partnership with management, boards can help define the planning process, contribute to the overall scan of the environment, set the priority areas of plan focus, and develop the goals for a successful plan. For health care provider trustees, who may not have formal business training, applying these concepts of planning to their work may represent a challenge. Because provider trustees have such a unique and valuable perspective, their contribution to the strategic planning process should not be curtailed by failing to understand the process.

This chapter should help to close that knowledge gap. By describing the basics of the strategic planning process and how the board contributes to its development, provider trustees will be able to more effectively engage in the planning dialog. The chapter will also assist provider trustees in understanding the key attributes of a successful plan and their unique role in contributing to its implementation. By understanding these planning essentials, provider trustees will more likely be able to reach their full potential of focusing the organizational strategies to the benefit of the patients and communities they serve. In doing so, provider trustees will extend their ability to improve the health and life of their individual patients to affect the health and well-being of their entire community.

What Is Strategic Planning?

What Is Planning?

Two of the key responsibilities of boards are to establish and support the organizational purpose and to provide points of view on what the organization should ultimately achieve in pursuit of that purpose. Health care providers who serve as trustees have a unique perspective and background that can assist the board in carrying out those responsibilities. Because their professional education and training do not usually encompass the concepts of strategic planning, it is essential for their trustees to acquire a basic understanding of the planning process in order to become effective contributors.

Strategic planning is an essential component of constructing the road map to the mission and the vision of the organization. Strategic planning is a discipline that enables the board and management to evaluate the present environment, the organization's position within that environment, and then to craft a plan to successfully fulfill the mission of the organization. Strategic planning demands commitments of time and talent from the chief executive officer (CEO), the board, and other stakeholders invested in the process.

Planning Definitions

Before beginning a discussion of the strategic planning process, it is important to become familiar with some basic planning terms and definitions. For purposes of this chapter, the following key terms and characteristics pertain:

Vision statements describe the desired future state of what the organization is attempting to effect beyond itself through its work and purpose.
   Characteristics:
   - Become a beacon of light that all staff move toward in organizational alignment
   - Should be inspiring
   - Are clear, challenging, and stand the test of time
   Example: "Hospitals and health care organizations that are trusted and held in high esteem by their communities."[1]
Mission statements describe the primary work and purpose of an organization.
   Characteristics:
   - Communicate the organizational purpose and make sure it is designed to say exactly what the organization anticipates it will achieve
   - Energize employees and stakeholders alike to pursue common goals
   - Should be unique to the organization
   - Are fairly broad, but cannot be all things to all people

Example: "To bring about excellence and accountability in governance by being the valued source, for health care leaders and trustees, of innovative governance thinking, information, tools and content."[1]

Value statements describe the core behaviors that guide the organization's relationships with employees, members, and other stakeholders.

Characteristics:

- Define how the organization will act, consistent with the mission, in the journey toward its vision
- Guide managers to hire and promote individuals whose outlook and actions are congruent with the values of the organization
- Reward and recognize those people whose work embodies the values of the organization

Examples:

"Integrity ... To be credible, reliable and genuine in our relationships and in the development and delivery of information, products and services to hospital leaders and the entire health care community.

Leadership ... To pursue our mission with courage and integrity, always striving to do what is right for patients and communities even in the face of adversity or controversy."

Diversity ... To foster a culture that enables people to grow and learn from each other by respecting, valuing and embracing difference— of people, of backgrounds, of ideas."[2]

Goal statements are the overarching intended outcomes of the organization.

Characteristics:

- Are general, broad, and fairly abstract
- Are intangible
- Are simply a clearer statement of the vision, but specific to the organization's planning horizon, the time frame during which the plan will be implemented
- May be followed by a descriptor statement that further clarifies the articulated concept

Example: "Advance a Health Care Delivery System That Improves Health and Health Care" descriptor statement: "To pursue strategies and advocate for models and resources that promote patients and communities receiving the right care, at the right time, in the right place."[2]

Strategies are the action plans that describe the individual steps required to achieve a particular goal.

Characteristics:

- Are the major components necessary to achieve the goal
- Close the gap between the current and desired positions

- Demonstrate a clear and direct relationship in support of the organization's mission
- Should include metrics so progress against strategies can be monitored and, as necessary, corrected
- May be followed by a descriptor statement that further clarifies the articulated concept

Example: "Improving Quality, Patient Safety and Performance" descriptor statement: "Support hospital efforts to develop systems of patient-centered care as the key to improving efficiency and effectiveness."[2]

Performance measures serve two purposes: (1) through a set of clearly defined metrics, mark the organization's progress in implementing the strategies and (2) ensure that the strategies collectively and directly support the mission. Characteristics:

- Are the specific, tangible deliverables necessary to achieve the strategy
- Are time sensitive

Example: "To publish and distribute a report based on the findings of a Blue Ribbon Panel of governance experts on the set of competencies for trustees, boards and CEOs building the case for the importance of incorporating these competencies in key board functions by 4th quarter."[1]

What Good Planning Does

Developing a strategic plan requires diligence in designing the planning process, including the assignment of clearly defined roles and responsibilities of the stakeholders charged with developing the plan. The planning process must capture the synergy of various and diverse stakeholder insights and opinions. It should also incorporate time to vet and test their assumptions about the organization and the environmental forces, as well as to explore future opportunities. A good strategic planning process should equip its leadership to achieve the mission and to move closer to the organization's vision, thus, fulfilling organizational destiny. A key benefit of a well-designed planning process is that it alerts the organization to risks associated with external and internal environmental forces. It also demands that the organization intimately understands and clearly articulates its competitive advantage in the market it serves.

A well-developed plan should succinctly communicate the major goals and strategies necessary to fulfill the organization's mission in pursuit of its vision to multiple and diverse stakeholder audiences. The performance measures serve to define the metrics used to evaluate the successful implementation of the strategies, and therefore, the overall strategic plan.

The strategic plan communicates the work and purpose of the organization, and should be employed to provide the nexus for the organization's operations by guiding those responsibilities and activities in pursuit of the mission. The result is an operating plan that complements the strategic plan and becomes an invaluable management tool to ensure that the operations and the strategic direction of the organization are aligned, and that management and staff are focused on accomplishing the same priorities. The synergy from everyone in the organization pulling together in the same direction to achieve its mission both strategically and operationally cannot be overstated. Moreover, good planning demands continuous work and dialog among management and staff, leading to more highly productive management–staff relationships.

What Planning Is Not

Strategic planning is a discipline, but it should not be viewed as an exact science or mathematical construct. Good planning is not developed in a vacuum or without the invaluable input and perspective of those charged with its implementation. Further, strategic planning must be viewed as a flexible process that both responds to environmental forces, yet remains true in pursuing the affirmed vision, mission, and goals of the organization. Strategic planning is not a substitute for actively managing an organization's operations, but it should be viewed as a tool to ensure operations are focused on achieving the bigger purpose.

Essentially, strategic planning must be a cultural imperative and embraced by those who are charged with its design, development, and implementation. Each stakeholder in the planning process must assume ownership and accountability for his or her respective role and responsibility in the process. This commitment is one that cannot be delegated.

Strategic Planning Process

Founded on the philosophical and cultural commitment from the CEO and board, the organization is prepared to embark on an exciting, meaningful, and purposeful journey in fulfilling its mission and pursuing its vision. The desired outcome is a formal, written strategic plan that clearly and succinctly describes the organization's road map that will be actively employed to guide the organization to its preferred future.

The major components of the strategic planning process that will be described throughout this chapter are development timeline; environmental scan; strengths, weaknesses, opportunities, threats (SWOT) analysis; planning assumptions; strategic framework; strategy development; and financial assumptions and plan.

Development Timeline

To organize the work of developing the strategic plan, the process begins with the development timeline. Strategic planning processes are incremental in nature with each component building on the next. The development timeline is helpful in highlighting the individual steps required to build the plan and in ensuring its timely completion. The timeline communicates the work to be done through the major process milestones, and it identifies the stakeholders responsible for developing the plan. To achieve organization-wide commitment to the process, it is imperative that the timeline also be clearly communicated to the staff charged with implementing its strategies.

Depending on the size of the organization and the complexity of the planning process, the development timeline might appear as a simple one-page Gantt chart (a chart in which horizontal lines illustrate the projected amounts of time involved in completing a particular process or deliverable) or a more detailed, multipage document that describes each step in each phase of the process (i.e., environmental scan, planning assumptions, strategic framework, and so forth) (Figure 12.1). Most important to the audiences employing the development timeline is its easy-to-use and understandable format. Without a visible timeline that all stakeholders have affirmed, the planning process can be left without focus or defined accountabilities.

Environmental Scan

The first phase of the planning process is the development of an environmental scan. The environmental scan is developed from both primary research and secondary sources and is a compilation of trends and issues occurring in the local market and in the broader health care landscape. It is important for organizations to become intimately aware of what is happening in the markets they serve. This can be done through formal research activities. To complement this knowledge and to gain a comprehensive appreciation of the broader health care landscape, organizations often turn to nationally recognized sources, such as the large health care consulting firms or accounting firms, to obtain trends and issues that these groups compile.

Strengths, Weaknesses, Opportunities, Threats (SWOT) Analysis

Once an environmental scan has been developed and vetted among the stakeholders, the second phase in the process is developing a SWOT analysis. A SWOT analysis is an exercise that evaluates both internal strengths and weaknesses of

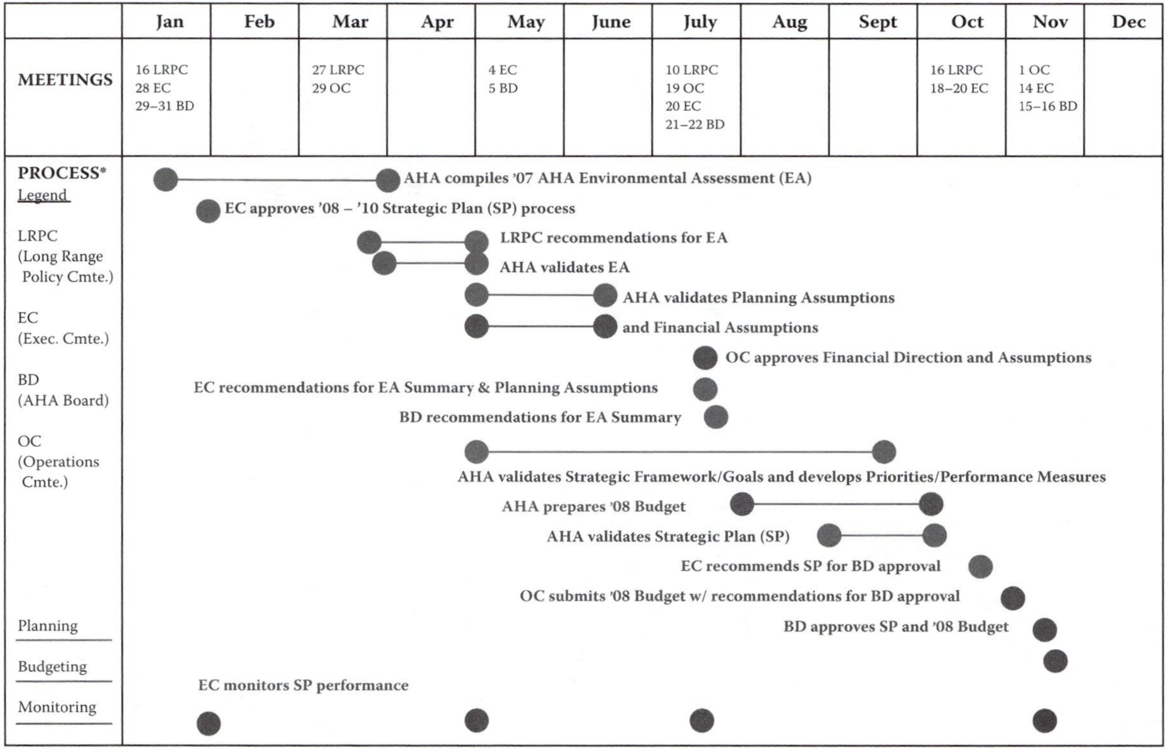

Figure 12.1 2008–2010 American Hospital Association (AHA) Strategic Plan *Development Time Line.* (*Source:* American Hospital Association, 2007, Chicago.)

the organization, as well as opportunities and threats imposed by the external environment. In evaluating an organization's internal strengths and weaknesses, it is critical that an open, honest dialog and assessment of the organization's operations be conducted. External opportunities and threats are best identified through research to validate consensus assumptions of the stakeholders and to alert them to emerging forces that might either positively or negatively impact the organization. There are several models for approaching a SWOT analysis, commonly found in planning literature and on the Internet. Organizations should evaluate the model that best serves their needs.

The objective of the SWOT is to create a short list of major internal strengths and weaknesses and external market opportunities and threats that the organization can then begin to affirm and prioritize.

Planning Assumptions

Planning assumptions are causal statements developed in response to selected SWOT findings that have a high probability of impacting the organization during the planning horizon.

Planning assumptions are also employed to test the validity and, as appropriate, to modify the strategic framework (i.e., vision, mission, values, and goals) of the organization. Although not discussed in this chapter, the organization should employ a similar process for developing a set of financial assumptions.

Strategic Framework

The strategic framework is generally understood to represent the vision, mission, values, and goals of an organization. If a strategic framework is absent for the organization, developing a vision and mission statement becomes the essential board task. Should a strategic framework presently exist, it should be reviewed annually and tested against the planning assumptions to ensure that it continues to be relevant to the organization in moving forward for the next planning horizon.

Strategy Development

The goals represent the broad, overarching multiyear intended outcomes of the organization in pursuit of its mission and vision. Once these have been developed as part of the strategic framework exercise, it is time to turn to strategy development. Strategies describe the annual action plans that will be implemented during the planning horizon to achieve the goals. Although the number of strategies to achieve each goal varies, identifying the top 6 to 10 required seems to work best and to be most manageable. The CEO and the management team should take the lead in the strategy development process. As supporting priorities and performance measures are created, it is imperative that staff closest to the work be involved in this process since they are likely to be given the responsibility and held accountable for implementing the priorities.

Performance measures are the individual metrics employed to determine if a priority has been successfully implemented and are communicated through a performance report that is shared with the board responsible for monitoring the organization's progress against the plan.

Performance measures should communicate what and when tangible actions are to be achieved. These should *not* include process-related items, such as creating a survey, convening a meeting, preparing materials, and so forth (Figure 12.2).

Strategic Planning Process: Thoughts on Effective Planning

Opinions vary on the significance of strategic planning, the board's involvement in strategic planning, and the importance of planning expertise as an attribute for trustee selection. However, most agree that an understanding of the organization's strategic planning process is a trustee asset. A trustee's working knowledge of the strategic planning process and how boards can most effectively participate maximizes the board's contribution to an organization's strategic success. The more trustees are familiar with the board's role in the planning process, the better prepared they are to guide their organization toward achieving success, and the closer their organization is to achieving that success.

As a critical link between the organization and its stakeholders, the board can play a key role in ensuring that stakeholder input is incorporated into the strategic planning process, and that stakeholder needs and expectations drive the organization's mission and goals.

It is a given that boards should be directly involved in establishing the strategic framework for the organization and for setting the overall strategic direction. A planning retreat often best serves to accomplish this work. A retreat location away from the interruptions of the daily work environment allows adequate time for the CEO and management to present planning material, and the opportunity for questioning by the board and for thoughtful dialog between the two. Providing board members with planning material in advance of the retreat goes a long way to promoting a productive and meaningful retreat experience. It is important that these sessions encourage and seek out diverse opinions and perspectives about where the organization is going and how it intends to get there. If board members only engage in deliberation with like-minded peers, a more homogeneous outcome may result, but they may also lose the value of a dissenting perspective.

2008 – 2010 AHA STRATEGY MAP

American Hospital Association

AHA's Vision for America
A society of healthy communities, where all individuals reach their highest potential for health.

Our Mission
To advance the health of individuals and communities; the AHA leads, represents and serves hospitals, health systems and other related organizations that are accountable to the community and committed to health improvement.

Our Values
People…Integrity…Leadership…Diversity…Collaboration

OUR GOALS

1. ADVANCE A HEALTH CARE DELIVERY SYSTEM THAT IMPROVES HEALTH AND HEALTH CARE

To pursue strategies and advocate for models and resources that promote patients and communities receiving the right care, at the right time, in the right place.

STRATEGIES:

1A) Improving Quality, Patient Safety and Performance
1B) Safeguarding Fair Reimbursement
1C) Transforming Health and Health Care
1D) Ensuring Accountability for Tax Exemption
1E) Increasing Health Care Workforce Capacity and Improving Employee Relations
1F) Strengthening Physician – Hospital Relationships
1G) Promoting Diversity
1H) Achieving Exceptional Health Care Governance

2. OPTIMIZE THE OPERATIONAL EFFECTIVENESS OF THE AHA

To sustain and enhance a member- and user-focused organization that promotes excellence, collaboration, innovation, growth and development.

STRATEGIES:

2A) Increasing Membership Recruitment and Retention
2B) Enhancing the Governance Process
2C) Empowering People and Organizational Strategies
2D) Optimizing Information Technology
2E) Maximizing Financial Strength

Figure 12.2   2008–2010 Strategy Map. (*Source:* American Hospital Association, 2007, Chicago.)

Once the plan is approved, boards need to take a leadership role in monitoring the performance against the plan through regularly scheduled, real-time progress reviews based on agreed-upon performance metrics with the CEO and the management team. An annual review that is largely qualitative is not sufficient. And if the plan is not on track, the board needs to understand why and what contingency plans, if appropriate, are being developed to address the change in course.

The Board's Role in Strategic Planning

The Decision to Plan

One thing is certain about health care delivery: there is very little that is certain. It is the ever-changing shifts in policy, regulation, technology, and reimbursement that make regular, structured planning an imperative for the success of a hospital or health system. The board must be aware of these changes and the resultant uncertainty, and it must hold the organization accountable to establish a rigorous planning process. Involvement in establishing the strategic plan, setting the goals, and monitoring its progress are among the chief responsibilities of the board.

Health care providers on the board have a unique perspective on the uncertainties of delivering care. They can understand the limitation of new health care treatments and technology, and they can appreciate the risks such changes bring to the health care system. Because they practice in the same regulatory and fiscal environment, they can also have a deep appreciation of the threats and opportunities offered by these external pressures. By working with nonprovider board members, provider trustees can help define a new vision of a delivery system that takes into account this uncertainty and provides a realistic assessment of the environment in which the organization operates. Using this vision, the entire board can hold the organization accountable to prepare for the future in a systematic way and can effect the initiation of the strategic planning process.

Strategic planning is the board and organization's attempt to create its future, to achieve its vision, and to exert its influence over an uncertain future. Both provider and nonprovider trustees bring their unique perspectives to the table and initiate the planning process with management, in order to secure the survival and future success of the organization's mission.

Contributing to Strategy Formation

Strategic planning is a team sport. It engages management, the medical staff, and the board in the process. However, it is the board that determines what level

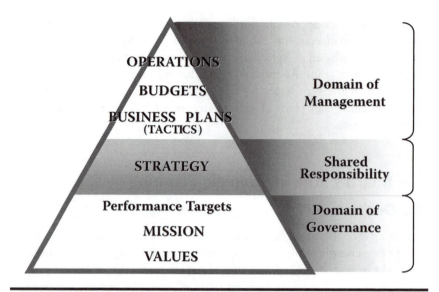

Figure 12.3   Strategy Formation. (*Source:* Mikhail, O., 2007, School of Public Health, University of Texas, Houston. With permission.)

of involvement each party will have, since the responsibility for the future of the organization is squarely in the board's hands. Despite the board's authority, each party brings to the process his or her well-defined responsibilities and account-abilities (Figure 12.3 and Figure 12.4).

Domain of Governance

The board is responsible for establishing the mission of the organization and driving its fulfillment. It ensures that the strategy is grounded in and consis-tent with the mission, and it drives the organization to accomplish the vision it describes. The board also formulates the organization's values. The board must be certain that these values are not compromised by the strategy, and that they form the basis for achieving the future envisioned by the successful achievement of the strategic goals. Finally, the board has the responsibility for establishing the goals for the plan. Only when the board clearly articulates these goals, along with significant accountability for their achievement, can success be realized.

Domain of Management

Management is responsible for developing the tactics to operationalize the strat-egy. It is through developing these tactics or business plans that management

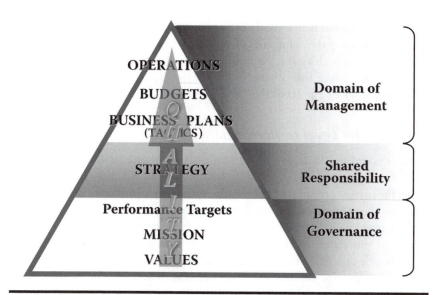

Figure 12.4 **Positioning of Quality. (***Source:* **Mikhail, O., 2007, School of Public Health, University of Texas, Houston. With permission.)**

contributes to the planning process and creates the mechanisms to advance the strategy. By tying budgets to the strategic plan, management develops the organizational commitment to turn the plan into reality.

Role of the Medical Staff

While the members of the medical staff have no formal accountability in the strategic planning process, it is essential for the success of the plan to have them actively engaged in its development. The medical staff is one of the primary stakeholders in the organization and has good insight into care delivery and the health care environment. Since the primary goal for health care strategic plans should be the advancement of the health and well-being of those they serve, the involvement of the medical staff as the principle providers of that care is critical to ensuring that the plan is well-focused, practical, and will achieve the desired results.

Shared Responsibility

While each party in the planning process has his or her own responsibilities and perspectives, it is the board that decides at what level it wants to be involved beyond its role in mission, values, and goal setting. The board may desire a role in defining the process, reacting to the environmental scan, and crafting the major strategies, or it may leave these tasks to management, providing input and approval only after the completed plan is delivered to them. There is, however, one area for the health care organization where the board must take the lead, and that is to ensure that a concern for the quality of patient care becomes a driving force for all aspects of the strategy.

Defining the Level of Performance

A major board prerogative in the strategic planning process is establishing the organizational goals, as well as the metrics to evaluate the progress of the plan. Given the current pressures on the health care system to improve its performance, boards must set organizational goals high enough to engender credibility, but not so high as to be unattainable. Achieving this balance and establishing "stretch" goals that move the organization forward require an intimate understanding of the health care field and its great potential to improve. Health care provider trustees can provide this needed understanding. These internal board experts should be resources to the entire board for the appropriate setting of strategic goals, as well as helping to define the measures of success of the overall strategy.

Once goals are established and measures of their successful accomplishment defined, the board has an important obligation to identify gaps between actual organizational performance and that required by the plan. The role of the board is to encourage management to move ahead with the established plan or to provide reasons why the plan or its goals are no longer appropriate for the current circumstances. The board is then required to weigh these responses against its own understandings and experiences and to determine their reasonableness. Once that determination is made, the board must hold all accountable to the execution of the original plan or its new modification.

Tying Budgets to Strategies

The old adage "put your money where your mouth is" sums up the idea behind tying budgets to the strategies outlined in the strategic plan. However, too often the costs associated with implementing individual strategies have not been thoroughly considered. Only when each strategy is subjected to a careful cost-benefit analysis can these be evaluated as prudent to pursue. As a rule, the importance of each strategy in relation to the others for the organization is indicated in its priority under each goal. Parallel to this are the sizes of the budgets assigned to each of the strategies.

The health care environment is ever-changing. Should environmental factors significantly change during the implementation of the strategies and require adjustments to the planning assumptions, then a contingency plan must be created. Although contingency plans should not be a focus in the planning process, occasionally a "Plan B" is necessary in order to accelerate reaction times in certain situations.

Implementation

As evidenced in this chapter, strategic planning is a time- and resource-intensive process; however, it will be ineffective if the organization fails to implement it properly. Implementation requires an understanding of the business environment, the appropriate timing of execution, and the proper reading of the business cycle. Budgets must not only support the strategy, but also be adequate to cover the expenses of the implementation, such as training, process redesign, and staff time.

A flawless implementation requires exquisite sensitivity to operations. Managers who are responsible for maintaining current operations will also be required to support implementation of the new strategies. Unless these additional responsibilities are recognized and managers receive support for their role, the plan will be seen as irrelevant to their personal success and satisfaction in doing their job. The handoff between senior management and the operational staff is the critical step in successful implementation. A process of continued feedback to these front-line managers through established performance measures and linkage to their individual performance evaluations and incentives needs to be established early in the implementation. Managers should also be consulted on how the implementation could disrupt their current operations and create a need for process redesign in their areas of responsibility. Engaging them in these discussions can ensure their buy-in to the implementation and maximize the likelihood of success. Board members with provider backgrounds can be helpful in identifying some of the clinical and operational obstacles to implementation while the process is still in the strategic plan development phase.

Successful implementation of the strategic plan also depends on how the plan fits into the organizational structure and culture. Unless these concepts are taken into account during strategy development, a plan may be designed that cannot be supported or implemented fully by the organization. Realistic assessment of the organization's capacity to execute the plan should be undertaken early in the process, and provider trustees, because of their experience, can be useful in this due diligence to help clarify the culture and organizational readiness.

Monitoring Plan Performance

In order for a plan to succeed, there must be continuous monitoring of organizational performance against the requirements of the plan. The responsibility for monitoring clearly belongs to the board. Before any attempt to hold parties accountable for performance against the plan, there must be agreement on what constitutes success between the board who monitors the plan and management who executes it. This *a priori* agreement allows management to embrace the plan by helping define what constitutes success according to the board. Agreement about key measures of success also ensures that mutual expectations will be clear and that any ambiguity in the plan is addressed.

For any monitoring function to be effective, frequent review of the performance measures should be undertaken. At least quarterly, the board should review these key measures and ask management for an explanation of any off-plan performance issues. With this type of regular feedback, management can make the appropriate adjustments to the plan and its implementation before overall organizational performance suffers.

The board should also conduct a review of the strategic framework at least annually. The health care environment is constantly changing, and this requires a reassessment of the planning assumptions that support the strategic plan. Significant changes in these assumptions may require that the entire framework be modified, and those changes could have a profound effect on implementation of and adherence to the plan. This periodic review allows the board to keep the plan flexible and responsive to environmental shifts.

Why Plans Fail

Obviously it is tremendous work and effort to develop and successfully implement a strategic plan. Sadly, too often strategic plans are created that end up sitting dormant on office shelves and only dusted off when the new planning cycle begins. Strategic plans should serve as a management tool to guide the organization's strategic and operational initiatives. Unless the organization is committed to the planning process and to successfully implementing the plan, the board's energy is frankly better employed in other pursuits.

At the forefront of successful strategic planning is the organization's cultural philosophy and seriousness of purpose, which begins with the CEO. This philosophical commitment must transcend the organization so that management and staff equally embrace their approach to their work and the importance of demonstrating success of the plan. Testing the organization's commitment to strategic planning begins by evaluating the CEO's commitment and role in the planning process.

Second, the board must have a working knowledge of the planning process and intimately understand its role and responsibility, as well as the roles of the CEO and management team. Further, the board should be familiar with the position in the organization charged with overseeing the planning process and plan development. Fundamentally, without an actively engaged CEO and a board that champions the planning process, the likelihood that a well-developed plan will be created, let alone implemented, is minimal.

In the most forward-thinking organizations the CEO is usually viewed as the "chief planning officer," while a senior management position is tasked with designing and overseeing the planning process.

For health care organizations, the strategic plan can also be jeopardized by failing to engage the medical staff early in the process. While management and front-line staff are responsible for implementing the plan, support from the organization's physicians, who in many cases direct the daily work of patient care, and who also may develop their own competing strategies, is critical to implementation success. Without physician support, or worse, with their resistance to it, even the most rigorous implementation attempts will be thwarted. Provider trustees can be invaluable in securing support from staff physicians.

Conclusion

Engaging in strategic planning is one of the most important responsibilities for boards. Organizations and their stakeholders rely on trustees to provide their insight and experience to help management assess the health care environment, envision the future, and craft the road map to successful health care delivery. Provider trustees can provide a perspective to this process that is unique, relevant, and much needed by the rest of the board. By understanding the basic concepts of strategic planning and becoming familiar with the planning process, provider board members can increase the effectiveness of their contributions and become exceptional trustees.

Planning is the first step in achieving the strategic goals. Boards must also be involved in overseeing the implementation of the plan and monitoring its progress in achieving those goals. Once again, provider trustees can play a unique role. From their professional experience, they can assist the board in the early recognition of cultural and organizational impediments to the successful implementation of the plan, and they can provide insights into the causes of poor plan performance as the implementation progresses.

This chapter serves as an introduction to the topic of strategic planning and the process for its effective execution. This knowledge, coupled with professional insights and experience, can lead to an even higher level of performance in service to the patients, families, and communities who depend on health care organizations.

Case Study

At a recent board retreat a long-serving board member, also a prominent private practitioner in the community, turned to the hospital CEO and asked, "Where are we headed, and how will we know when we get there?" The CEO responded, "Good question, we are working on the strategic plan right now. Would you like to join the committee?"

Study and Discussion Questions

There are numerous questions boards should ask about the organization's strategic planning process. Among others, here are some of the most important:

1. Do you have a working knowledge of the organization's strategic planning process?
2. What is the CEO's philosophy on strategic planning?
3. Is the board involved in approving the strategic planning development timeline? Are the steps (milestones) in the planning process clearly defined with roles and responsibilities assigned?
4. What is the board's role in developing the strategic framework (vision, mission, values, and goals)?
5. Is the planning process top-down, bottom-up, or a combination?
6. How do you engage the medical staff in the strategic planning process?
7. Is a formal, routine process in place for monitoring the organization's performance against the plan?
8. How are the community's needs and their input captured in the strategic planning process?
9. Who are the audiences to the strategic plan? How broadly is the plan shared?
10. Who is the strategic planner in the organization, and what is his or her relationship to the CEO and the board?

Suggested Readings and Web Site

Readings

Goldman, E. F. and K. C. Nolan. 1994. *Strategic planning in health care: A guide for board members.* Chicago: American Hospital Publishing.

Kaufman, R. A., R. Watkins, H. Oakley-Brown, and D. Leigh. 2003. *Strategic planning for success: Aligning people, performance and payoff.* San Francisco: Pfeiffer & Co.

McGowan, R. and A. MacNelty. 2007. Developing a physician-hospital alignment plan. *Trustee* 60:26–27.

O'Dell, G. J. 2007. AHA environmental assessment 2008. *Trustee* 60:19–30.

Orlikoff, J. E., and M. K. Totten. 2006. Trustee workbook 3. Strategic planning: Maximizing the board's impact. *Trustee* 59:15–20.

Rice, R. T. 2006. The board's role in strategic planning. *Trustee* 59:28–29.

Steiner, G. A. 1997. *Strategic planning: What every manager must know.* New York: The Free Press.

Web Site

Center for Healthcare Governance: http://www.americangovernance.com/

References

1. Center for Healthcare Governance. 2007. *2008–2010 Center for Healthcare Governance Strategic Plan.* Chicago.
2. American Hospital Association. *2008–2010 AHA Strategic Plan.* Chicago.

Chapter 13

Community Benefit: The Nonprofit Community Health System Perspective

Lawrence D. Prybil and Janet A. Benton

Contents

Executive Summary

Tax-exempt status traditionally was accorded to nonprofit hospitals and health systems on the premise that a commanding reason for their existence was to provide charity care to persons who required health care services but were unable to pay for them. The health care environment changed dramatically with the enactment of Public Law 89-97 in 1965 and introduction of the Medicare and Medicaid programs, which greatly expanded health insurance coverage for elderly and poor Americans. In 1969, the Internal Revenue Service issued a revenue ruling that established the so-called community benefit standard and spelled out the factors that would be considered in granting tax-exempt status to health care institutions.

In subsequent years, public debate regarding the community benefit standard and the requirements for achieving and maintaining tax-exempt status has accelerated. This chapter addresses emerging benchmarks of good governance with respect to oversight of community benefit programs and compares the current practices of 123 nonprofit community health system boards to these benchmarks.[1]

Learning Objectives

1. To better understand historical developments that led the Internal Revenue Service to establish the community benefit standard in 1969.
2. To learn about environmental changes and pressures that recently led to major changes in the Internal Revenue Service reporting requirements through revisions to Form 990, including Schedule H.
3. To explore emerging benchmarks of good governance for nonprofit health care organizations with respect to oversight of community benefit programs.
4. To better understand how current practices of nonprofit community health system boards compare to those benchmarks.

Key Words

- Benchmarks of good governance
- Community benefit
- Community benefit plan
- Community benefit standard
- Community health system
- Community needs assessment

Introduction

At federal, state, and local levels, there is a growing call for more accountability, greater transparency, and better performance by the boards that govern our nation's investor-owned and nonprofit organizations. This has been heightened by a number of factors, including the visible consequences of governance failures in the business sector,[2] higher education,[3] foundations,[4] and the health field.[5]

The General Accountability Office, the House Ways and Means Committee, the Internal Revenue Service, the Senate Finance Committee, a growing number of state legislatures, and bond rating agencies are among the bodies that are scrutinizing nonprofit health care organizations and their boards more closely than at any time in the past. Governance oversight of charity care and other forms of community benefit, executive compensation, and the quality of patient care are among the issues that are receiving attention. In effect, the requirements for maintaining tax-exempt status and the expectations for governing boards of nonprofit health care organizations are becoming more stringent.[6]

Not surprisingly, growing interest in the performance of nonprofit organizations and their governing boards has resulted in serious examination of governance practices. There is general agreement that proper governance of hospitals and health systems is important and, for a host of reasons, has become increasingly complex. It is also widely acknowledged that, on the whole, the governance of nonprofit organizations, including hospitals and health systems, should be improved.[7]

In recent years, these factors have stimulated reassessment of the characteristics and practices of effective boards. Except for requirements established by state statutes, the Internal Revenue Service, and the Joint Commission, formal standards for governance of nonprofit health care organizations have not been adopted in the United States. However, in recent years substantial efforts have been made by voluntary commissions, panels, and others to describe good governance practices and to provide guidance for boards and chief executive officers to consider as benchmarks in evaluating and improving governance performance.[8–18] Some of these benchmarks are well established and widely accepted; others are in their formative stages.

A study sponsored by the W. K. Kellogg Foundation and Grant Thornton, LLP, is currently examining selected aspects of governance in a group of non-profit community health systems. For the purpose of this study, *community health systems* are defined as:

> Nonprofit health care organizations that (1) operate two or more general–acute or critical access hospitals, or both, and other health care programs in a single, contiguous geographic area, and (2) have a chief

executive officer and a system-level board of directors who provide governance oversight over all of these institutions and programs.

Some community health systems that meet this definition are independent, while others are part of larger, nonprofit parent organizations. This study includes both categories. The critical characteristic is that the system includes an integrated governance and management structure that has oversight responsibility for the system's hospitals and other health care programs.

The overall purpose of this study is to examine the structures, practices, and cultures of community health systems' governing boards and compare them to selected benchmarks of good governance. The intent is twofold: (1) to identify areas where, on the whole, governance of these systems could be improved and (2) to provide information that will assist the systems' chief executive officers and board leaders in assessing and enhancing the boards' effectiveness.

One phase of this study involved a survey of the chief executive officers (CEOs) of the 201 community health systems that comprised the study population. Usable responses were received from 123 of the 201 CEOs (61%).[1] A major section of the survey sought the CEOs' perspectives on their boards' involvement in providing oversight over their system's community benefit plans and programs. This chapter summarizes the findings.

In deliberations on community benefit, the input of board members who are health care providers is vitally important. Their background and perspectives can enrich the dialog as the board members and senior management examine community needs, set priorities, and adopt system-wide community benefit policy and plans. This chapter gives health care providers benchmarks of good governance that will inform these deliberations.

Community Health System Board Oversight of Community Benefit Plans and Programs

Background

The landmark work of the Commission on Hospital Care during and after World War II led to the enactment of the Hospital Survey and Construction Act of 1946 (Public Law 79-725). This legislation, commonly referred to as the Hill-Burton Act, became Title VI of the Public Health Service Act. It represented the first large-scale policy instrument for shaping hospital and health services planning in the United States. To become eligible for hospital construction grants, states were required to establish hospital planning agencies, assess existing facilities and needs, and set statewide priorities. During the following decades, the

Hill-Burton Act stimulated several thousand hospital construction and renovation projects, reshaped the nation's health services delivery system, and introduced the concept that nonprofit, tax-exempt health care facilities should serve defined community needs.[19]

Historically, tax-exempt status was accorded to nonprofit hospitals and health systems on the premise that the fundamental reason for their existence was to provide charity care to persons who needed health care services but were unable to pay for them. The original Hill-Burton legislation required facilities receiving grants to provide free care for 20 years to eligible individuals unable to pay for their services; facilities funded with grants under Title XVI in later years were required to provide uncompensated care in perpetuity.[20] In 1965, Congress enacted Public Law 89-97, which established the Medicare and Medicaid programs and significantly expanded health insurance coverage for elderly and poor Americans. In 1969, the Internal Revenue Service (IRS) issued a revenue ruling that embodied a broader rationale for granting tax-exempt status to nonprofit institutions: the so-called community benefit standard.[21] In this ruling, the IRS reasoned that providing health care services for the general benefit of the community is inherently a charitable purpose and spelled out the factors that would be considered in granting tax-exempt status.[22,a]

As time passed and the health care field experienced major economic, legislative, and structural changes, questions began to arise about the adequacy and appropriateness of the community benefit standard as the basis for tax exemption. In 1991, the House Ways and Means Committee held hearings on proposed legislation designed to make a hospital's tax-exempt status contingent upon providing a defined level of charity care, and the IRS initiated a series of audits to examine the charitable activities of several large health care organizations. During the same period, prompted in part by a growing need for revenues, several states and local governmental bodies began to challenge hospitals' exemption from property and other taxes.[23] As stated in 1994 by J. David Seay:

> This public policy debate has led us to the point where non-profit hospitals must either concede their tax-exempt status or articulate in clear and convincing terms why they should retain this socially-important and fiscally significant form of social approbation.[24]

In subsequent years, the debates about the community benefit standard and requirements for maintaining tax-exempt status have escalated. Various forms of community benefit requirements, such as a specific level of charity care or standard reporting of community benefit activities, have been established in at least 22 states.[25] However, while it is vague and lacks the force of law, the community benefit standard has remained the principal federal guidance for nonprofit health care organizations regarding community benefit requirements. In 2005, the General Accountability Office (GAO) issued a report that critically assessed the level of charitable services provided by the nation's nongovernmental health care institutions. It concludes, in part, that

> current tax policy lacks specific criteria with respect to tax exemptions for charitable entities and detail on how that tax exemption is conferred. If these criteria are articulated in accordance with desired goals, standards could be established that would allow non-profit hospitals to be held accountable for providing services of benefit to the public commensurate with their favored tax status.[26]

In mid-2007, the national dialog about charity care and other forms of community benefit was informed by substantive reports on issues from the IRS and the Senate Finance Committee.[27] In brief, these included:

■ On June 14, 2007, the IRS issued a proposed revision of Form 990 that must be submitted annually by all tax-exempt organizations, including hospitals and health systems. The proposed form, specifically Schedule H, called for much more information about several topics, including charity care and other components of community benefit, executive and board compensation, and certain aspects of organizational governance. The IRS received voluminous comments about the proposal and, on December 20, 2007, published the version that will be used for the 2008 tax year. The IRS has sought public input on a draft version and plans to issue final instructions to assist in completing the updated Form 990 in 2008.[28]

■ On July 17, 2007, Senator Charles Grassley (ranking minority member of the Senate Finance Committee) released a minority staff discussion draft containing a host of potential changes to the standards currently applied to tax-exempt health care organizations, including the existing community benefit standard.

■ On July 19, 2007, the IRS issued an interim report on its Hospital Compliance Project, which studied community benefit activities in 487 hospitals. Among the principal observations set forth in the interim report was that 97% of these hospitals state they have a written policy on uncompensated care. However, the IRS found no uniform definition of this term and, in addition, found wide variation in the activities and levels of expenditure that hospitals report as community benefit.[b]

A number of voluntary associations, such as the American Hospital Association (AHA), the Alliance for Advancing Nonprofit Healthcare, the

Catholic Health Association (CHA), the Health Research and Educational Trust (HRET), the Public Health Institute, and VHA, Inc., have encouraged health care organizations to better document the services they provide and how they benefit the communities they serve. Historically, however, there have been no federal-level regulatory guidelines to be used by health care organizations to measure and report the full range of services that constitute community benefit. For the most part, nonprofit providers have been reluctant to adopt and implement uniform definitions and guidelines on a voluntary basis.[29] The lack of comprehensive, comparable data has been a cause of consternation for the Senate Finance Committee and other congressional committees for some time.[30] The updated Form 990, specifically the revised Schedule H, is intended to address this problem and provide more complete and consistent information for governmental officials, health care organizations, and the public at-large.[28]

Just as the long debate about requirements for tax-exempt status is beginning to yield more uniform definitions and reporting expectations, it also appears that some basic benchmarks for governance practices are beginning to emerge. The survey findings are presented in relation to several of these emerging benchmarks.

Findings

> *Engagement*: Proactive engagement and transparency are hallmarks of good governance. The Coalition for Nonprofit Health Care has called for trustees to be "more vigorous in exercising their oversight responsibilities" and "more inquisitive on matters requiring their attention."[31] The American Bar Association Task Force on Corporate Responsibility has stated that boards must engage in "active, independent, and informed oversight of the corporation's business and affairs."[32] Given the increasing pressure on non-profit health care organizations to demonstrate how their community benefit activities justify tax-exempt status, it seems clear that serious, ongoing dialog initiated by governing boards about community benefit issues is becoming a necessary and important governance practice.[33]

In this context, the CEOs of community health systems were asked whether or not their boards engage in "formal discussions on a regular basis about their system's community benefit responsibilities and programs."[c] The data in Table 13.1 indicate that 93% of CEOs who led systems that are part of larger parent organizations respond affirmatively, compared to 58% of independent-system CEOs. This difference is statistically significant. It appears that, on the whole, the boards of community health systems affiliated with larger parent organizations are more actively engaged

Table 13.1   Does the Community Health System Board Have Formal Discussions on a Regular Basis about the System's Community Benefit Responsibilities and Programs?

	Systems That Are Part of Parent Organizations (n = 44)	*Independent Systems (n = 79)*	*All Systems (n = 123)*
Yes	93.2%	58.2%	70.7%
No	6.8%	41.8%	29.3%
$X^2 = 15.0; p < 0.01$	100.0%	100.0%	100.0%

in dialog about their community benefit responsibilities and programs than the boards of independent systems. It is possible, perhaps likely, that the parent corporations are encouraging or requiring the leadership of their subsidiary units to place this important subject on their governance and management agendas.

Formal policy: Active board-level dialog is a necessary ingredient but, in itself, is insufficient to provide clear direction and priorities for the organization and its management team. To govern effectively, board deliberations must produce sound, well-constructed policies regarding vital areas of the organization's structure and functions. Given the importance of maintaining tax-exempt status and the increasing attention being given to community benefit issues, it seems evident that adopting policies that provide guidance for programs and services is emerging as a benchmark of good governance for all nonprofit health care organizations, including community health systems.[34]

In this survey, CEOs were asked if their community health system board has adopted "a formal written policy that defines overall guidelines for the system's community benefit programs." As shown by the data in Table 13.2, in community health systems that are part of larger parent organizations, 82% of the system boards have adopted formal written policies to guide the system's community benefit programs. In contrast, less than half (49%) of the independent-system boards have taken this step. This difference is statistically significant and indicates that a substantial segment of our nation's nonprofit community health systems presently are operating without formal board direction and guidance for their community benefit programs and services.

Community needs assessment: For years, many organizations, including the AHA,[35] CHA,[29] Public Health Institute,[36] HRET, and others, have

Table 13.2   Has the Community Health System Board Adopted a Formal Written Policy That Defines Overall Guidelines for the System's Community Benefit Programs?

	Systems That Are Part of Parent Organizations (n = 44)	Independent Systems (n = 79)	All Systems (n = 123)
Yes	81.8%	49.4%	61.0%
No	18.2%	50.6%	39.0%
$X^2 = 11.2$; $p < 0.01$	100.0%	100.0%	100.0%

encouraged hospitals and health systems to institute formal processes to assess community needs—preferably in partnership with other community agencies—to provide a solid foundation for setting priorities and allocating resources. As stated in the CHA's *Guide for Planning and Reporting Community Benefit*:

> Meeting the access and community health needs of our communities requires an assessment of community needs and assets and prioritization of needs and problems. A well thought out and systematic planning process is critical to having a community benefit program that builds on community assets, promotes collaboration, and improves community health.[29]

The Finance Committee minority staff discussion draft regarding potential community benefit reforms and proposed amendments to the existing community benefit standard released on July 17, 2007, called for assessment of community needs on a regular basis. The AHA has made a similar recommendation to the nation's hospitals.[33] It is apparent that board-level insistence on system-wide involvement in community needs assessment, preferably in collaboration with other community agencies, as a basis for setting community benefit priorities and allocating resources, is an emerging benchmark of good governance for nonprofit hospitals and health systems.

The CEOs who participated in the survey were asked if their community health system "engages in a formal assessment process designed to determine community needs in the system's area to which system resources should be allocated." The data in Table 13.3 show that more than half of these community health systems (54%) conduct formal assessments of community health needs on a regular basis, either independently or in

Table 13.3 Does the System Engage in a Formal Assessment Process Designed to Determine Community Needs to Which System Resources Should Be Allocated?

	Systems That Are Part of Parent Organizations (n = 44)	Independent Systems (n = 79)	All Systems (n = 123)
YES, the system conducts its own formal community needs assessment process on a regular basis.	18.2%	27.8%	24.4%
YES, the system collaborates with other local organizations in a community needs assessment process on a regular basis.	40.9%	22.8%	29.3%
YES, the system periodically engages in community needs assessment, but not on a regular basis.	25.0%	25.3%	25.2%
NO	15.9%	24.1%	21.2%
	100.0%	100.0%	100.0%

collaboration with other organizations. Collaborative approaches are more common among systems that are part of larger parent organizations (41%) than among independent systems (23%).

A quarter of all systems engage in assessing community health needs periodically, but not on a regular basis; one in five is not involved at all. It seems apparent that the absence of formal, board-approved policies regarding community benefit programs in 39% of these community health systems is reflected in lack of attention to formal assessment of community needs by a substantial proportion of them.

Formal community benefit plan: For all organizations, resources are limited and good stewardship by governance and management is imperative. As stated by Michael Porter and Mark Kramer, "No business can solve all of society's problems or bear the cost of doing so."[37] For nonprofit hospitals and health systems, adoption by the governing board of a formal plan for the organization's community benefit program is becoming a benchmark of good governance.[36] These community benefit plans should set direction and provide benchmarks against which performance can be assessed.

The CEOs were asked if their community health system's governing board has adopted a formal community benefit plan that provides measurable objectives for their system's community benefit program. The data presented in Table 13.4 show that on an aggregate basis, only 36% of these systems have a formal, board-adopted community benefit plan in place. Another 40% of the boards have established some priorities for their system's community benefit program but have not developed or adopted a formal plan. Of the community health systems that are affiliated with larger parent organizations, well over half (55%) have formal, board-adopted plans versus 25% of the independent systems. The difference is statistically significant. The adoption of a formal plan is a good governance practice; however, it is certainly possible that some systems without formal plans have robust community benefit programs.

Table 13.4   Has the Community Health System Board Adopted a Formal Community Benefit Plan That Spells out Measurable, System-Wide Objectives, for the Organization's Community Benefit Program?

	Systems That Are Part of a Parent Organization (n = 44)	Independent Systems (n = 79)	All Systems (n = 123)
YES, there is a formal board-adopted community benefit plan of this nature in place.	54.5%	25.3%	35.8%
The system board has established some priorities for the system's community benefit program, but at this point, there is not a formal plan in place.	31.8%	44.3%	39.8%
NO, not yet.	11.4%	30.4%	23.6%
Other	2.3%	0.0%	0.8%
$X^2 = 14.0$; $p < 0.01$	100.0%	100.0%	100.0%

Table 13.5   Is the Community Health System Board Regularly Presented with Performance Data on Measurable System-Wide Objectives Regarding Its Community Benefit Programs?

	Systems That Are Part of a Parent Organization (n = 44)	Independent Systems (n = 79)	All Systems (n = 123)
Yes	86.4%	58.2%	68.3%
No	13.6%	41.8%	31.7%
X^2 = 9.1; p < 0.01	100.0%	100.0%	100.0%

Performance reports: As with other facets of system operations, adopting a plan is important but, in and of itself, does not fulfill the governing board's oversight responsibility. Boards also should receive regular reports regarding the system's community benefit program, including performance data regarding progress in relation to established objectives.[33]

The findings presented in Table 13.5 show that 68% of community health boards regularly receive some performance data regarding progress toward system-wide objectives established for their organization's community benefit programs. Consistent with the pattern found on other community benefit issues, the figure for systems that are part of a larger parent organization is much higher than that for the independent systems (86% versus 58%). This difference is statistically significant. Without measurable objectives and evidence-based progress reports, it is difficult (if not impossible) for a board to fulfill its oversight responsibilities for its organization's community benefit program or to hold the management team accountable for results.

In general, the survey findings regarding community health system board oversight with respect to community benefit programs suggest there is a considerable gap between current practices and emerging benchmarks of good governance. The gap is significantly greater for the boards of independent systems than for those affiliated with larger parent organizations. There has not been extensive research regarding this subject; however, these findings are consistent with the results of a previous study by Shoou-Yih Lee, Jeffrey Alexander, and Gloria Bazzoli, who concluded:

> With few exceptions, a significantly greater involvement of system and network hospitals was found in providing community health services and inpatient services to Medicaid patients relative to

freestanding hospitals.... In general, affiliation with health systems and health networks appears to be positively related to community responsiveness in community hospitals.[38]

Conclusion

Based on the survey findings, it is clear that there are gaps between the current practices of nonprofit community health system boards and emerging benchmarks of good governance with respect to board oversight of community benefit plans and programs. This is not surprising because these benchmarks have been evolving in recent years in response to rapidly growing interest in the public and private sectors of society.

At this time, the gaps are greater for independent systems than for those affiliated with parent organizations, but they are evident in both groups. All of the benchmarks of good governance addressed in this chapter are attainable. According to information provided by the CEOs, each of the benchmarks is being met by numerous systems at this time.

It is believed that meeting these benchmarks places nonprofit health care organizations in a stronger position to warrant continuation of tax-exempt status. The benchmarks are reasonable and achievable. So, it is recommended that all community health system boards and their CEOs devote concerted attention and resources to meeting the emerging benchmarks of good governance with respect to their systems' community benefit responsibilities. Boards that have not already done so are urged to:

■ Adopt a *system-wide policy* regarding their systems' roles and obligations in providing community benefit.
■ Collaborate actively with other organizations in ongoing *community needs assessment.*
■ Adopt and regularly update a formal *community benefit plan* that states the system's objectives in clear, measurable terms.
■ Ensure that *reporting and accountability mechanisms* to monitor progress are in place.
■ Provide *thorough reports to the communities served* on a regular basis, at least annually.

Study and Discussion Questions

1. The Internal Revenue Service established the so-called community benefit standard and promulgated it in a revenue

ruling in 1969. Widely recognized as vague, why has it been allowed to remain for so long as the principal federal guidance for nonprofit health care organizations regarding community benefits requirements?

2. Given resource limitations and the importance of objective assessment of community needs as a basis for setting community benefit priorities, what could be the reasons why only 29% of community health systems collaborate on a regular basis with other local organizations in community needs assessment processes?

3. In an era when the basis for granting tax-exempt status to non-profit health care organizations is increasingly challenged at local, state, and national levels, why have only 61% of community health system boards adopted "formal, written policies that define overall guidelines for their systems' community benefit programs," and even fewer, 36%, adopted a "formal community benefit plan that spells out measurable system-wide objectives for their organizations' community benefit programs"?

4. What are the likely reasons that the boards of nonprofit community health systems that are part of larger parent organizations appear, as a group, to be significantly more engaged in community benefit planning, policy development, and evaluation than the boards of independent systems?

Notes

[a] These factors, which originally comprised the community benefit standard, included maintaining an emergency room on a 24-hour-per-day basis; providing charity care to the extent of the institution's financial abilities; granting medical staff privileges to all qualified physicians in the community, consistent with the size and nature of the institution's capabilities; accepting payment from the Medicare and Medicaid programs on a nondiscriminatory basis; and maintaining a community-controlled board comprised primarily of persons from the local community and not controlled by insiders. A later IRS ruling (Rev. Rul. 83-157, 1983-2 C.B. 94) stated that hospitals did *not* need to maintain and operate an emergency room to qualify for tax-exempt status *if* it showed that adequate emergency services existed elsewhere in the community and the hospital met the other requirements of the community benefit standard.

[b] In brief, *uncompensated care* generally is defined to include bad debt (i.e., hospital losses from unpaid bills for which they expected to receive payments) and charity care (i.e., the cost of services rendered to patients from whom no payment was anticipated). The term *uncompensated care* typically does not include underpayment

(that is, unreimbursed costs) from Medicare, Medicaid, and other publicly financed health care programs. However, as stated in the IRS interim report on its Hospital Compliance Project, hospitals presently employ a very wide range of definitions of *uncompensated care* and *community benefit*.

^c To provide a common frame of reference, the survey form sent to CEOs in this study provided a definition of *community benefit* based on one developed jointly by the CHA and VHA:

Community benefit is a planned, managed, and measured approach to meeting identified community needs. It implies collaboration with a "community" to benefit its residents by improving health status and quality of life. Community benefit responds to an identified community need and meets at least one of the following criteria: generates a low or negative margin, responds to the needs of special populations, and/or provides services or programs that would likely be discontinued if a decision were made on a purely financial basis.

Suggested Readings

Entin, F., J. Anderson, and K. O'Brien. 2006. *The board's fiduciary role: Legal responsibilities of health care governing boards*. Chicago: Center for Healthcare Governance.

Hospital charity care in the United States. 2005. St. Louis, MO: Missouri Foundation for Health.

Nonprofit, for-profit, and governmental hospitals; Uncompensated care and other community benefit. Testimony of David M. Walker, Comptroller General of the United States, General Accounting Office, before the Committee on Ways and Means, U.S. House of Representatives, May 26, 2005, p. 19.

Nonprofit hospitals: Better standards needed for tax exemption. 1990. General Accounting Office.

Present law and background relating to the tax-exempt status of charitable hospitals. 2006. Joint Committee on Taxation, U.S. Senate Finance Committee, September 12.

Rev. Rul. 69-645, 1969-2, C.B. 117.

Rev. Rul. 83-157, 1983-2, C.B. 94.

Young, G. J. 2004. Federal tax-exemption requirements for joint ventures between nonprofit hospital providers and for-profit entities: Form over substance? *Annals of Health Law* 13:329–35.

References

1. Prybil, L., S. Levey, R. Peterson, D. Heinrich, P. Brezinski, J. Price, A. Zamba, and W. Roach. 2008. *Governance in nonprofit community health systems: An initial report on CEO perspectives*. Chicago: Grant Thornton.
2. The role of the board of directors in Enron's collapse. 2002. July 8 Permanent Subcommittee on Investigations, Committee on Governmental Affairs, U.S. Senate.

3. Finder, A. 2005. Senate panel to review American U. board actions on spending. *New York Times*, December 3, Education sec.

4. Where's oversight of Oversight Foundation. 2007. *Des Moines Register*, March 21.

5. Burns, L. R., J. Cacciamani, J. Clement, and W. Aquino. 2000. The fall of the house of AHERF: The Allegheny bankruptcy. *Health Affairs (Project Hope)* 19:7–41.

6. Entin, F., J. Anderson, and K. O'Brien. 2006. *The board's fiduciary role: Legal responsibilities of health care governing boards*. Chicago: Center for Healthcare Governance.

7. Ono, N. 1998. Boards of directors under fire: An examination of nonprofit board duties in the health care environment. *Annals of Health Law* 7:107–38.

8. *Best practices: Nonprofit corporate governance*. 2004. Chicago: McDermott, Will & Emery.

9. Bjork, D. A. 2004. *Strengthening governance in hospitals and health systems: A survey of governance reform initiatives in not-for-profit hospitals and health systems*. Boseman, MT: American Governance and Leadership Group.

10. The Governance Institute. 2005. *50 practices of top-performing boards*. San Diego, CA.

11. Bader, B., E. Kazemek, and R. Witalis. 2006. *Emerging standards for institutional integrity: A tipping point for charitable organizations*. San Diego, CA: The Governance Institute.

12. Bryant, E. and P. Jacobson. 2006. Ten best practices for measuring the effectiveness of nonprofit healthcare boards. *Bulletin of the National Center for Healthcare Leadership*, December.

13. Internal Revenue Service. 2007. *Good governance practices for 502(c)(3) organizations*.

14. Center for Healthcare Governance. 2007. *Building an exceptional board: Effective practices for health care governance—Report of the Blue Ribbon Panel on Health Care Governance*, 68. Chicago.

15. The Governance Institute. 2007. *Boardsx4* governance structures and practices*. San Diego, CA.

16. Panel on the Nonprofit Sector. 2007. *Principles for good governance and ethical practice: A guide for charities and foundations*. Washington, DC.

17. Silk, T. 2007. Good governance practices for 501(c)(3) organizations: Should the IRS become further involved? *International Journal of Not-for-Profit Law* 10 (December).

18. Peregrine, M. 2008. IRS updates position on corporate governance. Letter to Corporate Governance Task Force, February 28.

19. Abbe, L. and A. Baney. 1958. *The nation's health facilities: Ten years of the Hill-Burton hospital and medical facilities programs, 1946–1956*, p. 616. Washington, DC: Public Health Service Publication.

20. Coleman, S. 2005. *The Hill-Burton uncompensated services program*. Congressional Research Service, The Library of Congress.

21. Rev. Rul. 69-645. C.B.117. 1969-2.

22. General Accounting Office. 1990. *Nonprofit hospitals: Better standards needed for tax exemption*.

23. Kuchler, J. A. 1992. Tax-exempt yardstick: Defining the measurements. *Healthcare Financial Management* 46:20–24.

24. Seay, J. D. 1994. From Pemsel's case to health security: Community benefit comes of age. A review of standards developed by the Voluntary Hospitals of America, the Catholic Health Association, and the Hospital Community Benefit Standards Program. *Journal of Health Administration Education* 12:373–82.

25. Evans, M. 2007. Caution: More scrutiny ahead. Regardless of federal standards on what constitutes adequate community benefits, hospitals still face close look from the states. *Modern Healthcare* 37:46.

26. Nonprofit, for-profit, and governmental hospitals; Uncompensated care and other community benefit. Testimony of David M. Walker, Comptroller General of the United States, General Accounting Office, before the Committee on Ways and Means, U.S. House of Representatives, May 26, 2005, p. 19.

27. 2007. *Community benefit debate escalates*. Chicago: McDermott, Will, & Emery.

28. Internal Revenue Service. U.S. Department of the Treasury. August 5, 2008. Update on 2008 Form 990 Draft Instructions.

29. Catholic Health Association. 2006. *A guide for planning and reporting community benefit*. St. Louis, MO.

30. Grassley, C. F. 2006. Memorandum to reporters and editors.

31. Coalition for Nonprofit Health Care. 2002. *Corporate responsibility handbook*, 9. Washington, DC.

32. Report of the ABA task force on corporate responsibility. 2003. *The Business Lawyer*, November, pp. 159–60.

33. *My brother's keeper: Growing expectations confront hospitals on community benefit and charity care*. 2006. PricewaterhouseCoopers, Health Research Institute.

34. Bilton, M. 2006. Community benefit: A new strategy. Presentation at the Hospital Association's Joint Board Retreat, Lake Okoboji, Iowa, August 11.

35. AHA, 2006. *Strengthening community trust: Strategies for CEOs*. Chicago.

36. Public Health Institute. 2004. *Advancing the state of the art in community benefit*, 15–43. Oakland, CA.

37. Porter, M. E. and M. R. Kramer. 2006. Strategy and society: The link between competitive advantage and corporate social responsibility. *Harvard Business Review* 84:78–92.

38. Lee, S. Y., J. A. Alexander, and G. J. Bazzoli. 2003. Whom do they serve? Community responsiveness among hospitals affiliated with health systems and networks. *Medical Care* 41:165–79.

Chapter 14

Culture, Ethics, and the Board

P. Michael Peterson

Contents

Executive Summary

A health care organization's culture is the cornerstone of its success. Culture influences personnel behaviors, management styles, organizational structure and system development, communication and decision-making patterns, hiring and firing practices, ways of delivering services, patient care quality, and safety. It will determine what is considered ethical and fair and what is not; what behaviors and outcomes are acceptable and what are not; what is viewed as good and what is not good. The underlying assumptions that define an organization's culture have the power to propel it toward or hinder it from success. Many systemic, workforce, and operational problems that health care organizations face are the result of not understanding or underestimating the culture's power to influence employees at all levels. The ability of health care boards and providers to measure, understand, change, and use their organization's culture will determine, to a large extent, how well they will perform in the health delivery arena.

Learning Objectives

1. To understand the relationship between organizational culture, ethics, behavior, and health within the organization.
2. To understand the role organizational boards and health care providers play in establishing, perpetuating, and reinforcing culture.
3. To understand the primary assumptions that define a culture.
4. To gain insights and actions that will help create an ethical culture.

Key Words

- Culture
- Health
- Ethics
- Leadership
- Fairness

Introduction

Organizational culture determines and defines how people behave and how the organization is structured. Organizational culture, however, is not defined by the behaviors and structures, but it is demonstrated in them. The essence of culture is in the underlying assumptions, values, beliefs, and ethics that have been jointly learned and taken for granted as the organization has successfully evolved.[1] These assumptions and values are often established by the board of directors and executives who run an organization; they (through various directives, objectives, decisions, and actions) instill them in management, who then act as gatekeepers of the culture. Over time they become shared and taken for granted by employees, both old and new.

These shared basic assumptions of an organization's culture act much like a software program—providing the foundational principles that guide behavior and thought within the organizational body. Culture's impact can be illustrated by a simple experiment that was done in a computer laboratory.[2] Since culture is based on simple, yet general assumptions, a computer program was written to test this idea with computerized birds called Boids. The Boids were given three very basic commands. First, "separation"—steer to avoid crowding other flock mates. Second, "alignment"—steer toward the average heading of other flock mates. Third, "cohesion"—steer to move toward the average position of other flock mates. Amazingly, the flight patterns that emerged were similar to the V-shaped pattern of migrating birds. Even when obstacles were thrown in front of them, the Boids would go through seemingly complex behavioral patterns, but ultimately return to the same basic pattern. Humans do the same thing. The simple cultural assumptions shared within an organization will determine how employees will work, perform, behave, communicate, relate, and think. The key for health care providers and board members is to have a clear understanding of the depth, breadth, and strength of culture, and how to work within it and shape it for the benefit of the organization.

Three Primary Cultural Assumptions

Organizational sociologists and psychologists have identified three foundational cultural assumptions: the nature of human nature, the nature of human relationships, and the nature of time and space.[1,3,4] These three general assumptions (which are often unconscious and taken for granted) are the ultimate source of espoused values and actions taken within the organizational body. The assumptions of founders, chief executive officers (CEOs), executives, and board members in these three areas will determine how the organization acts, how it is structured and organized, what it values, how it will work and behave, what will be rewarded or punished, and what is considered acceptable or ethical.

Assumptions about Human Nature

At the turn of the century, the basic assumptions that underwrote modern industry were enunciated by Henry Ford in 1922: "The average worker wants a job in which he does not have to put much physical effort. Above all, he wants a job in which he does not have to think."[5] Henry Ford had specific assumptions about human nature that were one-faceted, focusing only on physical labor, but he overlooked human psychosocial needs. This assumption also dovetailed into the academic and managerial notions at that time, being expressed as a concept of scientific management developed and espoused by Frederick Taylor.[6] Henry Ford aside, contemporary executive managers differ greatly on this dimension of human nature. Some assume that humans are basically lazy and work only when they are given incentives. Others assume that humans are basically motivated to work and only need to be given the appropriate resources and opportunities. These contrasting assumptions are exemplified in management as theory X and theory Y.[7]

Let us contrast two organizations with different cultural assumptions about human nature, as an example. In company A, people are viewed as responsible, motivated, and capable of organizing themselves. People are also seen as inherently interested in work and have a need to grow in their respective jobs. In contrast, company B believes that people are not capable of organizing themselves, are inherently lazy and tend to avoid work, and will take advantage of the company when given the opportunity. The assumptions behind each general theory have tremendous influence over how the organization behaves and structures itself. If people are viewed as lazy, irresponsible, and inherently evil, management will structure itself in a manner that centralizes control with management; will institute strict guidelines, policies, and rules to control worker behavior; will structure communication patterns so that decisions are made at the upper echelons of the company; and will treat workers in a more paternalistic manner.[8,9] In contrast, if workers are viewed more positively (i.e., responsible, motivated, and capable), the workplace will be structured far differently. Decision making will take place throughout the organization, rules and policies will be less constrictive and more flexible, and management will work more collaboratively rather than paternalistically with workers.[9]

Assumptions about Human Relationships

Workplaces and organizations are comprised of people, and work is accomplished through the combined interactions and efforts of individual workers.

The founder of a company institutes procedures and structures in the workplace in order to maximize the efforts of employees, and to minimize waste so that the business can profit and achieve acceptable levels of quality. If it is assumed that truth comes ultimately from older, wiser, and higher-status people, or that employees work best when they are told what to do, work will be structured linearly and vertically. Communication patterns will follow a hierarchical path, and decisions will occur from the top down. In contrast, if it is assumed that truth can only be arrived at by fighting things out in groups, then the workplace will be structured in a flatter manner, with communication occurring in all directions, and decisions will be made in a participatory manner.[9]

Assumptions about Time and Space

Cultural assumptions about time and space are the hardest to detect, but they can be the most decisive in determining how comfortable employees feel in the workplace. Assumptions about time vary in the degree to which they are viewed as a linear resource—once spent never to be regained.[10,11] Simply stated, "time is money," and it must be used carefully. Subsequently, only one thing can be done in any given unit of time. Assumptions about time also give meaning to being on time or late. Arriving at work early and leaving late can have different symbolic meanings in different contexts. It could be interpreted as high commitment or as an inability to be efficient.[1] In some industries and occupations, time is critical, because only certain windows of opportunity present themselves, requiring employees to schedule and plan their time wisely.

Space also has symbolic meaning. How an office or health care organization is laid out implies how people are to communicate with one another. Open-air office designs tend to facilitate interaction and coworker collaboration, while closed offices symbolize a need to think for one's self. Space also has to do with location and size of offices, as well as the furnishings that are contained within these spaces. We may jest about the "big corner office, with windows," but these jokes reflect serious cultural assumptions about the meaning of the physical environment. Failure to attain the appropriate space reward is interpreted negatively and can contribute to the development of distress and perceptions of unfairness.

Application of these assumptions within health care organizations would determine how a given organization or health care provider would answer the following questions:

- How do we communicate and make decisions about health care?
- How do we handle errors or problems?
- How do we structure and organize ourselves to maximize patient care and quality?

- What behaviors are we willing to accept or not accept among our workforce?
- What does an employee need to do to be successful?
- What do we, as an organization, need to do to be successful?
- What is patient safety, and how do we best achieve it?

Many health organizations do not know what their underlying cultural assumptions are, and thus, risk "flying blind" through the obstacles within a market-driven arena. Poorly articulated or formulated cultural assumptions will also lead to employees, work units, or occupations exercising their own independent cultural assumptions within the organizational body. They will do what they feel is necessary based on their own cultural assumptions. This can lead to chaos and a breech in ethics.[12–14] As Edgar Shein in *Organizational Culture and Leadership*[15] states, the fundamental fact for leaders is that if they do not become conscious of the culture in which they are embedded, those cultures will manage them.

Culture, Management Behavior, and Structure

Organizational culture has a profound effect on the behavior of managers.[16,17] Managers are the bearers and transmitters of the cultural assumptions and concomitant values and beliefs to the rest of the workforce.[18] Managers implement practices (behaviors) and organize themselves and the work (structure) based on their assumptions of the nature of the task and the employees. Their goal is to accomplish the task as successfully as possible. Task-driven assumptions are influenced by enterprise characteristics, including ownership status (private versus public), industry (service versus manufacturing), market competitiveness, and resource availability (human and technological resources). Employee-related assumptions are influenced by managerial assumptions about what employees are like and how they should best interact to achieve success for the business.[18] These assumptions will manifest themselves in the prevailing management style, including the degree of autocracy or participation practiced, ethics, and the expectations of employees.[19,20]

This discussion begs the question as to what management style or assumptions are best. Although some have purported specific management styles and assumptions to be better than others,[9] there is no consensus as to what the best style and driving culture should be. The variability in industry, occupations, and hopes and desires of employees (i.e., their personal cultural assumptions) suggests that diversity is a factor that should be considered when answering this question. Individuals often choose occupations because of an affinity with the goals and assumptions of the occupation. Those who value service and helping others will gravitate toward professions that value those characteristics, while those who do not value them gravitate toward less altruistic professions. The occupational values will also dictate what is viewed as acceptable management structure and behaviors, as well as appropriate employee or professional behaviors and practices.[21] Consequently, different occupations, industries, and sectors will vary in their perceptions of what is acceptable and what is not.

Occupational Cultures in Health Care

Within the larger cultural backdrop of the health care organization there are also subcultures that serve to enhance, modify, or compete with the culture of the corporate body. These subcultures are largely defined by the occupation in which the worker is engaged. Occupations shape and mold an employee's beliefs so that they often become internalized. Kohn and Schooler[22] consistently found that specific features of a given occupation related closely with occupational self-direction, perceived self-competence and self-efficacy, and self-control. This is very much the case within medicine and health care. According to Gillett,[14] medicine is a powerful subculture with its own language and understanding of the range of illnesses that affect human beings. It is defined by the following assumptions and beliefs:

- Medical truth is derived through scientific discourse.
- Knowledge of health and disease is constructed in terms of what might lead to effective interventions that can be mass produced and applied to the human body.
- Medical practice is determined by alliances made between big players in health care (i.e., pharmaceuticals, medical research, government).

These tenets give rise to the concept that good clinical practice involves the latest technology because reliance on one's own, perhaps experienced, judgment could leave one exposed to medico-legal risk if problems arise in patient care. In addition, medical professionals are responsible for the health of patients, and if necessary, they should sacrifice their health for that of their patient. Van Maanen and Barley[23] note, for example, that burnout is becoming a mark of occupational status among human service occupations such as nursing. Among resident physicians, it is common to subject them to a 48-hour shift as a "rite of passage" to becoming a doctor. Despite the potential for medical errors and lack of patient safety, it is important to prove one's willingness to sacrifice himself or herself (via sleep deprivation and exhaustion) to care for patients. The cultural tenet that good doctors are self-sacrificing can trump an organizational value of patient safety.

The cultural belief that good doctors also do not make mistakes, coupled with a fear of litigation within health care in general, can contribute to a climate of secrecy, a lack of honesty with patients, and reluctance to admit or learn from errors. Much has been written about the need for a safety culture within health care organizations, but often the prevailing organizational culture will prevent this from occurring. For example, Tucker and Edmondson[24] reported that in spite of increased emphasis on these issues, hospitals are not learning from the daily problems and errors encountered by their workers, and that process failures are common and an integral part of working on the front lines of health care delivery. Their study, which involved 239 hours of observation of 26 nurses at 9 hospitals, indicated that:

- Nurses are more accepting of problems than errors.
- Nurses prefer to implement short-term remedies that "patch" problems rather than seek to change underlying organizational routines that prevent recurrence.
- When one encounters a problem, do what it takes to continue the patient care tasks—no more, no less.
- When necessary for continuity of patient care—ask for help from people who are socially close rather than from those who are best equipped to correct the problem.

What causes these types of behaviors? The cause is organizational culture combined with occupational culture. Clearly, there is a greater value (and underlying assumption) in favor of individual vigilance, unit efficiency, and personal (nurse) empowerment over organizational learning and quality. Good (and successful) nurses are ones who take personal responsibility to resolve problems quietly on their own, who do not contribute to or highlight problems, and who maintain patient care during their shift regardless of whether that work adds value to the patient's experience.

These individualistic beliefs and subsequent actions may provide feelings of confidence and self-sufficiency, yet in order to resolve problems within the organization, it requires getting others involved. Unfortunately, in most hospitals organizational culture and management behaviors tend to reinforce this system of individual vigilance. Tucker and Edmondson[24] go on to say that 70% of the nurses interviewed believed that their manager expected them to work through the daily disruptions on their own, and that speaking up about a problem would be seen as a sign of incompetence.

These findings were also echoed by Hermann and Rowan,[25] who stated that in today's complex system of health care, medical accidents rarely result from a single error or individual. The traditional health care culture and its leaders have relied on blame-ridden investigations and punishment as a response to medical accidents, while allowing the systemic conditions (which are culturally determined) that gave rise to the accident to continue.

Managing boards of health care organizations need to be aware of the role that both organizational and occupational cultures play in determining employee behaviors and patient care. Failure to understand the cultural mechanisms at play will perpetuate problems and prevent quality improvement. Although health care cultures value healing, patience, self-sacrifice, individual vigilance, and personal responsibility, these same attributes can lead to lack of reporting, poor service quality, medical errors, and a fear of punishment and being honest. Provider trustees can give great insight into these issues for the better understanding of their nonprovider colleagues.

Culture and Ethics

Ethics is defined as the body of moral principles or values governing (or distinctive of) a particular culture or group.[26] Within health care organizations, ethics are the outcome of cultural values related to medicine and patient care, as well as what are permissible and acceptable behaviors and decisions for creating a successful business. Although many assume that ethics is a religious artifact, in reality it is an essential part of doing business because ethical principles and codes of conduct provide a framework for good decision making and organizational behavior. Ethics serve to link the personal beliefs of employees with the corporate cultural values and beliefs. Typically, cultures value honesty, integrity, trust, hard work, loyalty and commitment, and respect for one another.[13] Ethical tenets are learned through education (e.g., the organization publicly declares them as values) and observed behavior (e.g., we see what others do and do not do and the consequences of those actions). However, these attributes can be compromised if competing values of profit, market share, competition, and individualism are also espoused. Within any organization, a culture may promote competing values that serve to create ethical dilemmas for employees.

> "Do I provide the patient with all the medical options if it means costing the hospital money and time?"

> "Do I bring the misconduct of a coworker to management, or do I let it slide to protect the unit or team?"

In addition, pressure can be placed on employees to compromise ethics in an effort to achieve a greater good (or value).[27,28]

For health care organizations, it is important to answer the following questions:

1. Why might good people in this organization do unethical things?
2. What are our organization's values?
3. To whom is our organization accountable?
4. What do we mean by success?
5. Does the leadership of our organization support the idea of an ethical workplace?

The answers to these questions reveal much about the prevailing cultural values inherent within the organization, and what it will allow or disallow among its workforce.

In a 2003 National Business Ethics Survey, conducted by the Ethics Resource Center,[29] the most common types of misconduct observed were abusive or intimidating behavior toward employees, and lying to employees, customers, suppliers, and the public. These types of misconduct can be culturally reinforced, and thus perpetuate a difficult work environment. For example, a nurse supervisor who regularly berates new nurses as a means of controlling staff and achieving quality care creates a hostile work environment (unethical conduct), while achieving corporate goals (quality care). If she is rewarded by management for her performance (quality care), it simultaneously reinforces unethical management practices. Employees soon learn what is acceptable behavior within the greater corporate culture and what is truly valued. Mistreatment (perceived or real) of employees acts as a catalyst for unethical behaviors among a workforce and elicits retaliatory responses (e.g., stealing supplies, less productive use of time, backbiting, and noncompliance). In a study conducted by Harris Interactive on behalf of Deloitte & Touche USA,[12] 91% of employed adult workers stated that they would more likely behave ethically on the job when they have a good balance between work and the rest of their life, and 60% believe that job dissatisfaction is a significant reason for people to make unethical decisions at work. People do care about ethics, and they include it as important criteria for a healthy workplace.[30]

When an organization's culture drifts toward unethical practices, the end result is a work environment that is not professional, productive, satisfying, and safe.[31] Unethical cultures (or weak ethical ones) create a context in which ethical dilemmas are more common, and where personal values are consistently assaulted. This adds to the stress and emotional labor of the workforce that contributes to ill health, staff turnover, and lack of productivity and service quality.[32–34]

What Can the Board Do?

Employees listen to their leadership's messages and observe their behavior; therefore, it is imperative that any health care board set the example, in both word and deed, as to what is ethical, and the degree that ethics is a part of the organization's culture. Specifically, a board can work to make sure management:

- Talks about ethics at work
- Models ethical behavior
- Creates an environment where ethical issues can be freely discussed
- Upholds ethical standards via codes of conduct and disciplinary actions
- Provides ethical boards or groups that help employees make good decisions

Communication about ethics should become a regular part of performance reviews, staff meetings, and personal conversations. Consistent ethical reminders serve to strengthen the cultural value and create a safe environment that encourages employees to ask ethics questions and get the right answers.

Culture and Health

There has been greater attention given to employee health in light of the costs incurred by organizations to insure their workers, and to address illness-related absenteeism, lower productivity, errors, injury, and long- and short-term disability. It is not surprising that employee health has become a boardroom issue among the most progressive organizations. Given the wellness and illness issues associated with health care workers and organizations, health care cost containment is both important and necessary for success.

The relationship between an organization's culture and health is illustrated by the culture-work-health model[5,35] (Figure 14.1).

Organizational culture influences and determines how the business will develop and establish itself in terms of management behaviors, corporate structures, and administrative and policy systems. The culture serves to define how we should structure, organize, and behave to be successful. For example, a culture that values management control will develop an organizational structure and concomitant policies and regulations different from those developed by a culture that values employee involvement. In turn, the system will influence how workers behave and communicate.

Elements of the workplace that are influenced by the culture can be divided into two broad categories: environmental and behavioral. Environmental factors include company policies, rules, regulations, benefits, compensation, organizational structure, job design, and physical workplace. Behavioral factors include patterns of communication, including how departments or divisions communicate both quantitatively and qualitatively. Behavioral factors also include management style with subsequent decision-making processes, levels of worker control and autonomy, and degree of feedback and appraisal.

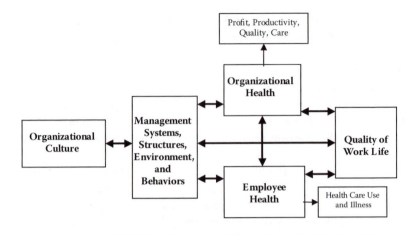

Figure 14.1   Culture–work–health model.

Both categories influence employee health and organizational health; therefore, it is conceivable that an organization can be sick or healthy depending upon its internal physiological functioning. Organizational health is often defined in terms of financial success and service or product quality. If the prevailing culture is sound, organizational health will occur, if it is unsound, it will not. Likewise, the culture influences employee health by establishing how people are managed, levels of support and communication, company policies, work-life balance, job design (including effort-reward and demand-control balance), and the physical workplace. All of these have been shown to have a direct impact on worker health through psychosocial stress.

The model also suggests that organizational and employee health will influence management systems and structures. For example, a healthy organization may tend to behave in a manner that is less restrictive and controlling, whereas in an unhealthy organization management may tend to clamp down on workers and exert more control over their jobs in an effort to keep "a lid on" the situation. The overall organizational health will also dictate the type and source of stressors that occur. Culture is most prone to change when organizational health and employee health become liabilities and require leadership to answer the question: What is going on, and why is it happening? This question is the catalyst for challenging long-held cultural assumptions and for determining whether they are appropriate for the corporation, employees, marketplace, and the age in which we exist.

When cultural assumptions create environments that prevent a balance between worker demands and control, and create an imbalance between employee effort and reward, employees begin to suffer greater levels of distress, which in turn makes them at greater risk for certain cancers, cardiovascular disease, and mental illness. In addition, increased worker stress has been linked to abdominal obesity, hypertension, and unhealthy or risky behaviors.[36,37] Ultimately, the context in which we work has a direct and powerful influence over our state of well-being. This concept is an important one that deserves attention as a boardroom topic of discussion. When boards fail to take their culture seriously, they often succumb to problems that derail their ability to function.

With work stress comes emotional labor, and recognition is growing that emotional responses to stress are closely linked to the origins and exacerbation of disease within workplaces.[32,38] For example, worker perceptions of stressors can mediate health-related behaviors such as smoking, drinking, substance abuse, and antagonistic behaviors. If workers perceive they have little control and excessive work demands, they will tend to exhibit behaviors that encourage negative emotional reactions (anger, frustration, boredom), problematic cognitive functioning (poor attention, concentration, and problem solving), and adverse interpersonal relationships (antagonism, defensiveness). If these reactions are widespread within a given organization, they can cause a severely negative impact on the organization.[39,40] Emotional reactions to work stress are critical components of both organizational and employee health.

When this occurs, it creates a phenomenon called a culture of stress, in which whole staff groups or organizations can experience a form of collective burnout.[4,41] In a positive work culture the group tries out various responses to solve a problem until something works. In a culture of stress, groups begin to make decisions that serve to minimize or avoid stress. Fear of doing something wrong and being punished for it overrides the motivation to try something new or to contribute to the organization. Within an environment, workers try to avoid inevitable pain. A culture of stress is created by cultural assumptions about human nature and human relationships that lead to an emphasis on negative feedback, punishment, and a climate of paranoia.

The role of the board is to monitor and identify the cultural assumptions that influence organizational and employee health. However, even that must be done carefully because there must be a balance between these two criteria. Overemphasis on employee health issues can impose restrictions and regulations that may compromise the health of the organization in the marketplace. Likewise, overemphasis on organizational health may create a masochistic environment that leads to short-term success but long-term chronic disease in terms of worker stress, ill health, lack of commitment, disloyalty, unethical behaviors, and poor performance.

The question is: How does one know whether these two health factors are in appropriate balance? The answer is actually very simple. Ask the workforce. The perceptions and attitudes of the workforce as a whole will indicate whether an appropriate balance has been achieved.

Culture and Fairness

Fairness and equity are hallmarks of Western culture. From childhood we all exhibit an inherent need for fairness and its judicious exercise toward us and others. But what is fairness? In its broadest sense, fairness is the perception that one's interests, claims, or rights are recognized, acknowledged, and given reasonable weight by significant others to whom one is affiliated in situations where the interests, claims, or rights of those others have to be reconciled.[42] In the workplace, this means that fairness is interpreted as an outcome that satisfies the claims and self-interests of both parties. Typically those parties are defined as the employee and the employer. Within work stress research, fairness has risen as an important construct to organizational and employee health. Effort-reward balance is based on the concept of fairness—that one's labor will be fairly and equitably rewarded, and that one's effort will be fairly applied to the needs of the organization. An imbalance in this area creates distress for both employee and employer, depending upon the nature of the imbalance.

According to Shain,[42] fairness is also an emotional response that may display itself as comfort, security, trust, mental well-being, and coherence (all is right with the world). When you perceive your employment situation as fair, you experience positive emotions. In contrast, a sense of unfairness may illicit feelings of anxiety, depression, anger, alienation, and disorder. For fairness to flourish, it requires a cultural context that promotes mutual regard, esteem, and respect, attributes that arise from our assumptions about human nature and human relationships.[43]

Two primary factors that inhibit fairness include "information failure" and "participation failure."[42] Information failure occurs when one party willfully withholds relevant facts from another party in a transaction. The purpose for this unethical behavior is to gain or maintain advantage. Often an individual perceives information as his or her property, and as such, he or she considers it his or her right to hold on to it and not share it, even if it creates a disadvantage with the other party. In our larger society, our laws draw boundaries around advantage, because beyond a certain point, such behaviors vitiate consent to bargains. In doctor–patient relationships, for example, free and informed choice with regard to medical or surgical procedures is a requirement and is central for a fair negotiation in decision making.

Participation failure refers to being left out or somehow excluded from decision-making processes in which one has material interest in the outcome.[42] When one party fails to gather input from another, or to seek consultation or advice in the process of making a decision that affects all parties, it creates a breach in fairness. This behavior vitiates the consent of disadvantaged parties because no opportunity is provided to exercise choice concerning outcomes that affect them.

An organization's cultural assumptions can work toward creating two extreme relationship patterns: power relations and relations of mutuality, regard, esteem, and respect.[42] According to Shain, in the former, the culture is manifest in behaviors and decision-making patterns that control and hoard information and resources. Often, threats or use of physical or psychological coercion are used to achieve objectives, and consistent efforts are put into gaining an advantage and position, and making independent, nonconsensual decisions about matters that affect multiple parties. In the latter, the cultural assumptions promote an environment where information and resources are shared, logic and reason are applied in making decisions, efforts to seek common ground and mutual advantage are employed, open communication and dialog about interests and needs are expressed, and relationship harmony is viewed as a worthy goal.[42]

Fairness also serves to motivate employees. Frederick Herzberg[44] espoused through his motivation-hygiene theory that recognition by the right person at the right time under the right circumstances satisfied a natural human need, which served to promote continued intrinsically motivated effort. However, when it was not provided, employees become increasingly unmotivated and retaliatory. He also stated that workers have an inherent need to achieve and accomplish something worthwhile, as well as to advance and grow in their work.[45] When these needs are not met, or are blocked through unfair behaviors, policies, and practices (perceived or real), workforce problems will arise. In describing a healthy workplace, Peterson found that both men and women listed fairness, equity, recognition and respect as important factors, with women ranking these attributes in their top 10 most important values in the workplace (significantly higher than their male counterparts).[30] With women occupying a greater percentage of the labor force, issues of fairness are becoming more central to corporate concerns.

Creating a Culture of Fairness

When talking about fairness in the workplace, often the issue focuses on race and gender. However, this is a mistake because it diverts the attention from behaviors to demographic issues, which have inherently led to further perceptions of unfairness via selective hiring and reward practices based on gender and race. Creating a culture of fairness requires addressing the major cultural constructs that govern management systems, structures, and behaviors and promote informational and relationship fairness.

To promote fairness, health care boards can provide leadership by example to:

1. Share information relevant to employees, stakeholders, and the public.
2. Provide opportunity for employees, stakeholders, and the public to voice concerns and provide input and counsel on matters that pertain to their work and relationship with the health care organization.
3. Hire and reward managers that behave in a manner conducive to a culture of fairness.
4. Regularly review policies to determine their level of fairness with respect to the twenty-first-century workforce realities.
5. Regularly review job descriptions and functions to determine if an appropriate balance between employee effort and reward is being achieved.

Culture, Ethics, and the Role of the Board

General Douglas MacArthur once said, "If your soldiers believe that you have their best interests at heart, they will follow you anywhere." This point is very appropriate to health care providers on boards. It is through the board that cultural assumptions and values are developed, instigated, and communicated to the organizational body. The questions for board members are whether these assumptions are truly in the best interest of the health of the organization, and do they demonstrate qualities of ethics and fairness that will serve to create a work context in which employees can succeed and thrive. When the board both reflects and determines healthy cultural values, employees will be more apt to follow in a like manner, starting with executive management and moving throughout the organization.

People learn by example, and we are perpetually observers of human behavior—both for the good and for the bad. We learn by watching how others behave, and how their behaviors are summarily rewarded. If good behavior, effort, values, and ethics are rewarded positively, employees will learn to behave, think, and value in the same manner. Likewise, if bad behavior, effort, values, and ethics are rewarded positively, they will learn to do the same—but with the additional burden of value conflict that accompanies a dichotomous outcome.

It is in the best interest of board members to be vigilant in their pursuit of a culture that is ethical and promotes health. Although health care providers on boards may not effectuate these values and beliefs in the workplace, they do set the course of direction that the organization will take and how employees at all levels will think, behave, and function. To this end, issues of fairness, employee health, organizational health, cultural values, and ethics should be boardroom items of discussion.

Creating an Ethical Board Culture

Paramount to creating an ethical board culture is understanding the organization's current culture.[5,35] It is difficult to know where to go if the organization's position is not clear. By taking a close, critical, objective look at cultural assumptions and how they influence the organization, areas for growth, improvement, and change become apparent. When assessing culture it is advisable to have it done by someone outside the organization who has not been influenced by it and who has no history or agenda within it. Internal cultural assessments often serve to downplay problems and fail to identify the major assumptions of importance. Someone external to the organization is in the best position to objectively evaluate the culture and to identify how it is either hindering or helping the organization.

The board should mandate systems that monitor (internally) for signs and symptoms of an unhealthy organization or unhealthy employees. For example, absenteeism rates, turnover rates, work stress, grievances, communication problems, sickness and illness rates, short- and long-term disability, accident and safety problems, ethics violations, patient care quality, and medical mistakes are measures that should be consistently monitored. This action at the organizational level can serve to prevent more chronic corporate diseases. Regular reports to the board on these matters should be requested and subject to discussion.

Leadership is vital for an ethical and healthy organization. Therefore, board members should self-monitor their behaviors, decisions, and practices to make sure that they align with healthy standards of conduct and cultural assumptions that promote a healthy organization and employee well-being.

Board members should not be afraid to challenge long-held cultural assumptions. The tendency is to perpetuate a given culture because it is known, safe, and comfortable. However, the culture could be the prime cause of institutional problems. The board should ask itself, "How is our culture impacting our success, or contributing to problems within the organization?" Culture is most effectively changed when it is determined to be contributing to a problem.

Conclusion

A health care organization's culture is the origin of its systems, processes, behaviors, and outcomes. It is defined by the underlying assumptions, values, beliefs, and ethics that have been jointly learned and taken for granted as the organization has successfully developed. These shared assumptions and values act like a software program dictating how employees (at all levels) will work, behave, communicate, and act day to day, and week to week. It defines what we should and ought to do in order to be a successful employee (doctor, nurse, social worker, dietitian), and to be a successful health care organization. Culture will be reflected in what it values, what is of prime importance at board meetings and in annual reports, and what matters are given the most attention and time.

The difficulty for any health care provider on a board is understanding the organization's culture because culture is not overtly recognizable, and it is often beyond our ability to easily grasp. Like gravity and laws of physics, we act in accordance with them, but we do not really give them much thought. We know they exist, but they operate in the background. Therefore, it becomes imperative to conduct regular cultural assessments, and to monitor employee attitudes and perceptions of the organization. It is through workforce assessments that cultural factors can be made known and linked to organizational performance measures.

Health care boards also need to take a greater leadership role when it comes to reinforcing and strengthening culture or when seeking to change it. It is important that board meetings include culture as one of the agenda items and work to establish a culture and subsequent values that transcend profit and monetary goals. The most successful twenty-first-century health care organizations have focused on their culture and have sought to establish it as one that primarily reflects a humane, ethical, and altruistic value system. Those that have successfully accomplished this task have reaped the financial benefits that those values have made available.

Case Study

In 1995, Baptist Health Care (BHC)[46] was facing abysmal patient satisfaction ratings, and recent corporate reengineering efforts had damaged employee morale. Discussions were also being conducted on possible mergers with larger hospital groups that could save BHC from going out of business. It was becoming painfully aware to the board and CEO that in order for the organization to survive, it was going to have to make some drastic changes. Although the focus of leadership discussions were on traditional financial and merger-related issues, Al Stubblefield, CEO, walked into the boardroom and said, "Let's build a service culture that will be very difficult to duplicate or compete with." He recognized that their current cultural values and subsequent ways of behaving were contributing to their unhealthy organization, and to turn things around the board was going to have to start with the most important part of any organization—the culture and the assumptions they had about how to run their organization, how workers would relate with one another, and how to manage the business.

The major transformation was the discovery that the key to patient satisfaction was to not focus on patients first, but on the employees. Patient satisfaction was directly related to employee satisfaction; only happy, fulfilled employees will provide the highest level of health care to patients. BHC's cultural change from a financial to a service excellence culture involved endowing the workforce with a sense of ownership, espousing consistent values, and creating systems, structures, and behaviors that built a strong, attractive culture. That cultural change resulted in increased recruiting power, created loyalty among employees and customers, reduced employee turnover, produced more word-of-mouth advertising, and affected the organization's immediate and extended family. They created their cultural change by balancing their five pillars of operational excellence: people, service, quality, financial, and growth. Key to their cultural change success was tapping into their employee passions. Employees choose health care to serve and care for others, not just to make money. By aligning BHC's vision and purpose with what their caregivers truly valued, they were able to fuel an employee-driven culture change—a change that employees felt a part of and improved both organizational and employee health. This also involved changing the culture to one that communicated openly and often, had a "no secrets" and "no excuses" environment, and made every employee an owner.

The end result of their cultural transformation was moving from the 18th percentile in patient satisfaction to the 99th percentile, being awarded the prestigious Malcolm Baldrige National Quality Award by President George W. Bush at a special White House ceremony, and being recognized as one of *Fortune* magazine's 100 Best Companies to Work For in America.[46]

Study and Discussion Questions

1. What value did BHC derive from an employee-first, patient-second culture?
2. How did BHC capitalize on the strengths of the caregiver culture?
3. How might BHC's culture influence behavior and ethics?
4. What do you think the BHC board discusses at its meetings?
5. How did BHC's cultural transformation influence its financial status?

Suggested Readings and Web Sites

Readings

Schein, E. H. 1999. *The corporate survival guide.* San Francisco: Jossey-Bass.
Stubblefield, A. 2005. *The Baptist health care journey to excellence: Creating a culture that wows!* Hoboken, NJ: John Wiley & Sons.

Web Site

Organizational and Cultural Assessments: www.stormindex.com

References

1. Schein, E. H. 1999. *The corporate survival guide.* San Francisco: Jossey-Bass.
2. Reynolds, C. Boids. Background and update. http://www.red3d.com/cwr/boids/ 2008 (accessed January 15, 2008).
3. Schein, E. H. Three cultures of management: The key to organizational learning in the 21st century. http://www.solonline.org/res/wp/three.html (accessed March 4, 1997).
4. Schein, E. H. 1996. Culture: The missing concept in organizational studies. *Administrative Science Quarterly* 41:229–40.
5. Peterson, M. and J. F. Wilson. 2002. The culture-work-health model and work stress. *American Journal of Health Behavior* 26:16–24.
6. Taylor, F. 1911. *Principles of scientific management.* New York: Harper Brothers.
7. McGregor, D. 1960. *The human side of enterprise.* New York: McGraw-Hill.
8. Herzberg, F. 1987. One more time: How do you motivate employees? *Harvard Business Review*, pp. 109–20.
9. Keys, P. 1998. The betrayal of the total quality movement in Western management: Managed health care and provider stress. *Family and Community Health* 21:1–19.
10. Hall, E. T. 1966. *The hidden dimension.* New York: Doubleday.
11. Hall, E. T. 1959. *The silent language.* New York: Doubleday.
12. Worthington, B. 2007. work/life balance influences workplace ethics. *Human Resource Executive Online.* http://hreonline.com/HRE/printstory.jsp?storyId=12614425 (accessed January 17, 2008).
13. Joseph, J. Ethics in the workplace. ASAE and the Center for Association Leadership. http://asaecenter.org/PublictionsResources/articledetail.cfm?I (accessed January 17, 2008).
14. Gillett, G. 2008. Medical science, culture, and truth. *Philosophy, Ethics, and Humanities in Medicine.* http://www.peh-med.com/content/1/1/13 (accessed January 15, 2008).
15. Schein, E. H. 1996. *Organizational culture and leadership.* 2nd ed. New York: Jossey-Bass.
16. Marsella, A. J. 1994. The measurement of emotional reactions to work: Conceptual methodological and research issues. *Work Stress* 8:28–31.

17. Gardner, R. 1999. Benchmarking organizational culture: Organization culture as a primary factor in safety performance. *Professional Safety* 44:26.
18. Aycan, Z., R. N. Kanungo, and J. B. P. Sinha. 1999. Organizational culture and human resource management practices: The model of culture fit. *Journal of Cross-Cultural Psychology* 30:501–26.
19. Thompson, N., S. Stradling, M. Murphy, and P. O'Neill. 1996. Stress and organizational culture. *British Journal of Social Work* 26:647–65.
20. Handy, C. 1985. *Understanding organizations.* New York: Penguin.
21. Trice, H. M. 1993. *Occupational subcultures in the workplace.* Ithaca, NY: ILR Press.
22. Kohn, M. L. and C. Schooler. 1983. *Work and personality. An Inquiry into the Impact of Social Stratification.* Ablex Publishing Corporation.
23. Van Maanen, J. and S. R. Barley. 1984. Occupational communities: Culture and control in organizations. In *Research in organizational behavior*, ed. B. M. Shaw and L. L. Cummings. Vol. 6. Greenwich, CT: JAI Press.
24. Tucker, A. L. and A. C. Edmondson. 2003. Why hospitals don't learn from failures: Organizational and psychological dynamics that inhibit system change. *California Management Review* 45:1–18.
25. Hermann, C. and L. Rowan. 2004. Managing culture: Building a blameless reporting system for the ambulatory care environment. *Group Practice Journal* 53(4):9–16.
26. Flexner, S. B., ed. 1987. *The Random House dictionary of the English language,* 2nd ed. Random House.
27. Ambrosio, E. and S. Walkerley. Broadening the ethical focus: A community perspective on patient autonomy. *Humane Health Care* 12, no. 2. http://www.humane-healthcare.com/Article.asp?art_id=619 (accessed January 19, 2008).
28. Leonard, B. 2000. Ethics has become a hot workplace topic. *HR Magazine.*
29. Ethics Resource Center. 2003. *National business ethics survey.* Washington, DC.
30. Peterson, M. 2004. What men and women value at work: Implications for workplace health. *Gender Medicine* 1:106–24.
31. Baker, L., S. Sara, D. Gaba, J. Geppert, A. D. Sinaiko, S. K. Howard, and K. Park. 2003. Patient safety culture in hospitals. Nashville, TN: Academy Health Meeting, abstract 706.
32. Pugliesi, K. 1999. The consequences of emotional labor: Effects on work stress, job satisfaction, and well-being. *Motivation and Emotion* 23:125–54.
33. Bates, D. W. and A. A. Gawande. 2000. Error in medicine: What have we learned? [See comment]. *Annals of Internal Medicine* 132:763–67.
34. Sexton, J. B., E. J. Thomas, and R. L. Helmreich. 2000. Error, stress, and teamwork in medicine and aviation: Cross sectional surveys. *BMJ* 320:745–49.
35. Peterson, M. and J. Wilson. 1998. A culture-work-health model: A theoretical conceptualization. *American Journal of Health Behavior* 22:378–90.
36. Peterson, M. 1997. Work, corporate culture, and stress: Implications for worksite health promotion. *American Journal of Health Behavior* 21:243–52.
37. Peterson, M. and J. Wilson. 2004. Work stress in America. *International Journal of Stress Management* 11(2):91–113.

38. Bergman, B., F. Ahmad, and D. E. Stewart. 2003. Physician health, stress and gender at a university hospital. *Journal of Psychosomatic Research* 54:171–78.
39. Marcoulides, G. A. and R. H. Heck. 1993. Organizational culture and performance—Proposing and testing a model. *Organizational Science* 4:209–25.
40. McTigue-Bruner, B. and C. L. Cooper. 1991. Corporate financial performance and occupational stress. *Work and Stress* 5:267–87.
41. MacLean, D. and R. MacIntosh. 1998. Health and disease in organizations. *Journal of Alternative and Complementary Medicine* 4:185–88.
42. Shain, M. 2000. *Fairness in families, schools and workplaces*. Toronto: Center for Health Promotion, University of Toronto.
43. Simons, T. and Q. Roberson. 2003. Why managers should care about fairness: The effects of aggregate justice perceptions on organizational outcomes. *Journal of Applied Psychology* 88:432–43.
44. Herzberg, F. 1986. Innovation: Where is the relish? *Journal of Creative Behavior* 21:179–92.
45. Syptak, J. M., D. W. Marsland, and D. Ulmer. October 1999. Job satisfaction: Putting theory into practice. *Family Practice Management*. http://www.aafp.org/fpm/991000fm/26.html (accessed January 10, 2008).
46. Stubblefield, A. 2005. *The Baptist health care journey to excellence: Creating a culture that wows!* Hoboken, NJ: John Wiley & Sons.

Chapter 15

The Future of Health Care Boards

Gary L. Filerman

Contents

Executive Summary

Boards must be prepared to change in response to an uncertain future. Drivers of change include the continuing advance of quality of care assessment that will place additional responsibilities on boards, growth in the role and responsibilities of medical group practices, organization of the labor force including health professionals, scrutiny of the role of physicians on boards and a changing legal environment reflecting public concern for transparency, and the stewardship of tax-exempt resources. Boards should anticipate more stringent regulations mandating organizational behavior and be proactively engaged in anticipating the mandate. Physician board members should be assessing their distinctive responsibilities.

Learning Objectives

1. To appreciate how the governance function has remained relatively stable for many years despite the many pressures on the health system, and why that stability is decreasing at an increasing pace.
2. To understand some of the most potent emerging issues that will shape governance, that future boards will be under greater scrutiny and will be more regulated than they are today, and the subsequent effects on operations of boards and their members.
3. To understand why the role of providers in general and physicians in particular will be subject to scrutiny, and why it may be the target of specific regulation.
4. To look forward to meeting the unique challenges and responsibilities of the provider as board member.

Key Words

- Autonomy
- Change
- Competency responsibility
- Emerging issues
- Regulation
- Scope-of-practice
- Social compact
- Unions

Introduction

> The times, they are a-changin'.
>
> **Bob Dylan, 1964**

It is striking to note how little the half-century-old literature of governance differs from what we read today. Fifty years ago the issues were board member recruitment and selection, conflict-of-interest, orientation, education, competencies, board size, use of time, structure, and relationships with the chief executive officer (CEO). In the intervening years, attention focused on community representation and physician board membership and, more recently, on oversight of quality of care, community benefit, and external reporting requirements. What the comparison with contemporary literature tells us is that the organization and content of the governance function have been relatively stable, predictable, and that the changes have been minor and incremental. Despite navigating through environmental white water, the governance function has remained a well-defined and comfortable outpost of tranquility in health care.

The premise of this chapter is that governance in the next 50 years, and more likely the next decade, will be uncomfortable and transitional. We are in a process of change that boards must recognize and proactively manage. The social compact that is the foundation of governance in both the private and public sectors is being redefined at an increasing pace. The essence of the compact is that society trusts boards to exercise stewardship on behalf of the stakeholders, be they the investors or the public. That trust has eroded, calling attention to the public policy gray area in which both for-profit and nonprofit governance functions.

The most significant driver of change is the tremendous expansion of the third sector, the nonprofit components of our economy, in recent years. What has become clear is the dependency of our society on the services they provide, the proportion of employment they account for, the resources that they control, and the impact that they have on tax revenue and expense. From this perspective, many events of the past decade take on a new meaning. Responses to abuses, the imposition of expanded reporting to the Internal Revenue Service (IRS), and the debate over the definition of community benefit are not isolated events. They are precursors of change toward a redefinition of the social compact. The emerging definition will narrow the gray by clarifying expectations for organizational behavior, accountability for results, and transparency of processes. In other words, the autonomy of governance will decrease.[1]

This chapter will clarify five of the most potent issues and challenges that face boards as they look forward: quality of care, medical work, the workforce, physicians and nurses on boards, and the legal environment.

Emerging Issues That Will Shape the Agenda for Change

Quality of Care

Two landmark court decisions, in 1957 and 1965, clarified the legal foundation of hospitals' responsibility for the quality of care provided within their walls. *Bing v. Thunig* and *Darling v. Charleston Community Memorial Hospital* dismantled the widely held belief that boards are not responsible for the actions of independent providers using the facilities.[2] Administration and practice are no longer autonomous domains. The 2000 report of the Institute of Medicine (IOM), *To Err Is Human*, said in effect that the health care system, that is, providers, including organizations and their governance, has failed to meet its responsibility to provide safe and high-quality care by not applying what we know.[3]

The 2000 IOM report, followed by others, has transformed the environment of medical care. Quality, the most fundamental objective of all health services, is now a public issue, no longer closely held by the profession. The attention has been focused by the intersection of the issues of quality and cost of care, aptly phrased as value for money.

In spite of all of the ensuing research into the many aspects of quality, the development of practice guidelines, tightened accreditation standards and enforcement, malpractice insurance costs, the application of measurement tools, public reporting, and other developments, progress has been slow and uneven. Barriers to improvement have been clarified, and many of them point directly to the responsibilities of governance. Too few boards have responded proactively. Managing to achieve optimal safety and quality will remain an emerging and dominant governance issue.

Medical Work

Medical work is changing rapidly in unpredictable directions. While changes due to discovery and technical advances have always propelled change in medical work, we are now experiencing an unprecedented convergence of developments that are expanding the parameters of change. The rapid emergence of the hospitalist is an example of a significant change in the organization of hospital practice, with implications for the financial and quality assurance relationship between the institution and community practitioners. The role of the organized hospital medical staff has declined as the identification and loyalties of physicians have shifted to medical groups. New systems of practice oversight have emerged, imposing accountabilities for processes and outcomes and raising the question of where the responsibility will lie for ensuring provider competence.

The growth of group medical practice continues to change the landscape of medical care organizations in the community. As groups increase in size, exposure to risk, and economic power, a new definition of responsibility for provider behavior is being forged. Quality of care assessment and pay-for-performance are highlighting the inadequacies of extant mechanisms to ensure the competence of providers. Board certification and licensure do not do the job of ensuring provider competence, on which the public has grown to rely. Where the responsibility for more effective competency assurance will ultimately rest is an open question. Will it be the hospital, the group, the individual, the professional, or regulatory bodies?

The question of ensuring provider competence is driving the issue of how to link the provision of services needed to the most appropriate provider. Boards have long held responsibility for approving scope of privileges, but the emerging question is: What is the relationship between privileges and scope of practice? Evidence is growing that many providers are competent to provide services, safely and cost-effectively, that are outside of their legally defined scopes of practice. New and established professions, access issues, and economic pressures are challenging the old boundaries. As a result, medical work will change in every organizational setting.

The Workforce

The workforce has been described as the "soft underbelly" of the organization, caught in the constant struggle to maintain quality and contain costs. The shortages of recent years and the projections all point toward the need for significant changes in the way that institutions respond to their workforce needs. Most recent efforts have been incremental short-term tinkering at the edges of the problem, such as enhancing nurse or pharmacist recruitment and retention and changing benefit packages. The problems of health services workforce supply and quality must be resolved in the context of the broader labor force issues facing education, industry, and the professions.

The expansion of organized labor in health care is an important trend with implications for the role of the organization in workforce development. Unions have become more sophisticated in their appeal to health workers and have raised the moral questions of wages and benefits in the public arena.[1] It is important to note that the line between professionals and nonprofessionals joining unions has disappeared with increased activity among nurses, physicians, and others. Unionization has traditionally been viewed as a negative reflection on management and an imposition on management prerogatives. There is increasing evidence that unions may contribute to a more stable workforce and that collaboration may address shortages and enhance quality of care improvement efforts. Boards will question whether traditional views of labor organization limit their options for solving workforce problems, as unions reassess their traditional relationships with health care organizations.

Physicians and Nurses on Boards

Over the past 30 years, the view of physicians as members of boards has changed. Today, they are voting members of the boards of the majority of community hospitals, as is recommended by the Joint Commission.[4] The case for physician representation is persuasive and has been reinforced as boards have become more engaged in monitoring and acting on quality of care information. However, as board involvement in quality issues expand, the physician board member's role has become clouded. Board actions that impinge upon provider incomes have the potential to represent significant conflicts of interest to physician board members. The question has become more complex as the economic relationship between hospitals and physicians has changed, with physicians' increasing participation in potentially competing enterprises such as specialty hospitals and imaging centers, among others.

Hospitals have worked hard to establish a governance culture that supports medical staff member participation, as opposed to the *ex officio* nonvoting participation of the chief medical officer or medical staff president. Most boards have clarified conflict-of-interest rules, and many have invested in the education of physician members. However, the relationship is drawing increased attention by regulators. They are likely to be concerned that decisions affecting access, such as starting or stopping services, or about which groups, and in what form, the organization may partner, may be compromised by the economic interests, however indirect, of physicians serving on boards. The question may have implications for the legal liability of the organization in the future.

The possibility of nurses who are staff members serving on boards has rarely been raised. In many cases, the nurse leader attends board meetings. Only 1.8% of hospital and health system boards have nurse members, and less than 1% are voting members.[5] However, the likelihood of scope-of-practice expansion will stimulate more attention to the possibility of nurses and other providers seeking parity with physicians on boards.

The Legal Environment

In the context of describing new IRS governance reporting requirements, the health sector has been described as "opaque and largely overlooked by regulators."[6] Regulators are usually defined as state attorneys general, the Congress, and increasingly, local authorities. Agreement that the tools available to them are inadequate to oversee the complexities of the expanded third sector domain is growing. It is important to note again the place of the third sector in the economy, and that the attention of these public officials also extends to such entities as universities and service organizations. All are being subject to increased scrutiny, usually from the perspectives of the return to society on their tax advantages and the transparency of their transactions and relationships.

There is only one way that such scrutiny can go. That is toward mandated specification of expectations, accountability for results, defined transparency, and the specification of operating policies and procedures. It is instructional to note the New Jersey law requiring 1 day a year of board education, with the state specifying the syllabus.[7] The gray area has now narrowed. The issue will be the level of detail of the specification, but based on experience and caution, it is likely to be outlined in the regulations with each board responsible for filling in the details. Compliance will be measured by the extent to which practice follows the board's own rules.[1]

The Coming Regulatory Environment

The convergence of these emerging issues presages a period of change for boards and their members. A new social compact for health boards will be the result. The Sarbanes-Oxley law applies to publicly traded companies, but it is the harbinger of the future for nonprofit boards. The source of regulations may be federal, state, or local legislation, and the responsibility for assessing compliance may be vested in the voluntary sector though deemed status. Sarbanes-Oxley-type laws have been introduced in several states, and a handful of hospitals are proactively moving to comply with many of the requirements.[8]

The assessment of the degree to which the organization complies with its own regulations will find a ready audience, including the media, organizations that advise prospective donors, and even bond rating services. It will certainly be of interest to prospective board members.

The template for such external evaluation will be the board's own codification of expectations for the behavior of the board and its members. The topics and issues to be addressed will be specified in the regulations. The old board manuals that gathered dust after orientation and which contain a few basic documents will not be sufficient. The board will have to commit substantial time and resources to the development of a comprehensive, living guide that members will be expected to carry into every meeting. Completing it may require the participation of legal and other experts. Tradition and informal agreement will no longer suffice.

The Mandated Guideline

Most of the topics mandated for inclusion in the board manuals of the very near future are familiar. The required detail of content and compliance is not so familiar. Critical topics for inclusion are listed below:

- The definition of board and board member independence.
- Responsibilities and processes for monitoring financial and quality of care performance, including the review of external reporting to governmental and nongovernmental agencies.
- Processes for establishing and overseeing executive remuneration.
- An explicit statement of the relationships of the board, officers, and committees to management.
- A delineation of the functions and limitations of the executive committee.
- A statement of commitment to public transparency and the procedures for ensuring it.
- Specification of composition of the board.
- Position descriptions for each board officer.
- Limitations of terms for board members and officers.
- Succession planning, processes to ensure turnover, and age limits for board members.
- Expectations for individual board members, including financial contributions and participation in development.
- Processes to ensure diversity in board membership.
- Processes for board recruitment.
- The process for appointing new board members, including review of credentials.
- Requirements for attendance at board and committee meetings.
- The guidelines and process for expelling board members.
- Rules governing board compensation and expenses.
- Definitions of conflict-of-interest by board members and employees, the process by which potential conflicts are reviewed, and requirements for annual statements of affiliations, including relationships with donors.
- Requirements for annual self-review and collective review of members and the board, including specific assessment instruments.
- Board education expectations, including specific allocations of resources, time, and processes.
- Explicit processes for board approval of medical staff bylaws and participation in provider credentialing.
- A description of how the board will develop and assess evidence for program evaluation.

- Rules for the conduct of open and closed meetings, including executive sessions.
- Rules delineating the roles of various categories of meeting participants, including specifying when members must recuse themselves.
- The process for periodic review and updating of the manual.

Obviously the development of these explicit policies and positions, and probably others to be added, will require a great deal of time and thought by the board, working together.

The Recurring Issue of Physicians on Boards

Conventional thinking is that the controversy of three decades over physician membership on boards has been put to rest. It will resurface in the emerging regulatory context. Physicians sit on a majority of boards,[9] and the current debate is over what proportion of the seats they should occupy. The question can be expected to reemerge because of the increasing role of the board in ensuring provider competence, as well as the myriad new and creative but confusing financial arrangements among them and with the organization. Segments of the profession may be expected to give voice to concerns about the effect of some arrangements on competition. Certainly regulators will be interested in the implications for public service and accountability objectives in both the non-profit and for-profit sectors.

The question of who the physician represents must be clarified in explicit terms and must be clear in all of the board processes included in the template. It will be useful to specify the category of physicians who may be board members, including members of the medical staff, employees, retired medical staff members, physicians who are independent (not related in any way), and *ex officio* medical group representatives, including the chief medical officer. Explicit clarification of the representational responsibilities and voting privileges of each is essential.

Pointer and Orlikoff take the position that "a physician board member is the same as any other member ... and [is] not supposed to represent any interests other than what is best for the organization and its stakeholders," and go on to cite the inclusive IRS regulations limiting the percent of "interested persons" on the board.[10] It may be anticipated that in the future, the percentage will be specified at a relatively low number per category. There continue to be too many situations in which the question of what interests are represented will be subject to scrutiny, if not question. Boards and especially physician members must be very sensitive to the issue and proactive in addressing it.

An Effective Board Member for the Future

The definition of an effective board member has changed over the past 30 years, but too slowly to position boards in general to appropriately function in the unpredictable future. The board is only as strong and effective as its members, that is, all of the members. There are boards that have made significant progress, but they are the exceptions, and the variation among boards calls attention to the weaknesses of the governance function.

The preceding chapters have identified desirable and essential characteristics of board members that must be carried forward and reinforced by the culture of the organization. In the future, they must be made more explicit. There are three fundamental tenets. First among them is loyalty to the welfare of the organization, which sounds obvious but must be reflected consistently in behavior. It is closely related to understanding and practicing fiduciary responsibility, the stewardship of resources, the second tenet. The third is independence, not only from external interests, but to a demonstrated but balanced degree from management. The three tenets reflect the values and ethics that the member brings into the boardroom and are the basis of the decision-making process.

In the future, the effective board member will be expected to reach beyond the board for intelligence and ideas. He or she will be expected to seek and pursue learning opportunities. Based upon this breadth of exposure, the effective member will be a source of new and creative ideas, not always depending upon the management and other members to create the agenda and enliven the discussion.

Each member will be responsible for the quality of the consideration of issues and topics, asking probing questions to raise the level of understanding and prevent bad decisions. The member will demonstrate team participation skills, encouraging differing opinions while respecting opposing views. In other words, the effective board member will leave each meeting confident of the quality of his or her contribution to constructive dialog.

Clearly, board membership will demand time, both in and out of the boardroom. Many extant patterns will have to change, including minimal preparation and minimal meeting time. Members will be expected to be well-prepared for meetings, participate in communications between meetings, and spend time talking privately with patients and families and representing the organization. It will not be possible to recruit new members with the promise of a minimal time commitment.

These characteristics will be explicitly addressed in the self and peer evaluation processes that the members will be expected to support. The criteria and how they are measured will be defined in the manual.

An Effective Board for the Future

This chapter began by reflecting upon the relative stability of the governance function in health services over the past 50 years through a white-water environment. The tranquility and comfort of board operations was also noted. That is a tribute to the commitment, energy, and talent that members have contributed to board operations.

This chapter is successful if it is clear about the predictability of the future, which holds little tranquility and much discomfort as boards adjust to the pressures for change. Coming face-to-face with the future will require some uncomfortable changes in governance processes and in the culture of all boards. No board now lives in the future.

A fundamental of adaptation is that the leadership regularly provokes uninhibited consideration of the extent to which the board itself (that is, members, structure, and processes) limits the adaptability and responsiveness of the organization. Resiliency depends upon what Paul Connolly labels adaptive capacity, "the ability to monitor, assess, respond to, and stimulate internal and external changes." Stagnant nonprofits have, in his characterization, "lost their adaptive capacity."[10] That capacity resides, or does not, in the board. Such a self-assessment will be difficult, uncomfortable, and necessary, especially for boards that think they are successful and unthreatened by the future.

As demanding as board business is today, the demands on time and energy are likely to increase, raising questions about the foci of board members' attention and the quality of consideration of decisions. Every claim on board members' time must be predicated on the judgment that it is really important. It is a matter of rationing. That means jettisoning processes and discussions that are reviews of the past and present and are mistakenly considered governance. Pointer and Orlikoff suggest that at least half of the board's time be focused forward.[9]

There is nothing new about the importance of quality consideration to good decision making. It is the higher stakes that challenge the board of the future to capture every possible creative and improved idea, every new and challenging insight, and every constructive and controversial criticism as consequential decisions are made. That is the value added of a culture of inquiry.[11]

Applying a strict time allocation rule does not mean that the content of all meeting time is fully structured. A culture of inquiry requires reflective space, time to think out loud, brainstorm, and float tentative ideas for constructive criticism. This is the place where the characteristics of an effective member will be tested. It is also a time when the board's definition of independence is tested. The CEO must be comfortable when not in control of the direction of the conversation, the options suggested, or the information brought forward.

Who participates in the discussion will also be an important consideration and subject to scrutiny. The underlying question will remain, "Who is not but should be represented at the table?" with intensified pressure from the board manual to explain, "If not, why not?" While the spirit, if not the content, of mission statements requires representation from the communities served, the reality of compliance is embarrassing. Among hospitals and health systems, 53% had no minority board members in 2007.[5] The vulnerability extends to the non-profit sector as a whole. Less than a third of trustees rate low minority board membership rates among their top issues.[12] There is no stronger stimulant for the regulated future.

The effective board will be comfortable in sunlight. A well-formulated statement of transparency philosophy and the procedures that implement it will provide a comfort zone covering the boardroom, the organization, and the community. Pay-for-performance will require public reporting of measurements of quality. If quality assessments go to the board, they will go to the public much to the ultimate benefit of the organization.[13] That fact mandates improved reporting systems, and it mandates the end of the expectation that only the provider members will understand quality assessments. All of the members of the board will be expected to master all of the information that flows into the public domain.

Conclusion

The social compact is being defined incrementally, and the prognosis is that the pace of change will accelerate. The role of providers on boards and committees will change as the effective board systematically addresses all of the challenges discussed in this chapter, revisits old ones, and engages those that will be mandated by the still hypothetical manual. Providers must be prepared to make important contributions to the spirit and content of the transition.

The first contribution is to be supportive, positive, and forward looking. Doing so will inevitably generate tensions among colleagues who will be uneasy about the implications of the changes for clinical work and economic relationships. Keep lines of communication transparent and predictable. Be prepared to invest time in communicating the necessity for changes and listening to the concerns. Do not minimize the sophistication of your fellow board members. Instead, work at bringing it to the level they need to fulfill the responsibilities of oversight.

The second contribution is to be well-informed and informative. Providers' views may have more credibility than they deserve, and that does not serve the organization well. Apply the same rule of evidence to the governance decision process that would be applied to clinical decisions. Providers should not accept the governance assignment unless they intend to do the extra homework. At a minimum, read the *Joint Commission Journal on Quality and Patient Safety*, *Trustee* magazine, and the *American Journal of Medical Quality*.

The provider members of boards or board committees will be central to the effectiveness of boards as they adjust to and live with the new social compact. It promises to be a challenging, demanding, and very rewarding role; in all respects, it will be an extraordinary opportunity to fulfill the promise of professionalism.

Case Study
Leadership for the Preferred Future

An article has landed on the boardroom table. The *Chronicle of Philanthropy* has given front page attention to the hospital and health system governance reform acts that have been introduced in many legislatures. It comes just as you, chair of the governance committee, have been charged with providing the strategic planning committee with a profile of the forces for change that will impact the hospital and its environment in 5 and 10 years. Professional organizations have been pushing back on the legislation without much success. The prognosis is that it will be law in your state in the next 2 years.

For the first meeting of your committee, you want to propose a work process and pose questions for discussion that will focus forward, stimulate thinking out of the box, and expand the horizon of the strategic planning committee. It is clear that the members of your committee need information about the forces that are shaping the future. Your first challenge is to identify background materials that will be informing without being so complex that the members will not read them. What would be a work process that will deliver what the planning committee needs to be effective? Where will you look to find these forward-looking articles?

Next, you will have to devise a scheme for listing the possible issues and developments that could be addressed. You know that it will not be useful to address all of the possibilities, so how do you narrow the list to a few that appear to be most relevant to your organization? It will be important for the committee to understand what you think are the most important challenges, but they should be presented in a way that encourages other viewpoints.

The strategic planning committee has asked for a progress report in a month that outlines the process of your committee and the product that they should expect.

Study and Discussion Questions

1. Have I, and the board, clarified the expectations, policies, and rules for provider members of the board?
2. Does our board have conflict-of-interest policies and procedures that proactively deter any foreseeable problem in practice or in perception?
3. How is our board responding to the mandate for internal and external transparency?
4. Have we reviewed how we spend board time to minimize time invested in reviewing the past and the present in order to devote more time and attention to the future?

Suggested Readings

Readings

Axelrod, N. 2006. Developing a culture of inquiry. *Board Members* May/June.

Briggs, E. L. 2004. *The governance factor: 33 keys to success in healthcare.* Chicago: Health Administration Press.

Chait, R. P. 2003. *How to help your board govern more and manage less.* Washington, DC: BoardSource.

Chait, R. P., W. P. Ryan, and B. E. Taylor. 2005. *Governance as leadership—Reframing the work of nonprofit boards.* Hoboken, NJ: John Wiley & Sons.

Conway, J. 2008. Getting boards on board: Engaging governing boards in quality and safety. *Joint Commission Journal on Quality and Patient Safety* 34:214–20.

O'Reilly, E. D. 2008. Put your board on high alert for Sarbanes-Oxley "creep." *Hospitals and Health Networks (H&HN),* April, pp. 57–60.

Robinson, J. C. 1999. *The corporate practice of medicine.* Berkeley: University of California Press.

The source: twelve principles of governance that power exceptional boards. 2005. Washington, DC: BoardSource.

Media

Ewell, C. M., director. 2005. *Physicians on the board.* San Diego, CA: The Governance Institute.

Kazemek, E. A. and C. M. Ewell, directors. 2007. *Physicians and conflict of interest.* San Diego, CA: The Governance Institute.

References

1. Studdert, D. M., M. M. Mello, C. M. Jedrey, and T. A. Brennan. 2007. Regulatory and judicial oversight of nonprofit hospitals. *New England Journal of Medicine* 356:625–31.
2. Stevens, R. 1989. *In sickness and in wealth.* New York: Basic Books.
3. Institute of Medicine. 2000. *To err is human: Building a safer health system,* ed. L. T. Kohn, J. M. Corrigan, and M. S. Donaldson. Washington, DC: National Academy Press.
4. Griffith, J. R. and K. R. White. 2007. *The well-managed healthcare organization.* 6th ed. Chicago: Health Administration Press.
5. The Governance Institute. 2007. *Boardsx4* governance structures and practices.* San Diego, CA.
6. Evans, M. 2008. Scheduling challenges with overhauled Form 990, hospitals are being asked for more specifics on governance, pay, perks, subsidized care. *Modern Healthcare* 38:6–7.
7. Kiely, R. 2007. How to educate a trustee. N.J. law only shows how far we have to go to adequately train board members. *Modern Healthcare* 37:24.
8. Becker, C. 2007. The latest board games. Not-for-profit governance evolves—including a trend toward corporatization—all in the name of quality, transparency! *Modern Healthcare* 37:28–30.
9. Pointer, D. D. and J. E. Orlikoff. 1999. *Board work governing health care organizations.* San Francisco: Jossey-Bass Publishers.
10. Connolly, P. M. 2005. Navigating the organizational lifecycle. *BoardSource,* pp. 6–7.
11. Axelrod, N. R. May/June 2007. Culture of inquiry: Healthy debate in the boardroom. *Board Member* 15(3).
12. Schwinn, E. 2007. Fund raising and lack of diversity are key challenges for trustees. *The Chronicle of Philanthropy,* November 29.
13. Colones, R. 2005. Team effort. McLeod uses "patient rounds," leadership meetings to boost quality. *Modern Healthcare* 35:24–25.

Editors

David B. Nash, MD, MBA

David Nash is the Dr. Raymond C. and Doris N. Grandon Professor and Chairman of the Department of Health Policy at Jefferson Medical College of Thomas Jefferson University in Philadelphia. Jefferson is one of a handful of medical schools in the nation with an endowed professorship in health policy. Dr. Nash, a board-certified internist, founded the original Office of Health Policy in 1990. From 1996 to 2003, he served as the first associate dean for health policy at Jefferson Medical College. In 2004, he was named codirector of the master's program in public health at Jefferson, and was named as a finalist in the 15th Annual Discover Awards for Innovation in Public Health by *Discover* magazine.

Internationally recognized for his work in outcomes management, medical staff development, and quality of care improvement, his publications have appeared in more than 100 articles in major journals. He has edited 17 books, including *A Systems Approach to Disease Management* by Jossey-Bass, *Connecting with the New Healthcare Consumer* by Aspen, *The Quality Solution* by Jones and Bartlett, and most recently, *Practicing Medicine in the 21st Century* by American College of Physician Executives (ACPE). In 1995, he was awarded the Latiolais (Lay-shee-o-lay) Prize by the Academy of Managed Care Pharmacy for his leadership in disease management and pharmacoeconomics. He also received the *Philadelphia Business Journal* Healthcare Heroes Award in October 1997, and was named an honorary distinguished fellow of the American College of Physician Executives in 1998. Finally, in 2006, he received the Elliot Stone Award for leadership in public accountability for health data from the National Association of Health Data Organizations (NAHDO).

Repeatedly named by *Modern Healthcare* to the top 100 most powerful persons in health care list, his national activities include the CIGNA Physician Advisory Committee, membership on the board of directors of the Disease

Management Association of America (DMAA), and chair of a National Quality Forum (NQF) Technical Advisory Panel—three key national groups focusing on quality measurement and improvement. He continues as one of the principal faculty members for quality of care issues of the American College of Physician Executives in Tampa, Florida, and the developer of the ACPE Capstone Course on Quality. Dr. Nash was recently appointed to the board of the West Virginia Medical Institute (WVMI), the Medicare QIO for Pennsylvania. For the last decade, he has been a member of the board of trustees of Catholic Healthcare Partners in Cincinnati, Ohio—one of the nation's largest integrated delivery systems—and he chairs the Board Committee on Quality and Safety.

Dr. Nash is a consultant to organizations in both the public and private sectors, including the Technical Advisory Group of the Pennsylvania Health Care Cost Containment Council (a group he has chaired for the last decade) and numerous corporations within the pharmaceutical industry. He is on the board of directors and advisory board of multiple health care companies. From 1984 to 1989, he was deputy editor of *Annals of Internal Medicine* at the American College of Physicians. Currently, he is editor-in-chief of four major national journals, including *P&T, Disease Management, Biotechnology Healthcare*, and the *American Journal of Medical Quality*. Through his writings, public appearances, and digital presence, his message reaches more than 100,000 persons every month.

Dr. Nash received his BA in economics (Phi Beta Kappa) from Vassar College, Poughkeepsie, New York; his MD from the University of Rochester School of Medicine and Dentistry; and his MBA in Health Administration (with honors) from the Wharton School at the University of Pennsylvania. While at Penn, he was a Robert Wood Johnson Foundation Clinical Scholar and medical director of a nine-physician faculty group practice in general internal medicine.

Dr. Nash lives in Lafayette Hill, Pennsylvania, with his wife, Esther J. Nash, MD, fraternal twin 21-year-old daughters, and 17-year-old son. He is an avid tennis player. Please visit www.jefferson.edu/dhp/ (E-mail: David. Nash@jefferson.edu) and his new blog at http://departmentofhealthpolicy. blogspot.com/.

William J. Oetgen, MD, MBA, FACP, FACC

William J. Oetgen received his undergraduate degree in psychology at Marquette University in 1969. He was a *cum laude* graduate of St. Louis University School of Medicine, where he was elected into Alpha Omega Alpha, the national medical honor society. He served his internship and pediatrics residency at Walter Reed Army Medical Center in Washington, D.C. He subsequently completed his internal medicine residency at Walter Reed and volunteered to serve at the U.S. Army Hospital, Seoul, Korea, as an internist and flight surgeon. Completing his tour in Korea, Dr. Oetgen returned to Walter Reed for his fellowship in cardiovascular medicine. Dr. Oetgen was director of the coronary care unit at Walter Reed, and he completed his active-duty Army service as assistant chief of the cardiology service in 1986. He retired as a colonel in the U.S. Army Reserve in 1999.

Entering private practice in 1986, Dr. Oetgen was appointed chief of cardiology at Greater Southeast Community Hospital in Washington, D.C. In 1996, he graduated from Georgetown University School of Business with a Master of Business Administration. In 1997, Dr. Oetgen cofounded Maryland Health Care Associates, a large multispecialty medical practice, and Apollo Medical Management Company, a management services organization in the southern Maryland suburbs of Washington.

Dr. Oetgen has served on the board of directors of HealthScribe, an Internet-based medical transcription company, which was featured in Thomas L. Friedman's *The World Is Flat*. He is a current director of Integra Health Services, an Ohio-based medical business process service provider.

Since 2005, Dr. Oetgen has served as a director of MedStar Health, Inc., the largest integrated health system in the Washington, D.C.–Baltimore, Maryland corridor, with eight local hospitals under management. In his tenure, Dr. Oetgen has been a member of the corporate Quality and Professional Affairs Committee, the Finance Committee, and the Audit and Compliance Committee. He is currently vice chairman of the Executive Compensation Committee.

Dr. Oetgen is a clinical professor of Medicine at the Georgetown University School of Medicine and an adjunct professorial lecturer at the Georgetown University McDonough School of Business. Dr. Oetgen is the author or coauthor of more than 100 articles in the medical literature. He is a fellow of the American College of Cardiology and a fellow of the American College of Physicians. He and his wife of 38 years, Phyllis M. Oetgen, JD, MSW, have three children and two granddaughters. Dr. Oetgen's avocations are golf, skiing, U.S. history, and the bluegrass banjo. (E-mail: oetgenw@georgetown.edu)

Valerie P. Pracilio

Valerie P. Pracilio is a project manager for quality improvement in the Department of Health Policy at Jefferson Medical College, where she is responsible for organizing efforts on various research projects primarily related to health care quality improvement.

At Thomas Jefferson University, she is currently facilitating performance improvement initiatives in each of the Jefferson University Physician (JUP) ambulatory practices and serves as a member of the Jefferson Clinical Care Subcommittee. Pracilio is working to implement a smoking cessation initiative across all JUP practices through funding from Pfizer, Inc., and has been involved in evaluating provider participation in pay-for-performance programs.

Outside of Jefferson, she completed an initiative to improve quality at two rural hospitals in Pennsylvania through funding from State Representative Todd Eachus. Pracilio was recently selected as a 2008–2009 Health Research and Educational Trust (HRET) Patient Safety Leadership Fellow. Through this experience she will implement an initiative aimed at developing a process for medication reconciliation at Jefferson, with the goal of advancing patient safety and health outcomes.

Pracilio's research interests include health information technology as well as cancer and value-based purchasing. Her research efforts have included a project focused on the capacity for colorectal cancer screening in Pennsylvania, which was submitted to the Legislative Budget and Finance Committee, and a study on the effects of a workflow management system on quality within an identified health care system.

Pracilio has a bachelor's degree in health care administration from the University of Scranton and is currently enrolled in the Masters of Public Health Program at Thomas Jefferson University. (E-mail: valerie.pracilio@jefferson.edu)

Index

B